Paul Monk (www.paulmonk.com.au) was born and grew up in Melbourne, and took out a BA in European history at the University of Melbourne and a PhD in international relations at the Australian National University. He joined the Australian Department of Defence in 1989 and the Defence Intelligence Organisation in 1990, where he later headed first the Japan and Koreas desk and then the China desk.

Between 2000 and 2017, he was a director and principal consultant for Austhink Consulting, specialists in applied cognitive science, whose clients included ASIO, the CIA, the ANZ Bank and the Hawthorn Football Club. He has written eleven other books, including *The West in a Nutshell* (2008) and *Dictators and Dangerous Ideas* (2018) and is a regular commentator on China and international affairs more generally in national print and electronic media.

Books by the same author (available through Echo Books):

Sonnets to a Promiscuous Beauty (2005) (eBook only)
The West in a Nutshell: Foundations, Fragilities, Futures (2009)
Darkness Over Love: A Complete Fiction (2014)
Opinions and Reflections (2015)
Credo and Twelve Poems (2015)
The Secret Gospel According to Mark (2017)
Dictators and Dangerous Ideas (2018)
The Three Graces: Companionship, Discretion, Passion (2022)

First Published in 2005 by Scribe Publications.
This edition published by Echo Books.
Echo Books is an imprint of Superscript Publishing Pty Ltd, ABN 76 644 812 395
Registered Office: Registered Office: PO Box 997, Woodend, Victoria, 3442.
www.echobooks.com.au
Copyright © Paul Monk
Creator: Monk Paul, Author
Title: Thunder from the Silent Zone : Rethinking China
ISBN: Paperback 978-1-922603-14-2

A catalogue record for this book is available from the National Library of Australia

Book layout and design by Peter Gamble, Canberra
Set in Garamond Premier Pro Display, 12/17, and MinervaModern.

Original cover image by Badiucao, exiled Chinese artist and dissident.

Thunder from the Silent Zone:

Rethinking China

Paul Monk

To the tens of millions of victims of communism in China: those executed, tortured, starved to death, set to forced labour, imprisoned, abused, deprived of the most elementary human rights, in the name of revolution.

and

To Wei Jingsheng (mainland dissident), Peng Mingmin (centenarian Taiwanese activist), Martin Lee Shuming (doyen of Hong Kong democrats) and young Joshua Wong and Jimmy Lai (defiant Hong Kong democratic activists).

May their cause prevail.

Table of Contents

A Note on Chinese Spelling — vii

Preface to the Second Edition — ix

Why this book has been republished. — ix
My four scenarios analysis and where it stands now — xi
What has changed since 2005? — xiii
Taiwan — xv
Cai Xia and the critique of the Xi regime — xix
Danger Zone: The Shorter Term and Longer Term Futures — xx

Preface to the First Edition — xxiii

Part One: The Grand Strategic Perspective

1. The Clash of Civilisations and the Chinese Empire — 3
2. Chinese Grand Strategy and American Hegemony — 23
3. Variations on the LAM: plotting China's futures — 33

Part Two: China and Taiwan

4. Kinmen and Kinship — 47
5. Conceiving a Paradigm Shift — 59
6. Looking at the Taiwan Strait from 'Down Under' — 71
7. Can Rationality Save Us? — 93

Part Three: Chinese Culture and the Modern World

8. Ancient History, Modern Cinema and Political Allegory — 109
9. Overcoming the Confucian: rethinking Chinese tradition — 119
10. Hu's Rhetoric: A Chinese 'Stolypin' in Australia — 131

Part Four: Democracy and Human Rights in the Chinese World

11. Wei Jingsheng and the Communist Party — 143
12. The Truth about Tiananmen — 155
13. Green Island: from prison camp to memorial — 171
14. Of Beethoven and Chinese Democracy — 183

Conclusion. Setting China Free — 197

Endnotes — 205

Index — 231

Acknowledgements — 239

A Note on Chinese Spelling

The spelling of many Chinese names, including that of both people and places, has changed under the so-called Pinyin system introduced in China in the 1950s. A number of older systems for romanising Chinese names, including the Wade–Giles system, long antedated the Pinyin system; and their renditions of many names are entrenched in both the historical literature and common usage.

To avoid confusion, I have followed a fairly standard practice: names are used in the familiar old form when they are Taiwanese, and with some exceptions in the newer Pinyin form when they are Chinese. Thus, Mao Tse-tung is rendered Mao Zedong, and Peking is rendered Beijing, since these have become standard. But Chiang Kaishek, for example, is preferred over Jiang Jieshi, because the Pinyin alternative has not been widely adopted for his name.

Whereas Chinese personal names under the Wide–Giles system generally had hyphenated given names, such as Tse-tung or Kai-shek, the Pinyin system compounds the two into a single form, such as Zedong or Jieshi. For the sake of consistency, I have adopted the practice of compounding the given names even when using the older Wade–Giles spelling. Thus, Sun Yat-sen appears as Sun Yatsen, and Chiang Kai-shek as Chiang Kaishek.

Preface to the second edition

Why this book has been republished.

Until the late 2010s, around the developed world and beyond, there was a widespread view that China's rapid growth and even its political and economic model would make China the number one power in the world by around 2030. That changed, as it became apparent that Xi Jinping was pulling back from the reforms of Deng Xiaoping and that China was facing growing problems of slowing growth, debt, corruption, dissent and demographic maturation. It had also become apparent, by then, that Xi Jinping was intent on preparing China for war and was militarizing his country's foreign policy. The central argument of this book, when first published, was that just such developments might well occur.

Thunder from the Silent Zone: Rethinking China was originally prepared for publication in 2004 and published in 2005. It has been reprinted in 2023 for two reasons:

1. The argument advanced in it all those years ago has been strongly vindicated by what has happened in between, but more importantly,

2. The methodological approach urged in the first edition is now more necessary than ever.

By 'argument' here I do not mean *prediction*. Pundits are addicted to making bold predictions, both short and long-term. As Philip Tetlock brilliantly demonstrated, in a book that was published at the same time as *Thunder from the Silent Zone*, in 2005, such predictions have a very poor hit rate, but the pundits rarely admit their errors.

His book, *Expert Political Judgement: How Good Is It? How Can We Know?* (Princeton University Press, 2005) was a remarkable study, which went far towards demonstrating the need for serious methodological overhauling of how geopolitical and economic forecasting are done. He gave me a copy at a conference at Wye River, Maryland, in September 2005, and I reviewed it back here, praising its fascinating insights, while observing that the overhauling would likely prove problematic, but that the need was painfully clear.

My own argument, in 2004-05, was that the future was importantly indeterminate, especially looking out more than a quite short time frame, and that far too many pundits—intoxicated by China's then two decades of rapid growth—were making projections of soaring growth far into the future and ignoring a number of divergent economic and geopolitical scenarios which seemed to me highly germane to any realistic strategy to hedge against China's futures. It will be immediately apparent why Tetlock and I hit it off at Wye River.

As far as I can ascertain from outside—and without having done a rigorous longitudinal study of the kind Tetlock did before 2005—the performance of Western governments, including their intelligence agencies, and of international conglomerates, has not appreciably improved in the years since. Doubtless, some have done so here and there. But the rhetoric of public policy and economic debate seems to suggest that all the intractable biases that bedevil human predictive and probabilistic forecasting remain endemic. In a world beset by major, interactive challenges, this is a serious problem.

Squatting square in the middle of all those challenges is China itself. What are the challenges? The escalating and daunting issue of nuclear armaments, the problems of climate change and pollution, the matter of population and productivity, the matter of pandemic disease and its genesis, the matter of potential great power conflict over China's military challenge to the seventy-year-old Pax Americana, the question of human rights and accountable governance. One could go on, the workability of the international trading system and the viability of the American dollar as the pivotal currency in global markets are also at stake.

We, collectively, need to understand and interact with China on all these matters. *Thunder from the Silent Zone: Rethinking China* was conceived and first published as an accessible handbook less on *what* to think about China, so much as on *how* to think about it. I had come out of working inside the Australian government as head of China analysis in the Defence Intelligence Organization deeply disillusioned with how the intelligence and policy arms of that government did their thinking, as a process. My grounds for this state of mind are set out in the preface to the first edition and there is no need to go back over them here.

There has, clearly, been a 'sea change' in judgements about China, both in Australia and across the developed world, over the past five years or so. That has been a heartening sign that key analysts have not been asleep at the wheel. But the need for better critical thinking and communication, about how futures evolve and what it make sense to do in both hedging against uncertainty or danger and acting as adroitly as possible to bring desirable futures into being, remains clear. This book is being reissued not with the pretension to having 'all the answers', but in order that it will be available as a point of reference.

My four scenarios analysis and where it stands now

The book covered and still covers a lot of historical and conceptual ground. It could have been updated, but the purpose of reissuing it is not to offer a current intelligence briefing. It is, rather, to put into ongoing circulation the briefing that the book delivered at its inception. The chapters on democracy and human rights, in Part Four, far from having been overtaken by events, have gained in importance given the trends in China since 2004. The reflections, in Part Three, on Chinese culture in the modern world likewise. Chapter 10, on Hu Jintao in Australia, serves to throw into high relief the challenge with which the dictatorial politics of Xi Jinping confront us.

But Part One, 'The Grand Strategic Perspective' and Part Two, 'China and Taiwan' are the parts of the book which, in their original and unedited versions, most urgently need reading now. I have quite deliberately not updated them, because updates are easy to come by. Depth of perspective and the examination of deep and often unexamined presuppositions or assumptions are much harder to find. My work in this book offers both. Towards the end of this Preface, I shall offer a basic update, based on current data and developments. But here I want simply to draw attention to the absolutely central arguments advanced almost twenty years ago, since I believe they have both stood up well over time and warrant close consideration now.

There are three chapters in Part One. The first is a sustained critique of the 'clash of civilizations' thesis advanced by the late Professor Samuel Huntington (1927-2008), of Harvard University, in 1996. The second is a reflection on the rise of China and the challenge it seems to present to American hegemony, or what is commonly called the Pax Americana, which began with the defeat of Nazi Germany and militarist Japan in 1944-45. The third chapter 'Variations on the LAM: plotting China's futures' is, however, the key essay in the book and the most compelling reason for republishing it now.

There are a number of passages, between pages 47 and 60, which call for re-emphasising in the present context:

> Thinking through China's possible futures requires deep critical analysis, grounded in first class scholarship, and the testing of mental models and basic assumptions. It cannot be achieved through superficial extrapolation of barely understood statistical trends, or reactive briefing on moment-to-moment or year-to-year crises. *p. 47*
>
> For the purposes of argument, I shall refer to the simplistic and overawed linear way of thinking involved here as the Linear Ascent Model (LAM). *p. 49*
>
> The question of how rapidly China is likely to continue growing, and to what dimensions, tends to disappear over the horizon of about 2030 on a simple and unbounded curve of astounding economic growth. *p. 52*

Those three remarks lead into a long, three paragraph conclusion to the chapter on the LAM:

> It would be irresponsible to rule out the possibility that China will fail to negotiate some critical thresholds in the early decades of the twenty-first century. Instead of being awed by simple statistical extrapolations, we would do better to make more complex calculations about the impediments to China's continued growth and political cohesion, and think seriously about the mutations that both China's polity and economy must undergo, if its growth is to be sustained and managed. And, let there be no mistake about it: if it cannot sustain rapid growth for a long time to come, it faces very serious political and social problems. Even a serious downturn could have dramatic repercussions.
>
> In place of the LAM, we should think of four models for change in China over the next generation. These might be labelled mutation, maturation, metastasis and militarization. None is linear and none entails uninterrupted ascent, or a Chinese dominated twenty-first century. Mutation would involve a fundamental reshaping of the polity to cope with internationalisation and a complex economy. Maturation would involve a flattening of the growth curve, but only to a level enabling China to cope with the enormous demands of a population that is unlikely to stabilise short of 1.7 billion by mid-century. Metastasis would occur if the multiple and formidable challenges facing the Chinese polity prove overwhelming and result in a collapse of the undertaking to modernise a unified China... The fourth model, Militarisation, would involve a nationalist effort to cope with the stresses of rapid change and uncertainty through a massive increase in military power, much as Germany undertook before 1914 and Japan before 1941.
>
> The mutation model is the one the rest of the world should be seeking to support and encourage. It has been foreshadowed, in part, by the mutation of polities elsewhere in East Asia over the past half-century—notably in Japan, South Korea and Taiwan. It would entail a substantial furthering of the withdrawal from power by the Communist Party and substitution in its place of more democratic norms and, even more crucially, a far more sound and reliable rule of law. *pp. 59-60*

The statement about China's population stabilising by mid-century, at about 1.7 billion, needs correction. It has begun to fall already, from a highpoint of 1.41 billion and is projected to fall to 700 million by the end of the century—a phenomenon with extraordinary socio-political and economic implications. The other datum which needs correction here is an historical one. At several points, in the original edition, I cited figures of 30 million deaths from the Great Famine under Mao in 1958-62. That was then the best estimate available. The best evidence now, based on path-breaking archival research in China, suggests that the death toll may have been as high as 55 million, a mind-numbing figure.[1] I have updated this estimate in the text, except where I am quoting someone else's claim.

There was considerable debate, in the 1990s and 2000s, even in the 1980s, about whether China would reform and open politically; and even whether it ought to be the concern of Washington, or the outside world more generally, to seek to bring that about. Would it happen naturally, as China's economy grew? Was such political opening alien to Chinese political culture, at a deep level? Would any attempt to engineer it from outside be counter-productive? Or was such a mutation scenario crucial to China finally assuming a place as a leading and responsible stake-holder in a global liberal order?

Xi Jinping has swept all these questions off the table, as a matter of both declaratory ideology and political action. And we have come to realize, a little belatedly, that his manner of rule, like that of Vladimir Putin, is inimical to the global liberal order of the Pax Americana. While the mutation scenario was a plausible subject for debate for many years, it is now off the agenda. The other three scenarios, however, are very much in the mix in the 2020s and have been for a decade now. The policy of 'constructive engagement' adhered to in Washington and the rest of the OECD since 1989 must be deemed to have failed at this juncture. It was premised on the mutation scenario. A serious reframing of how to deal with the China of Xi Jinping and his communist regime is now very much needed.

Had I updated the book, it would have been open to many readers to think or even assume that I had developed this four scenario analysis with the wisdom of hindsight. That would, I believe, have deprived the book of much of its latent power. Leaving the text as it was (save for a small number of merely typographical corrections) shows that deeper thinking and the questioning of assumptions and projections was perfectly possible in the early 2000s, when almost no-one of whom I am aware was doing this.[2] That means it is also possible now. I would like to believe that the wider availability of this book will help to stimulate it.

What has changed since 2005?

There are vital data, of course, that must be taken into account in any update. They can be readily summarized here, if only because they serve to demonstrate why the maturation, militarization and metastasis scenarios were well-conceived many years ago and require searching analysis now. What we know, to a certainty, is that China's military expenditure has increased by leaps and bounds this century, generating the largest and swiftest military build-up during peacetime in history.

We also know that Xi Jinping has militarized the South China Sea, despite explicit undertakings not to do so. We know that he has threatened to use force to subdue Taiwan and that he has called for the country to be ready for war. Moreover, he is Chairman of the Central

Military Commission and, far from professionalising the army as the instrument of the state, he has reinforced its function as the instrument of the Communist Party for furthering its agenda. This is all, of course, very much what the militarization scenario forecast.

At the same time, however, expenditure on internal security—the secret police, the armed police, the great firewall, censorship, surveillance—has grown gigantically. It has increased by 300 percent in just the last decade and has now overtaken military expenditure in gross terms. In 2021 the Party state spent 1.38 trillion Yuan ($US203 billion) on internal security as against 1.268 trillion ($US186.5 billion) on the military. But those are official exchange rate figures. If converted into Purchasing Power Parity terms, as GDP often is, they are much larger. In 2022 PPP terms, China's internal security budget comes out at $US328 billion and its military budget at $US302 billion.

And even that is not the complete picture, since China does not include in its defence budget, which is markedly opaque, a number of things that are included in the US defence budget. Moreover, the United States spends to maintain a global network of alliances, bases and security guarantees. China spends solely to enhance its own national power. What, therefore, do these raw figures tell us? That the Party is deep into militarization, but is also clinging to power and legitimacy by its teeth. It fears internal instability, dissent and civil society even more than it fears external enemies. This is grist for the mill of the metastasis as much as for the militarization scenario. We are, analytically, in very interesting territory here.

It gets better. During those same years, the Party's macro-economic policies, hailed briefly, in the wake of the Global Financial Crisis, as a new model for development—the Beijing Consensus[3]—perhaps more viable than the much-touted Washington Consensus[4], began to run into increasing problems. The first was massive misallocation of capital through huge subsidies to loss-making state-owned enterprises (SOEs), channelled through the state-owned banking system[5]. The second was further massive misallocation of funds, chiefly by provincial and city authorities and speculators, into the construction of vast quantities of superfluous housing or infrastructure, due to poor coordination between national, provincial and city policies. The third was massive imbalance in the financial system due to the private sector—starved of capital by the state owned banks—having to create a shadow banking network of its own. None of this was path-breaking or even competent macro-economics.

Overall, debt levels skyrocketed in the decade between 2010 and 2020. This led to a series of studies, published in 2017 and 2018, which anticipated the end of the Chinese boom and the failure of the Party's model of governance.[6] Growth rates in GDP began to flatten and all this even before COVID-19 broke out in Wuhan and added stress to the global, as well as the national, economic order. Here was both material for the maturation scenario and indicators that the metastasis scenario might, also, have legs. What was not in evidence was a set of further macro-economic reforms that could have eased the pressure on the system and streamlined China's transition to a more open and sustainable market economy.

Does all this mean that the immediate, to say nothing of the longer-term trajectory of China, whether economic or political, is now readily predictable? It certainly does not. What it means is simply that it was demonstrably possible, in the early 2000s, to anticipate that some of these scenarios were plausible and that we should think hard about them and perhaps hedge against them. The critical assessments of 2017-18 were belated and addressed only part of the picture. What is required now is not more feckless predictions, but more fine-grained and acute analysis, paying attention, in particular, to those variables that will—depending on subtleties in how they evolve—go far to determining what happens from here.

Taiwan

The matter of prediction and scenario planning has, of course, come to the fore in recent years with regard to whether China, under Xi, will finally go to war in an attempt to subdue Taiwan and force it to accept integration into the People's Republic of China—something which the overwhelming majority of its citizens clearly do not want. There has been mounting concern that, if the United States and its allies dig in to defend Taiwan against such an assault, we could end up embroiled in World War III—in a heavily nuclear-armed world.

The danger of such a war, when this book was first being written, was appreciably less than it has since become. That is for three main reasons: China's military power has grown enormously over the past two decades, China's political regime has moved decisively towards dictatorship and away from even the vague pretence of democratic norms; and the United States has been weakened -by its fruitless 'forever wars' in Iraq and Afghanistan, by the Wall Street engineered Global Financial Crisis and by its political deterioration, culminating in the rise and erratic one term presidency of Donald Trump.

Having visited Taiwan many times between 1994 and 2004, I developed the clear view that the determination of the Communist Party to take the island from its people was a mistake from the point of view of China's own national interest. This was not and is not the same as stating that it is a mistake from the point of view of the interests of the Chinese Communist Party. Therein lies the challenge. But until the death of Mao Zedong and the ascent of Deng

Xiaoping to primacy, one might have argued that economic reform and opening were not in the Party's interest, though they might well be in the national interest of China.

Such reform and opening—up to a point—took place, because the Party under Deng decided that it was indispensable to the national interest and that, therefore, the Party must find a way to engineer it[7]. My argument in this book, when it was first published, was that a thought experiment needed to be pressed home as to whether and why the de jure recognition by Beijing of Taiwan's full independence might actually be in China's national interest—and to such an extent that the Party could, conceivably, be brought around to accepting and even embracing that idea. I have left that argument—in chapters 5, 6 and 7—unchanged, precisely because the urgency of the matter has grown so much in the intervening years.

I framed the matter, in the original Introduction, as follows:

> In a number of ways, the future of Taiwan will tell the story of the future of China, which is why it has a disproportionate place in this book. Geopolitical concerns about China centre on the question of whether it will use force in an effort to assert its sovereignty over Taiwan. Economic hopes for China amount to the idea that it will become, over the next generation or two, a gigantic Taiwan—peaceful, prosperous and fully modern. Political concerns about China centre on the fact that it has failed, thus far, to achieve the political reform that has occurred in Taiwan. But Taiwan is a clear demonstration of what is possible in moving from dictatorship to democratic constitutionalism in the Chinese world.[8]

Those observations have only become more correct since 2004/05, with the ascent to the presidency of Tsai Ingwen and the maturing of the Democratic Progressive Party as a democratic force. Taiwan as a secure, prosperous and well-disposed sister state would be of far more value to China than Taiwan as a brutalized, resentful and poorly governed province[9].

But the argument in this book always allowed that this seems counter-intuitive and that, in any case, there seemed and seems no possibility that the Communist Party would step back and reconsider its position so radically. Given the relentless suppression of Hong Kong by the Party since 2020[10], including its repudiation of the most fundamental principles of the Basic Law put in place before the city state was handed over by the UK to the Communist Party, in 1997, why would one hold out any hope of its attitude regarding Taiwan being turned on its head?

In order to show how fundamental assumptions can mislead one as to the nature of observable and testable reality, I made use of the idea of a Necker Cube[11] and suggested it be used to frame the thought experiment about what is really in China's national interest. This is a Necker Cube of the kind I described, without diagramming it:

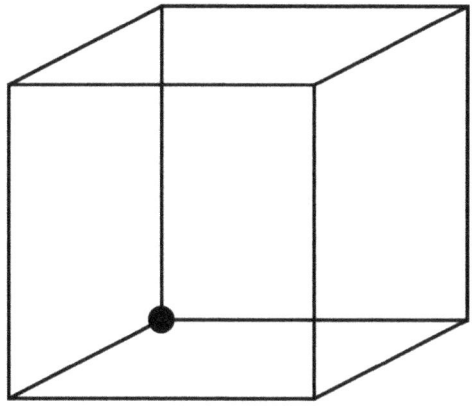

Example of a necker cube

Observe the dot. Is it at the front corner or the rear corner of the Cube? That is indeterminate. It's a matter of visual perspective, not fact. Assume one visual perspective and you see it at the front. Reframe your perceptions and it appears in a back corner. This offers a disarmingly simple demonstration of how perceptions and assumptions can mislead us. Historical cases of strategic misjudgement have demonstrated, again and again, that this happens. The challenge is to ferret out the assumptions before they lead to disaster—and then shift them.

Pivoting on this conceptual *coup de main*, I argued that it was both necessary and possible to reframe the Taiwan problem in such a way that it would make as much sense to Chinese strategists as economic reform made in the wake of Mao Zedong's demise. I will not reiterate the argument in this Preface, since it is in the body of the book. Two points warrant emphasis here, however: that the argument for a paradigm shift needs to be given oxygen, needs to be a matter of advocacy, if it is to end up solving the Taiwan problem for us; and that such paradigm shifts have occurred, in very major geopolitical cases in the recent past, so they can and do happen.

Three cases of them happening are the Soviet withdrawal from Eastern Europe in 1989, the peaceful abandonment of apartheid by the South African white minority regime in 1994 and the withdrawal from East Timor by Indonesia, after the holding of a genuine plebiscite there in 1999. Were any of these seen as realistically likely five years before—in 1984, 1989 and 1994, respectively? They were not. They were, in fact, seen by strategists and statesmen alike as chimerical ideas, extremely unlikely to occur. As late as 1988, Paul Kennedy (as I point out in this book) argued that the Soviet Union would not withdraw from Eastern Europe or countenance the reunification of Germany. He was proved wrong within twelve months.

What makes this intervention important is that the danger of conflict and even of catastrophic conflict has manifestly risen. Before his death in mid-January 2023, my friend of thirty years, retired Major-General and Senator Jim Molan, laid out an apocalyptic scenario, in which China chose to go to war not merely by attempting an amphibious invasion of Taiwan, but by launching a multiple Pearl Harbors assault on American bases critical to any possible US defence of Taiwan[12]. His point was less to predict that such an assault would happen, than to alert policy makers to the reality that it could—and that we are utterly unprepared for what would follow.

The Chinese Ambassador to Australia, Xiao Qian, stated frankly, in 2022, that China would retake Taiwan whatever that required and would then 're-educate' the people of Taiwan to understand their subordinate place within the Chinese world. These are the stark realities of the strategic situation as this book goes back into print. Jim Molan's concern was plainly that China might do, in the near future, what Japan did in December 1941—and be far better equipped to carry it through than was Japan. Any such idea was a distant and abstract possibility in 2004. It isn't any longer. Alarms have been sounded and alliance systems—the Quad and AUKUS—are forming to discourage China from going to war.

This was also the approach of the Reagan administration and Margaret Thatcher's Britain in the 1980s vis a vis the Soviet Union, seen as a formidable adversary, with tank divisions poised at the Fulda Gap to invade West Germany and a nuclear arsenal of gigantic proportions that could, if used, wipe out human civilization. The West increased its commitment to deterrence and the Soviet Union not only did not invade Germany, but first, in 1989, withdrew voluntarily and peacefully from Eastern Europe, which it had occupied since 1944-45, then disintegrated completely, in 1991. Though no one wants to end up in a confrontation with China, we are now in a situation with regard to it comparable to that which at least appeared to face us in Europe in between 1945 and 1988.

As I remarked in reviewing Molan's book[13], he lays out his scenario for the imagined war in enough detail to make it sound compelling. It is reminiscent of a book published in 1925, *The Great Pacific War*, by Hector Bywater, a naval analyst with *Jane's Fighting Ships*. In that book, Bywater spelled out a scenario for a war between Japan and the US eerily similar to what unfolded between late 1941 and August 1945[14]. But that was an era before satellites or nuclear weapons, ballistic missiles, drones, cyber-monitoring or the forward basing of US forces in East Asia. For China to attempt, on the scale Molan projected, what Japan had undertaken in 1941 would involve it in the most incalculable risks.[15]

We stand, therefore, at a pivotal point in the history of China, of Asia and of the world. This book might have been allowed to languish in obscurity had it been overtaken by events. It is being republished now because, on the contrary, it has been vindicated by events in several ways. Its vision for change, however, is far from having been vindicated or fulfilled. In that regard, everything lies ahead to be accomplished or, failing its accomplishment, everything ahead looks grim and potentially disastrous. All the more reason to give this clarion call for critical reasoning and deep rethinking of embedded assumptions a fresh set of legs.

Cai Xia and the critique of the Xi regime

Whom should we trust when it comes to assessments of the condition and future of China? When it comes to predictions, almost no-one would be my counsel. But when it comes to wisdom and insight there are certainly those whose work we should elevate well above the Party's propaganda and so-called 'Xi Jinping Thought'. Among them, Cai Xia stands out for three reasons: she was, until 2020, a leading professor at the Party's own Central School for cadres; she is a veteran, at 70, with a long view of China's internal politics; and she argues, now in exile, against the current, that China for its own sake needs to move to a constitutional democracy.[16]

She is very much the kind of reader with whom I would feel pleased to share this book and with whom discussion of its arguments would be fruitful and interesting. In a leading article in *Foreign Affairs*, in 2022, she argued that the regime under Xi is weak and brittle[17]. This was before the mass demonstrations against his COVID lockdown policies in 2022, which included calls for him to step down and for the Communist Party itself to give way to sweeping political reform. Both her argument and those calls resonate strongly with the arguments I made in this book in 2004/05, notably in the Conclusion, which remains unchanged in this new edition.[18]

Cai Xia has advocated a hard line on China by the United States and its allies, both in the Quad and elsewhere. She should be heeded, not least in the current political climate in Australia. The Party's hold on power, she insists, is more fragile than is widely believed. In June 2021, she argued, in a long paper about Sino-American relations at the Hoover Institution, that China needed to be foiled and confronted, not cajoled or appeased. Larry Diamond, a Hoover Institution specialist on democratic transitions, affirmed her remarks as being of historic significance and declared that they should be heeded in Washington.

Writing in *The Economist*, in late 2021, Cai declared that one-party dictatorship is now a major obstacle in the path of China's further development. 'Only', she stated explicitly, 'by ending this totalitarian system of governance and moving towards a constitutional democracy will the country be on course for good and durable economic and social development.' So much for the Beijing Consensus as a competitor with the Washington Consensus. In fact, in September 2022, in *Foreign Affairs*, she went even further, declaring bluntly that the CCP is 'more of a mafia organization than a political party.'[19]

Danger Zone: The Shorter Term and Longer Term Futures

There has been a growing debate across Asia and around the world in the Xi Jinping era as to how democratic states should respond to the ambitions and the aggressive behaviour of the Beijing regime. Australia is in the forefront of these debates, because it has a massive economic relationship with China, to which it has become a huge supplier of commodities, and because it is an integral part of the Anglo-American world order, without which it would not have come into existence as a modern state at all.

The debate within Australia has, for at least a decade, been cast in terms of what former Deputy Secretary of Defence for Strategy and founding Director of the Australian Strategic Policy Institute, Hugh White, called 'the China choice'. Very substantial business interests and their intellectual acolytes have lobbied for Australia to 'accommodate' China's rise and nudge the United States to do the same, by stepping back from North East Asia and accepting that Asia is as much China's natural sphere of influence as the Western Hemisphere is deemed to be that of the United States itself, ever since the Monroe Doctrine.

Opinion shapers such as Hugh White, Geoff Raby (a former ambassador to China), Stephen Fitzgerald (no relation of John Fitzgerald), another former ambassador to China, diplomatic historian James Curran, former prime minister Paul Keating and numerous others have vigorously challenged the idea that China poses any kind of strategic or hegemonic threat to Australia, while arguing in varying degrees that those expressing concern about China and the bellicose behaviour of the Xi regime are racists, Sinophobes, sycophants of Washington and or London, and in any case deluded as to the possibilities of 'containing' China's rise. There has never before in the country's history been a debate so important or one that has so clearly divided the nation's political, business and intellectual elites.

I have been one of the most consistent challengers to their school of thought. The republication of this book is a conscious move in the great debate. It takes place at a time when the ALP government, under Prime Minister Anthony Albanese, has both emphatically declared itself to be aligned with the US, Japan and India in the Quadrilateral Security Dialogue (Quad), which is all about concern at China's militarization and its geopolitical ambitions; and declared that Australia will greatly strengthen its military preparedness to confront China should that be necessary. It has also, however, unlike the Morrison government which preceded it, sought a stabilization of the relationship with China and taken a very cautious stance on the question of relations with Taiwan.

All this merits close attention in its own right. But it can only be understood in a far wider geostrategic context—one which the critics of our alliance relationships and defence planning tend to get rather muddled. The only one of them to write a monograph length analysis of the situation that makes much sense is Geoff Raby[20]. Reviewing his book, in October 2020, for *The Weekend Australian*, I praised the quality of his analysis of China, but was critical of his unsubstantiated assertions that Australia will have to bow to a new Chinese dominated world order and will not have the option of remaining an ally of the United States.

Two seminal books, both published in 2022, have taken the strategic debate to a new level and ought to inform any future public (or indeed classified) discussion of Australia's place in the international strategic scheme of things. The first is Michael Green's *Line of Advantage: Japan's Grand Strategy in the Era of Abe Shinzo* (Columbia University Press, New York, 2022) and Hal Brands and Michael Beckley's *Danger Zone: The Coming Conflict With China* (W. W. Norton and Co., New York, 2022). The first shows that Japan has moved to shape the strategic environment in such a way as to resist Chinese hegemony and align with the United States, while still seeking to deter China from actually going to war. The second argues that China will be increasingly tempted to go to war in the next decade, because in reality its rise has peaked and it faces a very challenging future.

One would hope that both books will be read by, among many others, every member of the now forty strong China desk staff in Australia's Defence Intelligence Organization. The first is richly illuminating for Australians because it takes them outside the rather incestuous domestic debates in this country and shows another and very significant country acting on similar lines to our own for well-considered reasons. The second is a wake-up call. It makes two arguments which, taken together, should reshape how we frame our sense of China's possible futures and the strategic behaviour that may flow from them.

The first argument is that China faces a number of massive domestic challenges, already looming, which will curtail its ascent and could derail its economy and its political order altogether. Far from a 'China Dream' being fulfilled in the second half of the 21st century, what is rather more likely, on current settings, they observe, is a China Nightmare: an aging and shrinking population, a shrinking workforce, the need to choose between massive welfare expenditures and massive military and security expenditures, all but insoluble environmental problems, political sclerosis and a ring of distrustful neighbours who have been antagonized and alarmed by the moves Xi Jinping has wilfully made in the recent past.

The second argument is that, precisely because China faces crisis and decline, not ascent and dream-come-true riches from 2030 onwards, it could be tempted to go to war in the very near future, believing that territorial gains are a 'now or never' proposition and resource security likely to become more precarious a decade and more out. This line of argument runs clean counter to the rather well-known argument by Graham Allison about the so-called 'Thucydides Trap'—a declining hegemon being drawn into a war with a rising power, on the (supposed) model of Sparta and Athens in the Peloponnesian War (431-404 BCE). It holds, instead, that wars are more often triggered by a rising power perceiving that it's opportunity is limited and that time is actually against it.

Brands and Beckley do not urge that China be reassured or conciliated. They argue that it will have to be deterred and, if necessary defeated in the 2020s. Thereafter, it is likely to remain a major challenge for decades, but the real danger to the American led world order will come in the near future. There is no need in this Preface to examine their argument in detail. I have done that elsewhere. What is salutary about their argument is its originality and the manner in which it compels us to rethink what remain widespread assumptions about where things are heading and why and what can or should be done about it.

From a purely analytical point of view, it is deeply heartening to see so cogent an argument being made at all. But its being made absolves none of us from the task of thinking analytically and rigorously ourselves. On the contrary, it should spur us to greater intellectual and strategic seriousness. The republication of this book, after eighteen years, seems all the better warranted for the fact that *Danger Zone* has just been published. I am very comfortable in the company of Brands and Beckley—as in that of John Lee, James Mann, Aaron Friedberg, Jonathan Fenby and that circle of thinkers in this country with whom, for some years, I have been sharing strategic concerns. They know well who they are.

Paul Monk
Melbourne
23. 02. 2023

Preface to the First Edition

The West has been intensely interested in China for a long time, but never more so than now. The reason is simple. China has not been such an economically significant and diplomatically confident nation since the eighteenth century, and almost everything has changed since then. There are, in short, good reasons to be interested in China. Many simply have to do with understanding its place in the world, and making sense of the phenomenon of China's rise in recent decades. Others, of a more specialist nature, have to do with the strategic interests of business and of government. Although written from a background of strategic interest, this book is intended to appeal not only to China-watchers but to anyone simply trying to make sense of China.

My own efforts to do so go back to my early school years, which happened to coincide with the Cultural Revolution (and the Vietnam War). As an eleven-year-old, I bought and read Stuart Schram's then-new biography of Mao Zedong, and I gave a school speech on the May Fourth Movement at twelve years of age. But China did not become my chief focus until, having completed doctoral studies in international relations, I went to work for the Australian government as an East Asia analyst in the Defence Intelligence Organisation (DIO). This work culminated with my appointment as head of China analysis in 1994. The DIO years were instructive, in a number of ways, and provided the grounding for this book.

My doctorate was not about China; it was a study of United States interventions against communist-led peasant insurgencies in the Philippines, Vietnam, and El Salvador throughout the Cold War. Of course, China loomed in the background, but it was not a central concern. The focus of the enquiry was the 'intelligence' exhibited by the American government in its efforts to suppress such insurgencies, between the early 1950s and the early 1980s. As my enquiry deepened, I developed a fascination with the nature and uses of field intelligence, and the institutional problems that made it difficult for even the best intelligence or desk-level analysis to impact on high-level foreign and security policies.

As a direct result of this interest, I decided, around 1988, that I wanted to work in my own country's intelligence system to see whether the same institutional problems existed, and to test whether any of the academic knowledge I had acquired was of use in the fabled 'real world'. The idea of working as an intelligence analyst held a certain appeal, but it was not my prime motivation. Indeed, I was not at all committed to a long-term career in intelligence, or in government. I just wanted to explore the system and test my ideas. Had I been more prudent about a firm career choice, I might have gone on to do post-doctoral studies at a good American university. But I was not prudent. And, in any case, had I taken the academic road, I would never have been in a position to work on China. Academia requires long-term intellectual specialization; government service demands an altogether different set of skills.

The first institutional problem I encountered was not one I could have anticipated. Having been offered a job in the Department of Defence, I was required to undergo what is known as 'security vetting' before I could take up the position as a graduate trainee. To my astonishment, and that of the department's recruitment staff who had offered me the job, I was denied what is known in the trade as a 'Negative Vetting' (NV) clearance. Denial of such a clearance was rare, and normally occurred only if you had a criminal record, a drug problem, links with subversive political organisations, or a comparable question mark against your name. Since none of these explanations applied in my case, the denial came as a bolt out of the blue. The mystery deepened over the following weeks as the security-vetting people refused to inform either me or the recruitment staff of the reason for the denial.

After quite a bit of bureaucratic arm-wrestling on my behalf, the clearance was finally granted. Following further enquiries, I was informed I had been denied it initially because of my 'interest in Russia'—not 'sympathy for', not 'obsession with', but merely an 'interest in'. This was in early 1989, less than a year before the Berlin Wall was toppled. I was deeply intrigued by this strange judgment—the more so because, when I did arrive in Canberra to work, the first security briefing I received consisted of solemn warnings that the KGB remained the biggest security threat in Australia. The briefing officer earnestly asserted that I should not believe 'all this glasnost and perestroika stuff' because the Soviet Union remained bent on world domination, and was simply trying to pull the wool over the eyes of the West. The briefing was capped off with the even more curious statement that Australia's security services had 'only recently' realised that the Eastern European intelligence services were, for the most part, controlled by the KGB. Yet my 'interest in Russia' had been a problem.

Such was my rather inauspicious introduction to the Australian intelligence service. Around the same time I came across a charming passage in the memoir of Malcolm Muggeridge, concerning his own induction into the world of intelligence (Britain's MI6), back in 1941. Having been tapped on the shoulder, the future editor of *Punch* readily agreed to join the service. When he was taken to a rather large building on Broadway and shown around, he quickly formed the impression that 'the whole place was so absurd that it had to be a façade'. As Muggeridge relates, he then thought, 'Aha! They're testing me! They're waiting to see how I respond and, if I behave appropriately, they'll say, "Well, this man's sound. Now we'll show him the *real* intelligence service'. Then I realized this was the real intelligence service!" I laughed heartily at Muggeridge's anecdote, only to then discover that it had real and depressing relevance in Australia, even in 1989.

The story of that discovery began with a Kafkaesque twelve-month quest for admission to what was then called the Joint Intelligence Organisation (JIO). (It was to be renamed the Defence Intelligence Organisation in 1990). Having started work as a Defence trainee, I applied for a position as an intelligence analyst in JIO in mid-1989. Taking up such a position required what is known as a 'Positive Vetting' (PV) clearance—something much more detailed and intrusive than a NV clearance. Despite everything that had already happened, I assumed, a little naïvely, that this would be plain sailing. I could not have been more mistaken.

Although I eventually obtained the clearance, the process was to drag out over almost twelve months and, during the last six months, I was left without any specific work to do. I later learned that a number of bizarre rumours about me were spread through the Defence Department in those months: for example, that I would never be granted a PV because I had supposedly blown the cover of an ASIS (Australian Secret Intelligence Service) agent in the Philippines while doing field work there. I never learned the origin of this strange rumour, but I thought it grossly unfair—considering I had not, to my knowledge, ever known any ASIS operatives in the Philippines.

Finally, after an appeal via a senior journalist to the secretary of defence (over the heads of the security vetting people), I was granted my PV clearance in June 1990. I remember thinking to myself that if security vetting was like this for someone of my background during peacetime in Australia, God help anyone under a dictatorship during a crisis! Still, I was through the door into the intelligence world. While undergoing security vetting I had published a monograph on land-reform debates in the Philippines, under the title *Truth and Power*. This—truth and power—had become my key interest, and I was ready to get down to the business of understanding Australia's place in the world, through the lens of its intelligence collection and analysis agencies.

My arrival coincided almost exactly with the reforms under which JIO was renamed the Defence Intelligence Organisation (DIO). I was assigned to Asia Section, which dealt with East Asia (China, Taiwan, Hong Kong, Japan, and the Koreas) and South Asia (India, Pakistan, Bangladesh, and Sri Lanka). My first position was as a junior analyst of East Asian geopolitics. I was delighted with this assignment, because it was apparent, by 1990, that Australia's economic and strategic future was closely bound up with the extraordinary economic development happening in East Asia. This was the place to be.

My initiation into the real intelligence service, however, was just beginning. One of the first things I discovered was that the knowledge management of the intelligence system was unimpressive, to say the least. Shortly after my induction to DIO I was shown the secure vault in Asia Section, where all the classified documents were kept, and was dismayed to discover that it was an absolute shambles. These precious 'secrets' that all the vetting was about were stored in such a mess as to be all but useless as a resource for learning or analysis. There were jumbled heaps of disordered and neglected papers and reports on the lower shelves; an absence of any coherent indexing system for the files; and, in such files as there were, I found a mind-boggling accumulation of ephemera, bearing no relation to any identifiable analytic tasks. I spent many evenings over my first six months in the job working in the vault and, at my own initiative, imposing order on chaos. I introduced what was supposed to be already in use: a bibliographic indexing system known as the Defence Intelligence Thesaurus.

Some time after I had begun this little labour of Hercules, I was given the task of writing an analysis of China's territorial claims in the South China Sea, on the grounds that the DIO did not have a paper on this important topic. As there was nothing on file in the secure vault, I went across to the Menzies Library, at the Australian National University, and quickly discovered the best work in print on the subject. Within a fortnight I had written the report and presented it to my section head, who declared it the best thing he had read on the subject. Because it was a DIO product, it was, of course, classified. Subsequently, as I completed my reordering of the secret files, I found not one but two substantial, classified reports on the same topic, buried in the vault under piles of bureaucratic detritus. They had been completed in the previous few years, then 'filed' and forgotten.

However, it was not simply the filed-and-forgotten secrets that were in disarray; the heads of even senior analysts appeared to suffer from the same problem. Not long after I had arrived in DIO, a draft report on China's international position a year after Tiananmen came across from the country's peak intelligence analysis body, the Office of National Assessments (ONA). It had been written by ONA's senior China analyst, who shall remain anonymous. Three DIO officers—all my seniors—had read the draft without taking issue with it in any way. When it was shown to me, I was stunned by the incredible number of errors of fact and reasoning it contained. I wrote a blistering set of comments on it and took it in to the section head. I asked him whether he had seen the ONA draft. He confirmed that he had, adding that he thought it was basically sound. 'Well', I declared, 'I think it's an absolute crock.' Then I showed him why.

A comical game of bureaucratic politics ensued before the ONA analyst was induced to come across to DIO to discuss our differences of opinion. He rather pompously informed the section head that we at DIO plainly did not know very much about China. For instance, we had challenged his assertion that the United States had ceded hegemony over South-East Asia to China when it withdrew from Indochina, in 1975. 'It might be a nice, romantic view of the Vietnam War,' he responded, 'to say that the United States was defeated by a bunch of local, nationalist revolutionaries, but we all know, in the cold light of day, that it was China the US was fighting, and that it lost.' The section head heard him out, on this and a litany of other points before commenting on how healthy it was for us to meet and discuss our differences. He did not, however, take up the cudgels with him on any of them.

Given leave to do so, I challenged the ONA analyst on many points. The Alice-in-Wonderland conversation went like this:

> 'When you say that the US ceded hegemony over South-East Asia to China in 1975, I take it that by "hegemony" you mean political domination. Over what—the Philippines? Indonesia?'
>
> 'Oh!' he replied. 'What I really meant was continental South-East Asia.'
>
> 'Ah!' I came back. 'Thailand, Malaysia, Singapore?'
>
> 'Well, er, what I actually had in mind was Indochina.'
>
> 'Indochina?' I queried. 'Well, that's not exactly co-extensive with South East Asia, is it? But, correct me if I'm mistaken, it was the Soviet Union, not China, that supplied the North Vietnamese with the weapons to overrun South Vietnam. It was the Soviet-backed Vietnamese who exerted control over Laos and then overthrew China's ally, Pol Pot, and occupied Cambodia for a decade. Where does that leave Chinese hegemony?'
>
> 'Well,' he sniffed, 'I don't see that this affects the substance of my argument.'

Was this the real intelligence service? I wondered. What was even more remarkable was that, after our little exchange, the ONA paper was published and circulated throughout the usual cleared channels of government without a word being altered—including the howler about Chinese hegemony over South-East Asia. I was so thunderstruck that I went to see a friend who was head of intelligence coordination for the Department of Prime Minister and Cabinet (PM&C). Had he seen this ONA report? It appeared that he had, but only in passing. And, I realised, its flaws had been no more apparent to him than to my senior colleagues at DIO, or the senior analysts at ONA who had cleared it for publication.

As I was new to the game, I concluded that one of three things must follow from this disturbing episode. Possibly, ONA reports were in general not taken seriously, so that it mattered little what sweeping claims they made, however ill-founded; or they were taken seriously only when an urgent matter was in hand, which did not include this particular report; or they were routinely taken seriously and shaped the way policy was framed in the Department of Prime Minister and Cabinet (PM&C) and the Department of Foreign Affairs and Trade (DFAT). Each of these inferences was deeply unsettling, and I had no idea which was correct.

Part of the problem was that Asia hands in DIO were almost entirely cut off from the best academic Asia specialists in the country. 'The biggest security threats in this country are not the KGB or the Chinese … they are journalists and academics,' the DIO's chief security officer had warned me when I first arrived. 'You're an academic!', he exclaimed, jabbing a finger at me accusingly. Given that kind of mentality, it was not altogether surprising that, in all too many cases, DIO analysts and managers did not even seem to know who the recognised academics were. Undeterred by the security officer's paranoia, I worked the phone from the start, making contact with as many East Asia scholars as I could.

I spoke first to James Cotton, then working on Korean affairs at the Australian National University's Research School of Pacific and Asian Studies. When I told the section head I was meeting Cotton for lunch, his response was 'Who's he?' When I replied that he was one of the few people in the country who knew much about Korea, I was told, 'Well, be very careful what you tell him.' Needless to say, I didn't think that, at that point in time, I had anything at all that I could tell Cotton. I wanted to learn from him—and fast.

A second thing I discovered within a short time of joining the real intelligence service was that fundamental perceptions and assumptions—prejudices, to put it bluntly—could be as tenacious there as anywhere else. One of my very first assignments was to prepare and deliver a paper for the annual Q Conference—a gathering of intelligence analysts from the around the English-speaking world. The paper was to be on relations between South Korea and the two (then) communist giants: the Soviet Union and China. In the weeks of August and early September 1990 during which I was preparing the paper, the Soviet Union established full diplomatic and economic relations with South Korea. The South Korean president, Roh Tae-woo, was quoted in his country's press as saying that within two years the same could well happen in relations between South Korea and China.

At the Q Conference I advanced the argument that China could indeed establish full diplomatic relations with South Korea by September 1992, and I explained why. Of the 100 or so intelligence officers in the room—from the United States, Canada, Britain, and Australia—there was not one who voiced agreement. The dominant opinion was that because the hardliners in China had won, China and North Korea were inseparable; the diehards on both sides would stick together like lips and teeth. I was rather perplexed by this point of view, given that the South Korean president himself had flagged the possibility, and that the Soviet Union had just set the precedent. As it happens, the establishment of full diplomatic and economic relations between South Korea and China did take place in August 1992—two years, almost to the day, from Roh's statement.

Not only was knowledge management pretty ordinary and critical thinking somewhat under-exercised at DIO (and ONA), but doing anything much about these things was next to impossible for those who, like me, had to do the analysis. A single example will help to illustrate this. Having learned early on through Professor Mark Elvin, at ANU, that Professor David Goodman (then at Murdoch University in Western Australia) had developed a 'who's who in Chinese politics' in the form of an integrated relational database, I made contact with Goodman and arranged to meet him to learn more. What transpired from the meeting bemuses me still.

When I asked Goodman what he had created, he described his computer database in some detail. If you plugged the name of a Chinese political figure into it, it would spit out his entire career profile; if you plugged in the name of a city, you could get a list of all the mayors back to the late 1940s, and so on. It sounded like a marvellous tool. Having completed his description, Goodman said to me, 'But I assume that DIO has something very similar to this already'. Rubbing the side of my nose, I responded, 'Well, let's just say that what you have produced seems to me likely to be of considerable interest to the government.' DIO, in fact, had nothing remotely like his database. So far as I was able to establish, neither did any other government agency in Canberra.

Eager to see if we could acquire access to Goodman's work, I had the temerity to arrange an inter-agency luncheon, to which I invited Geoff Raby (then head of the newly formed East Asia Analytical Unit, in DFAT), as well as China hands from across the intelligence community, the DFAT North Asia Division, Immigration, AUSAID, and Defence. My own section head was among the guests. It quickly became apparent that most of those present did not know each other. Notwithstanding this lack of propinquity, once I had described the Goodman database it was readily agreed that it would be a useful tool on an inter-agency basis. The problem was that no one present could conceive of a way in which the small sum required to purchase access from Goodman's university could be put together on an inter-departmental, collaborative basis.

Being a junior officer, I could not take the running on a matter of this nature, and so I let it go. Five years later, a colleague from elsewhere in the intelligence community approached me, asking about the database. I passed on Goodman's details, but I never heard whether such contact was made. In the meantime I had been promoted, more or less annually, to become head of China analysis for DIO in 1994. Along the way, I discovered another institutional problem in the intelligence service, best illustrated with an anecdote from my time running the China desk.

The problem was in getting the authorisation to meet interesting foreigners and talk seriously with them about international security affairs. This being the secret world, it turned out that the more they knew, and the greater the stake they had in talking to us, the harder it was to get permission from my own side to meet them. The anecdote that I shall relate concerns Taiwan, but similar things occurred in regard to China and even the United States.

Between 1992 and 1994, I twice received invitations to visit Taiwan. The invitations came unofficially, via Professor Mark Elvin at ANU, from Jason Hu (then head of Taiwan's Government Information Office (GIO) and a former graduate student of Elvin at Oxford University, who went on later to become Taiwan's ambassador to the United States and then its foreign minister). I had no success in persuading the powers that be at DIO that there was any merit in allowing an East Asia hand to visit Taiwan, even though Jason made it clear that he would arrange for me to meet anyone I requested—up to and including the president, then Lee Tenghui.

Then, in mid-1994, I received a third invitation—this time from a think tank in Taipei—to attend a conference in Hong Kong co-hosted by the RAND Corporation, and then to visit Taiwan. I faxed my reply stating that my request would almost certainly be rejected on the grounds that the conference was merely 'academic' and that Taiwan was out of bounds. I suggested that the organisers instead invite the director-general of DIO, with a note saying that if he was unable to attend, he could perhaps send his senior China analyst. Next thing, my immediate boss informed me that the director-general wanted to send me to a conference in Hong Kong. The stratagem had worked. I got to Hong Kong—and Beijing and Shanghai and Taipei.

When I did visit Taiwan, though, I went there under strict instructions issued not by DIO, but by the China section in DFAT: I was not to meet any government officials or military personnel, only academics. That a senior intelligence analyst should have this kind of stricture placed upon him by his own government seemed to me to rather defeat the purpose of having intelligence officers in the first place. As it happened, both government officials and military personnel in Taiwan were eager to meet me, and it was only with the greatest effort that I prevailed upon them to conduct such meetings in a manner even minimally consistent with my instructions from Canberra. The minimalism consisted in not meeting government officials (except Jason Hu, at GIO) and not meeting military officers (except Major-General Henry Tsai, at military intelligence headquarters).

I have since been to Taiwan in a private capacity on many occasions, and have been far freer to enquire than if I had remained an intelligence officer. On one such visit, in the company of the ANU's Professor Peter Van Ness, a group of foreign scholars and I met a wide range of people, and shared remarkably frank and open discussions about security affairs. When we came out of one meeting—a round table on missile defence at Academia Sinica—I exclaimed to my colleagues, 'You've no idea what a relief it is not to be a government official!' I think it is rather a pity that an intelligence officer should reach this conclusion—though, of course, I am hardly the first to do so. Nonetheless, it has been my experience that it is far more difficult to use one's intelligence to any effect inside the real intelligence service than outside it.

This experience has led me to write these wide-ranging and uncensored reflections on China, including analyses of the Taiwan question that directly challenge the conventional wisdom and will, quite certainly, nettle the gatekeepers of current policy. Neither my reflections nor my analyses are the product of my work at DIO, and they do not draw upon any classified information. They are the work not of an intelligence agent, but of a free agent using his intelligence. In writing this book, I have drawn upon the work of a great many first-class scholars, some of whom I first met, or whose work I read, when I was in the real intelligence service.

Others were absorbed into my thinking when I lectured on Chinese politics at La Trobe University in 1999, at the invitation of the Levenson Prize-winning China specialist Professor John Fitzgerald. I centred my lectures that year on the life of Hu Yaobang, who joined the Chinese communist movement in 1929 at the age of fourteen, and at the end of his life became a champion of political reform and humanism inside the party—for which he was sacked. The purpose of my own writing is to stimulate free and fresh thinking, and to assist those around the world who, whether they are working inside or outside the secret world, are trying to come to grips with China's past, present, and future.

In the wake of the brutal repression of the student protests across China in June 1989, a national survey conducted by the government's Xinhua news agency found that the mood of university students all over the country was one of terror and an inclination to resistance, but that this mood was smothered in silence. Fear of the Communist Party's secret police induced both the mood and the silence. Some remained defiant and wrote graffiti on campus walls with slogans such as 'China is dead!', 'Where is justice?', and 'The government caused the turmoil!' One of the most striking pieces of graffiti was 'Thunder from the Silent Zone!'[1]

The source of that rather poetic turn of phrase, and this book's title, is an untitled poem from 1934 by Lu Xun (1881–1936), one of the most famous and independent-minded of modern Chinese writers. It is a short poem, written in Shanghai, two years before Lu Xun's death, during the White Terror—Chiang Kaishek's effort to extirpate the Communist Party, which had begun in 1927. The poem was a protest against the suppression of dissent and the failure of the Chinese revolution to uphold the rights of the individual.

While translating poetry is a notoriously difficult thing to do, this poem might be rendered into English as follows:

> *Ten thousand ashen faces stare mutely from the undergrowth. Who will give them a voice; pour out their sorrows to the Earth? My heart aches for the unending tribulation of my land; And in its very silence I hear the rumble of thunder.*[2]

This mood was used by the communists after Lu Xun's death in 1936 to suggest that he was a supporter of the communist revolution. He was not. He was, instead, an admirer of the liberalism of John Stuart Mill, as introduced to the Chinese world by the great translator and man of ideas Yan Fu, in the late nineteenth century. Mao Zedong described Lu as 'a man of unyielding integrity, free from all sycophancy or obsequiousness ... a cultural hero without parallel in our country's history.' For this very reason, he could not have worked with Mao Zedong himself.

Had Lu Xun lived long enough to flee to Yan'an in the late 1930s or the 1940s, he would have found a very anti-liberal spirit at work. Had he survived into the 1950s, he would have been appalled by the communist terror and propaganda, and would quite certainly have been arrested during the Anti-Rightist campaign of 1957. He would have been staggered by the catastrophe of the Great Leap Forward, and would have been lucky to have survived the Cultural Revolution.

It was Lu Xun's spiritual and intellectual heirs who were suppressed by Deng Xiaoping in the 1980s and by his successors in the 1990s and 2000s. Individuals such as Hu Yaobang,[3] Hu Jiwei,[4] Qin Benli,[5] Wei Jingsheng,[6] Fang Lizhi,[7] Liu Binyan,[8] Yan Jiaqi,[9] Ruan Ming,[10] and ten thousand others who have been silenced or suppressed, were the heirs of Lu Xun. That, ultimately, is why his protest poem gives this book its title and its inspiration.

It was as one of the heirs to Lu Xun that Yan Jiaqi, then director of the Institute of Political Science in the Chinese Academy of Social Sciences, gave a speech in 1988 titled 'China Is No Longer A Dragon'. In it he argued that the symbol of the dragon gave China the image of imperial authority and unrestricted power, but that this was 'inappropriate for a nation seeking to be a democracy'. It should be replaced, he urged, by a symbol more consistent with the idea of the rule of law. 'We want to change the concept of the worship of authority represented by "dragon culture" so that governments at all levels, various enterprises and every individual … can make their own decisions under conditions permitted by the "optional norm" in the law.'[11]

This book is dedicated to the idea of the democratic liberation of China and the Chinese people. Lu Xun used the expression 'thunder from the silent zone' to mean 'explosive anger within a repressed society.'[12] However, I am not using it only in Lu Xun's sense. I am certainly concerned with the suppression of human rights in China and, in particular, with the Tiananmen Square brutality of 1989. I have a broader concern, too, with the Communist Party's long-standing suppression of all dissent and potential opposition in China. But I am also referring to 'the silent zone' surrounding the general understanding of China's place in the world, and unexamined assumptions about what is possible both within China and in relations between China and the rest of the world.

Within 'the silent zone', too many people outside China avoid saying things that might cause offence to 'China' (almost always meaning offence to the Chinese Communist Party, which presumes to speak on behalf of the Chinese people), particularly regarding the appalling state of human rights in China, and unreasonable insistence by the powers-that-be in Beijing that Taiwan must accept that it is an inalienable part of the sovereign territory of the People's Republic of China. Both the continuing abuses of human rights and the mounting pressure on Taiwan, as well as the orchestrated campaign against Japan early in 2005, make it clear why this silence is intolerable and, indeed, dangerous for the world at large. It must be broken.

Lu Xun was writing of explosive anger about the suppression of democracy and human rights in the Nationalist China of Chiang Kaishek. He was not alone in doing so, and the democratic dissidents of that time were the forerunners of the far larger numbers who have struggled against the arbitrary rule of the Communist Party since 1949. In the 1930s and 1940s there were many critics of the Nationalist (Guomindang) dictatorship in China. Liberal intellectuals such as Hu Shih, Luo Longji, Sun Fo, and Zhang Junmai argued that the dictatorship had to give way to democracy, and that human rights, beginning with the right to freedom of speech, had to be respected.[13] Their arguments bear a striking resemblance to those advanced against the communist dictatorship ever since the Hundred Flowers campaign of April to June 1957.[14]

In the 1930s, the response by the regime of Chiang Kaishek, when it was not outright repression, was that China needed a period of 'political tutelage' before it would be ready for democracy. This still appears to be the response from authoritarians now, seventy years after Lu Xun wrote his poem. The retort of the proponents of democratisation in the 1930s was that, even if political tutelage was necessary, there was no self-evident reason why the Nationalist Party should have a monopoly on it. Nor should it occur without a constitution that would enshrine and protect human rights, since otherwise the tutelage would be in submitting to an arbitrary dictatorship, not a democratic government.[15]

The demands for democratisation had their roots in the reform movement under the late Qing Dynasty, and in the 1919 May Fourth Movement. They were reinforced from 1929, in opposition to the Nationalist dictatorship imposed by Chiang Kaishek as he sought to unify China by force and crush the communist movement. Those demands, as articulated by Hu Shih and Luo Longji, were not made because of a few abuses of human rights by the Nationalists and certainly not out of covert support for the communist revolution, but because of fundamental principles of political philosophy. It was a fellow liberal, Zhang Xiruo, who wrote to Hu Shih in July 1929, praising him for having the 'rare courage and seriousness' to lecture the government on behalf of 'the silent majority'.[16]

The Nationalists were no more inclined to heed their critics than the Communist Party has been. The staunch anti-communist Chen Qitian warned in 1932 that there were disturbing similarities between the Nationalist dictatorship and the late Qing Dynasty in their resistance to constitutional reform, and that the Nationalists would meet the same fate as the Qing.[17] Chen was proven right. Unfortunately, they met their fate at the hands of Mao Zedong's Communist Party, which then put in place a dictatorship more complete and more ruthless than anything the Qing or the Nationalists had so much as contemplated.

The dictatorship is still in place, despite all the changes that have occurred since the death of Mao Zedong in 1976. Remarkably, it still defends its monopoly of political power on the basis that China is not ready for democracy, or that democracy is not compatible with Chinese culture. Given the Communist Party's history, these are truly extraordinary claims. It is not the Chinese people who require tutelage from the Party, but the party which requires tutelage, at the very least, from the Chinese people. It requires correction by the ballot box, by a free press, by an independent judiciary, and by a citizenry able to defend its rights without being imprisoned, shot, or crushed beneath tanks.

The basic reality from which any reasoned assessment of the Communist Party's dictatorship in China must proceed is that its history is heaped with the corpses of tens of millions of Chinese people. There were the terror campaigns in the early 1950s in which as many as three million people were executed.[18] There was the anti-Rightist campaign of 1957 in which some 300,000 of the nation's intellectual elite were arrested, imprisoned, and subjected to 're-education' for criticising party policies.[19] There was the gigantic famine in 1959–61, directly caused by party policies, in which an estimated 45 to 55 million people died of starvation.[20] And there was the upheaval of the Cultural Revolution, in which the country was reduced to chaos, perhaps two million people were killed, and a whole generation was denied a systematic education.

By what right can any party with such a history remain in power and talk of 'political tutelage'? The party claims not only a monopoly on power, but a monopoly on the 'correct' interpretation of its own history. Yet, had China been a democratic state, it is inconceivable that Mao Zedong could ever have launched the campaigns of terror, mass repression, catastrophic economic policy, and social upheaval that he inflicted on his country. The party's leaders know all this, as did the many party members in the 1980s who called, in vain, for political reform. Yet the party still asserts that, fundamentally, its legitimacy derives from Mao Zedong and the communist seizure of power in 1949. On Mao's 110th birthday, 26 December 2003, Hu Jintao lauded Mao's 'outstanding achievements', while omitting to so much as mention the Great Leap Forward or the Cultural Revolution.[21]

Lu Xun, had he lived in these times instead of under Chiang Kaishek, would without any doubt be a dissident and would be, therefore, either in exile from China or in prison there. At best, he would be under constant surveillance and harassment, as are so many of his kindred spirits and intellectual grandchildren. Likewise, Hu Shih and Chen Qitian. This is the reality concerning which no-one who is free to speak should be silent. Yet many are, chiefly because they seek to do business with a China still dominated by the party and do not wish to incur its displeasure. Such ill-conceived tact does not bode well for the future of democracy in China or of geopolitics as China's power grows. The true interest of the world at large and of those who seek to do business in the Chinese market is in speaking to the party with the voices of Hu Yaobang and Zhao Ziyang, Hu Jiwei and Qin Benli, Wei Jingsheng and Yan Jiaqi; or, in short, in speaking with the voice of Lu Xun to those who still practise tyranny in the name of 'people's democracy.'

Economic growth in China has been explosive since the party began to allow market forces to work, but it is an illusion to believe that this growth has occurred because of party rule. On the contrary, it has occurred to the extent that the party has relaxed its ideological domination of the economic life of the country. There is every reason to demand that its political rule be abolished altogether and replaced by a genuine democratic constitutionalism which would, at long last, give the Chinese people the freedom they have sought for the last century.

A generation of economic growth has produced a country that has the potential to play an immensely constructive role in the world at large, for the first time in its history. The danger is that either the party will finally implode and the country will go through yet another cycle of regime breakdown, economic disorder, and violence; or that, in seeking to justify its monopoly of power, it will veer in chauvinistic directions and drag the country and the region into war over its claim to Taiwan or its inclination to bully Japan. It would be in no-one's interests for either of these scenarios to occur. But if they are to be avoided, political reform in China is vital.

In a number of ways, the future of Taiwan will tell the story of the future of China, which is why it has a disproportionate place in this book. Geopolitical concerns about China centre on the question of whether it will use force in an effort to assert its sovereignty over Taiwan. Economic hopes for China amount to the idea that it will become, over the next generation or two, a gigantic Taiwan—peaceful, prosperous, and fully modern. Political concerns about China centre on the fact that it has failed thus far to achieve the political reform that has occurred in Taiwan. But Taiwan is a clear demonstration of what is possible in moving from dictatorship to democratic constitutionalism in the Chinese world. It set China an economic example a generation ago, and has now set it a political example. It would be a tragedy for the whole Chinese world if Yan Jiaqi's dragon was now able to crush the democratic freedom of the people of Taiwan, instead of being prompted by it to bring such freedom to China as a whole.

What is most likely to bring about political reform in China and restrain it from attempting to impose its will by force on Taiwan? There is no simple answer to this question and no guarantee that either can be achieved. However, both are more likely to be achieved if the case for each is made as lucidly, as forcefully, and as widely as possible. There is too much silence surrounding these issues, which is caused by nothing other than undue deference to the dictatorial regime in power in China. The silence must be broken. Voices that are too seldom heard, that the dictatorship seeks to suppress, need to be listened to. Not angry voices, but voices speaking reason and truth. The thunder is a dull rumble in the background—portending storms if such voices go unheeded.

Part One

The Grand Strategic Perspective

Chapter 1

The Clash of Civilisations and the Chinese Empire

In the military confrontation between the Han and the Hsiung-nu, Sima Qian became a faithful observer of a dramatic escalation that caused widespread misery and threatened to plunge the nascent empire into economic chaos.

—Nicola Di Cosmo, *Ancient China and Its Enemies: The Rise of Nomadic Power in East Asian History.*

No aspect of China's recent resurgence has provoked more commentary than the idea that it could shift the balance of world power in the twenty-first century, and perhaps even challenge the United States for world primacy. Myths and imaginings proliferate in this domain, but there has also been some serious scholarship. It is vital for China-watchers in the next couple of decades to keep a clear sense of perspective in sifting myth from reality. Yet not even senior scholars are always good at doing this: Samuel Huntington is a case in point. His controversial book *The Clash of Civilizations and the Remaking of World Order* (published in late 1996) mixed the plausible with the fanciful, the cogent with the incoherent. A critique of this book is a good starting point for thinking through the geopolitical significance of the rise of China in our time.

'The emergence of new great powers is always highly destabilising', Huntington wrote, 'and if it occurs, China's emergence as a major power will dwarf any comparable phenomena during the last half of the second millennium.'[1] These were dramatic and foreboding words. Yet, for a while in the mid-1990s, they became the 'buzz' in strategic and economic thinking alike. Though Huntington was widely criticised, the kind of thinking he provoked is still common a decade later. China analysts need to critically reflect on what basis there was—if any—for such extraordinary predictions. They certainly stir the geopolitical imagination. Yet there are serious problems with the conceptual underpinnings to Huntington's prognosis: it suffers from internal incoherence, historical confusion, and geopolitical naïveté. There is, of course, much else in *The Clash of Civilizations and the Remaking of World Order* which might be addressed, but it is this central idea of the dramatic reshaping of the geopolitical order that we should tackle head on.

In anticipating the rise of China to truly awesome stature, Huntington was adding his voice to a considerable chorus. Speaking in 1994, Lee Kuan Yew—whom few, I think, would accuse of being prone to light-headedness or bombast—declared:

> The size of China's displacement of the world is such that the world must find a new balance in 30 or 40 years. It's not possible to pretend that this is just another big player. This is the biggest player in the history of man.[2]

Viewed in such terms, the world of the mid-1990s was not the post–Cold War world, but the pre-Sinocentric world. Contrary to the famous proclamation of Frank Fukuyama in 1992, history had not—and has not—come to an end at all. Indeed, just when one might have thought it safe to go back into the water of liberal internationalism, a behemoth was stirring in the deeps, and water was about to be displaced on such a scale as to generate a gigantic tsunami. It seems quite odd to contemplate such prophecies alongside more sober estimates of China's condition and prospects—one thinks, for instance, of Gerald Segal's last essay, 'Does China Matter?'[3], published in 1999—but the continuing rapid growth of China's economy and its increasing willingness to flex its geopolitical muscles demand that we think through some of the more unsettling scenarios.

This is particularly evident in Australia, a country that will be markedly affected if anything resembling the Huntington (or Lee Kuan Yew) prognosis should come about. Indeed, what should be of concern to the United States is the way in which influential Australian voices have begun to openly talk of China coming between the U.S. and Australia. Stuart Harris, former secretary of the Department of Foreign Affairs and Trade, authored a monograph several years ago under the title *Will China Divide Australia and the US?*[4] More recently, a former deputy secretary of defence for strategy and intelligence, Hugh White, went so far as to envisage China defeating the U.S. Pacific Fleet, displacing America in East Asia, and becoming Australia's new great and powerful friend.[5]

Two former Australian prime ministers added their voices to the Huntington chorus following the publication of his book. Malcolm Fraser (prime minister from 1975 to 1983) observed that China's 'economic strength' meant that global power is 'up for grabs'. He declared confidently, 'America is doomed to be passed by China, which will become the world's number one economic power within a foreseeable time frame. It may be in ten years; it probably won't be longer than fifteen.' Bob Hawke (prime minister from 1983 to 1991) commented that China had been the 'dominant power in the world for most of the last 2500 years' and was about to resume this role.

Similar talk has also been heard, at times, from Chinese officials and military officers of the more hawkish kind, especially in the variant that, after 200 years of weakness and humiliation, China is about to put things to order and, in the words of one senior military officer, 'nobody is going to stop us'. By 'nobody', of course, one must assume that he meant the United States. Until a few years ago, however, it would have been all but unthinkable for serious people in Australia to publicly contemplate the possibility that it might defect from the American alliance and move into China's orbit. Such a move would be fraught with the most serious consequences. It would be especially unfortunate should it occur due to a misconception of the nature and foundations of China's resurgence.

How has all this become the subject of discussion, or even a matter for speculation? China was ragged and poverty-stricken after thirty years of Maoist communism. In December 1978 (at the Third Plenum of the Eleventh Central Committee) its political leaders committed themselves to a program of economic and political reform aimed at mending China after the disasters of the Mao years—from the Anti-Rightist Campaign of 1957–58 and the Great Leap Forward, with its catastrophic famine (1959–61), to the Cultural Revolution (1966–76). The individual at the forefront of this program of change was Deng Xiaoping. By putting Maoism behind China, and the destructive Gang of Four behind bars, this tiny, tough, chain-smoking party machine boss opened the way for basic economic reforms that unleashed an astonishing process of growth in China and began to turn it into what looked increasingly like the engine of growth for the whole Asia-Pacific region.

Perceiving this, but clearly not sharing Huntington's apprehensions, Ross Garnaut—one of Australia's leading economists and himself a former Australian ambassador to China (1985–88)—observed after Deng Xiaoping's death:

> the economic reforms he engineered and the huge response to them in China (have) transformed the outlook for the Asia Pacific region and the strategic outlook for the Western Pacific and the Eurasian continent. For Australia, the transformation is immeasurably for the better.[6]

Immeasurably for the better? This judgement stands in stark contrast to Huntington's ominous premonitions. For, if Huntington is even approximately correct in his forecast, the implications for Australia—a thinly populated, continental-sized Sybaris out on the 'exposed' fringes of the 'Greek' world as a new empire rises—are highly unlikely to be beneficial. And this should make Australia the 'canary in the coal mine' as far as the level of threat to the West by a renascent China is concerned.

The very title of Huntington's book, *The Clash of Civilizations and the Remaking of World Order*, made future violent conflict seem inevitable. This was accentuated by his explicit remark that the rise of China will be on a scale that will 'dwarf' any precedent for such phenomena in the past five hundred years, and that such developments 'have always been highly destabilising'. His choice of the 500-year time frame looks very much like an allusion to Paul Kennedy's high-impact book of 1988, *The Rise and Fall of the Great Powers: Economic Change and Military Conflict from 1500 to 2000*.[7] That half-millennium saw several such clashes, in which the ideas and technology of the West consistently triumphed.

Huntington argued that such supremacy was only ever a sort of illusion based on very temporary conditions. Such views, which are now rather fashionable, need to be contested, quite apart from whether or not further clashes lie ahead of us. In particular, it is necessary to critically examine these underlying suppositions: that Western civilisation has simply enjoyed a sort of fortuitous ascendancy, and that it is illusory to believe that its ascendancy has been based on ideas which are universally applicable or prescribable.[8] In the final analysis, the whole debate about a 'clash of civilisations' turns on these principal issues. If China's resurgence is based on principles and capacities that are incommensurable with those of the West, we could be in trouble. If, on the other hand, there is a strong convergence between what the West has achieved and the path on which China has embarked, there will be a quite different future than the 'clash' rhetoric suggests.

As it turns out, Huntington's position is internally incoherent. His account of civilisations—Western civilisation, not least—is flawed. His policy prescriptions are, in turn, both poorly conceived and less than compellingly argued for. The incoherence of his definition of civilisations and their clashes undermines the policy suggestions he makes, and would do so even if it were possible to justify his prediction about the extent of China's rise. Compounding all this is the fact that the prediction itself is open to serious question.

Examined in the perspective of 500 years, the rise of the West—and the belated response of other civilisations to that rise—is overwhelmingly due to the accelerated development of human material civilisation. What has called for explanation is why Western Europe initiated and dominated this process, while the other great centres of civilisation—most notably the Ottoman empire, the Mughal empire in India, and the Ming and Qing empires in China—stagnated by comparison and became geopolitically and economically subordinated first to the Europeans and then the Americans.

As late as 1800, the Chinese economy was still the largest in the world, in aggregate terms,[9] and its population was, by a wide margin, the greatest of any polity in the world. Yet in the nineteenth century it sank into decrepitude compared with the industrialising West. The famous work of Joseph Needham, *Science and Civilization in China*, was prompted by curiosity about this decline. Similarly, as late as the seventeenth century, the Ottoman empire was still seen as a major threat to the security of Western Europe, but in the nineteenth century it also sank into such a position of weakness that it became known as the 'sick man of Europe'.

The perceived decadence of the old civilisations 'all points East' was notably expressed by Alfred Tennyson in 1842, in the early days of the British industrial revolution and in the immediate wake of the First Opium War against China. In his lyric poem Locksley Hall he wrote:

> *Not in vain the distance beacons. Forward, forward, let us range*
> *Let the great world spin forever, down the ringing grooves of change.*
> *Thro' the shadows of the globe we sweep, into the younger day.*
> *Better fifty years of Europe than a cycle of Cathay.*

Tennyson's bold Occidentalism stood only at the late morning, as it were, of the long upward sweep of Western ascendancy. By the noontide of that ascendancy, just before World War I—and even more in its aftermath, when they partitioned the Ottoman empire—the Europeans and their colonists controlled something like an astonishing 75 per cent of the world's land surface, and dominated all its oceans.

Even a few decades of hegemonic wars—climaxing in the devastation of Europe itself by World War II—did not seem to shake this domination, since it was America and Russia (both in important respects European powers) who emerged to take the place of the exhausted Western European powers as hegemons on the world stage. However, by the last decade of the Cold War, the economic rise of Japan and the beginnings of China's economic transformation under Deng Xiaoping gave rise to the idea that a new epoch of Asian resurgence was under way.

It is a commonplace to remark that this change dates back to the Meiji Restoration in Japan. In fact, that earlier impulse disintegrated with Japan's total defeat in the Pacific War. The phenomenon so much in evidence by the early 1980s was much more the product of Japan 'embracing defeat' (to borrow the title of John Dower's 1999 book) and charting a different course within the American-dominated Pacific basin after 1945.[10] This is something which must be emphasised, since comparison of Japan's behaviour from 1868 to 1945 with the anticipated behaviour of China over the next half century or so could be systematically misleading. Japan's remarkable resurgence under the Pax Americana is far more notable than the Meiji Restoration—and may well provide, for compelling reasons, a more appropriate model for what to expect of China in the next few decades than the 'massive displacement of the world' prophesied by Lee Kuan Yew and Samuel Huntington.

As Japan rose further and further in the 1970s and 1980s—to the extent that it replaced the United States as the world's largest creditor nation in the wake of the Plaza Accord,[11] and the United States became the world's largest debtor nation—a number of commentators suggested that Japan was on the verge of displacing the United States as 'number one'. As early as 1973, Herman Kahn, of the Hudson Institute, had hailed the rise of Japan and anticipated its 'successful and peaceful integration into the international system'.[12] His sober-minded forecast has been borne out by events. During the 1980s and early 1990s, however, other observers (perhaps with less robust nerves than Kahn) began to see Japan—and its way of doing business with massive trade surpluses and a putatively hidden agenda—as increasingly threatening. In 1991, George Friedman and Meredith Le Bard (by then editors of the well-known international security affairs website Stratfor) published a book called *The Coming War With Japan*, in which they warned of the dangers of a second Pacific War. They foretold generations of struggle between Japan and the United States for mastery of the Pacific basin, commenting ominously, 'If there is any hope of avoiding a second US–Japanese war, it rests in our leaders becoming frightened.'[13] Of China, they made no mention.

The real significance of the rise of Japan was not that it represented a threat to America, but that it inspired emulation elsewhere in Asia, starting with its own erstwhile colonies in Taiwan and South Korea, and culminating in the China of Deng Xiaoping, Zhao Ziyang, and Zhu Rongji. It is just as significant that, even as these East Asian economies truly 'took off' in the 1970s and 1980s, communist economies everywhere—starting with the Soviet Union—were clearly running into intractable developmental bottlenecks, rooted in their command economies. In China's case, this problem had been seriously compounded in the 1960s by the irrational and uncontrollable tendency of Mao Zedong to try radical politics and anti-intellectual flying leaps in economic development.

As Dali Yang has argued, it was the catastrophe of the Great Leap Forward (and the consequent famine that claimed the lives of 45 to 55 million Chinese peasants), even more than the subsequent catastrophe of the Cultural Revolution, which convinced masses of Chinese—both inside and outside the Communist Party—that Mao's communism could not work, and that both economic and political reform were imperative.[14] The examples of Japan,

South Korea, and Taiwan loomed large in the thinking about what precise reforms could make a difference.

Summarising the measures adopted by China's leadership in the late 1970s, William Overholt (a protégé of Herman Kahn) remarked in 1993 that the core ideas amounted to a common policy-package across East Asia, comprising seven key elements:

1. A reduced military budget;
2. The subordination of political ideology to the imperatives of economic growth;
3. A strategic reliance on the United States to keep the peace;
4. The acceptance of foreign corporations and technologies;
5. An increasingly market-oriented economy;
6. The encouragement of domestic economic competition; and
7. An outward-looking economic and social posture.[15]

This is a rather neat summary of what came to be the reform agenda of Hu Yaobang and Zhao Ziyang. It remained the agenda of premiers Zhu Rongji and Wen Jiabao, though the military budget rose rapidly under these two. And it was, in all its essentials, the brainchild of Deng Xiaoping, who held course against considerable ambivalence within some sections of the Chinese polity. Though its military reforms have occasioned some regional misgivings, China did hold to this broad policy prescription with notable consistency and tenacity for a generation.

Nonetheless, it is this agenda, and not any particular virtues of the Chinese Communist Party or traditional Chinese culture, that has made possible its growth over the past twenty-five years. It is precisely the transformation of both the party's ideas and traditional Chinese culture that has made the recent resurgence of China conceivable at all. This is a point that seems to elude those who, like Huntington, see in China's recent economic revival the resurgence of a traditional civilisation. To grasp this point is, already, to see beyond the more ill-considered kinds of geopolitical rhetoric that tend to cloud conversation about the nature of China and its future direction.

The economic upsurge in China has, indeed, been astonishing. Yet the potential was always there, once the policy settings were put in place to enable the Chinese people to enter the modern, market-driven world. In the early 1970s—before there was any indication that reform and opening would occur at all, much less within a decade—Mark Elvin wrote a path-breaking study, *The Pattern of the Chinese Past*, in which he concluded:

> The technological creativity of the Chinese people has deep historical roots and slumbered

for a while, mostly for practical considerations. As it slowly reawakens, we may expect it to astonish us. Chinese agriculture, however, can only grow fast by using a vast and ever increasing quantity of industrial inputs and can, therefore, never be a leading sector. If industry is to advance rapidly enough to let agriculture, and the economy as a whole, break out once and for all from the old high-level equilibrium trap [Elvin's highly original theory about why China had stagnated for centuries], it almost certainly needs to enter the international market to a far greater extent than hitherto. It is capable of doing this with an effectiveness that will come as a shock, if the decision is taken to do so. The consequence, however, will be a disruption over the control of information and thought which is essential to the survival of the Chinese Communist regime. Whether this latent contradiction is potentially lethal or merely troublesome is, perhaps, the riddle of the longer term future of the country. *Felix qui potuit rerum cognoscere causas*.[16]

The final phrase translates as, 'Fortunate are those who understand the causes of things'.

Given what has transpired in China since 1973, it would have been fortunate indeed had more people read and reflected on these lines in the intervening years. In fact, the contradiction pointed out by Elvin has yet to be fully resolved, and goes to the heart of current debates about political and economic reform in China, as well as its way of dealing with the external world. Yet in the years after 1979 China's economy began to grow at an astonishing pace, in response to the market signals triggered by the reform initiatives of Deng Xiaoping and his colleagues.

Dwight Perkins, at Harvard University, estimated in 1980 that China might grow at an average annual rate of 6 per cent for a decade or so, but claimed that the 10-per-cent growth rates achieved for a time by Japan and South Korea were 'beyond China's reach'. As it happened, its reported annual growth rate hovered around 10 per cent for much of the period from 1981 until 2005. Its real GDP increased from a miserable $106 billion in 1970 to $1.3 trillion in 2003,[17] at which point it was growing at reported rates of 8 per cent to 9 per cent per annum. This is what gave rise, by the mid-1990s, to the Huntington species of projection about China's future wealth and power.

The scale and implications of China's rapid economic growth are the subject of Chapter 3 of this book, so I shall not cover them in detail here. It is enough to remark that, on the basis of the raw economic data, Huntington subscribed to the most alarming and ill-founded sort of estimate as to the rate of China's progress in military modernisation. Ignoring the falsified expectations of the 1980s that Japan was about to become 'number one', he sketched out an image of China as a civilisation with the weight and mass to displace the West on the world scene. The fact that China is geographically and demographically so much larger than Japan seems to contribute considerably to such apprehensions—as if these things, in themselves, lend it great advantage.

Yet when Britain rose to its extraordinary global pinnacle in the eighteenth and nineteenth centuries it was no bigger geographically than it is now, and had a population a fraction of its present sixty million or so. China, conversely, was, even then, as large as it is today and had a population of several hundred millions, none of which made it dynamic or immune to foreign intervention. The sheer size of its population and a number of demographic trends actually pose very serious problems for China in the decades ahead. While its geographic size appears to make it formidable, it is by no means clear that its cumbersome imperial structure and vast population give it net advantages in the twenty-first century.

If anything, the importance to economic and political power and influence of those vital energies that China lacked in the nineteenth century—and which the Communist Party continues to suppress—is greater than ever in this century. Yet it is precisely the Chinese 'civilisation', which sank into torpor in the many centuries between the downfall of the Southern Song and the upheavals of the twentieth century, that Huntington sees as arising to threaten us all in the twenty-first century. He has it exactly wrong. It is the vital energies of modern civilisation, science, and open markets—not China's old, imperial civilisation—that are the engines of its current and prospective resurgence.

It seems probable that Huntington borrowed the very term 'clash of civilisations' from an essay in *The Atlantic Monthly* in 1990 by Bernard Lewis, the distinguished scholar of Middle Eastern affairs. The essay was called 'The Roots of Muslim Rage', and in it Lewis wrote:

> It should now be clear that we are facing a mood and a movement far transcending the level of issues and policies and the governments that pursue them. This is no less than a clash of civilizations—that perhaps irrational but surely historic reaction of an ancient rival against our Judaeo-Christian heritage, our secular present and the world-wide expansion of both.[18]

While my concern here is China, events since 11 September 2001 have done much to put Islam on centre stage for the very reasons Lewis was describing. But the question of Islam and the West was, in any case, important for at least three reasons. First, Huntington himself saw the Islamic resurgence and the rise of China as a dual—and even allied—challenge to the West. Second, Islam was, pre-eminently, the civilisation that nearly overwhelmed the West in the European Dark Ages, after the fall of the Roman empire. It was also the great obstacle that the

Europeans needed to negotiate, one way or another, in order to get to India, China, and the fabled spice islands of the East.

Third, the question of what clashes of civilisation are, and how we are conditioned to look at their histories, begins, for the West, with the huge threat that Islam was seen to pose in the decades after the fall of Constantinople (1453) and the Battle of Lepanto (1571). The sense of superiority that the Islamic world enjoyed over Europe in 1500 is easy for Westerners in the twentieth century to forget, but it is very much comparable to the sense of superiority the Chinese felt in regard to the Europeans when the bearded 'barbarians' arrived off Cathay. The comparison is useful to the purpose of understanding what may be at stake in the coming century, should Huntington be correct in his prophecy. There is a fourth reason, but I shall come to that presently.

Writing of the Islamic world of the Arabic caliphs in the centuries before it was devastated by the Mongol conquests, Lewis commented:

> While Europe was caught between Islam in the south, the steppe in the east, the ocean in the west and the frozen wastes in the north, the world of Islam was in contact ... with the rich and ancient civilizations of India and China. From the one they imported positional, decimal notation of numbers; from the other paper, with immense effect, both on their sciences and on their humanities, as well as on government and business. The Islamic world enjoyed a rich and diverse culture, vast lands and resources and a complex and flourishing economy. It also had a sophisticated and law-abiding society, in such contrast to Europe that, as late as Ottoman times, European travellers marvelled at the city of Istanbul, where gentlemen and even soldiers walked without swords.
>
> The Islamic oecumene was one society ... united by one language and the culture which it expressed. In the Arabic language, the Islamic world possessed a medium of communication without equal in pre-modern Christendom—a language of government and commerce, science and philosophy, religion and law, with a rich and diverse literature that, in scope, variety and sophistication was as unparalleled as it was unprecedented. The ossified Greek, debased Latin and primitive vernaculars of Europe in the early medieval centuries could offer nothing even remotely comparable ... Compared with Islam, Christendom was, indeed, poor, small, backward and monochromatic ...[19]

This still sounds startling to many Western ears in the early twenty-first century. But much the same might be said of Tang and Song China, by comparison with Europe between the seventh and thirteenth centuries. Indeed, Marco Polo remarked of Yuan China—even as it had been reduced from its Song apogee by the depredations of the Mongols—that it was wondrous, opulent, and sophisticated beyond the imaginings of his thirteenth-century Italian contemporaries. 'All the world's great potentates put together have not such riches as belong to the Great Khan alone,' he wrote.[20] Jonathan Spence reminds us, however, that Marco Polo's account of China was 'a combination of verifiable fact, random information posing as statistics, exaggeration, make-believe, gullible acceptance of unsubstantiated stories and a certain amount of outright fabrication ...'[21] So much so, that Spence was prompted to ask, 'Was Polo there at all? And was he writing about China or about something else?'[22]

Nonetheless, well before Polo's time, under the Tang and Song dynasties of the eighth to eleventh centuries CE, China had attained a level of material development that altogether surpassed that of Europe at the time. Indeed, by common agreement, China and Islam alike had attained a level of cultural development by the end of the first millennium that Western Europe conspicuously lacked. Or, rather, *inconspicuously* lacked, because the Islamic world paid Europe scant attention, and the Chinese world was, more or less, oblivious to it entirely.

Writing in the early 1550s from the court of Sultan Suleiman the Magnificent (to which he was the ambassador of the Holy Roman Empire), Ogier Ghiselin de Busbecq commented to his master, Emperor Charles V, that the Ottoman empire would surely conquer Christendom, since the latter—being divided, irresolute, and debauched—would be incapable of withstanding the disciplined might of the Turks. Istanbul was detained only by the need to deal with Persia, he averred, and then it would turn its attentions to Europe, drawing upon the resources of the whole of the Middle East.[23]

Yet, even as he wrote, the geographers and strategists in the Ottoman court were becoming concerned by reports of European conquests in the New World, their penetration of the Indian Ocean, and their advances in navigational technologies and naval artillery. They were urging the Sultan to construct a canal through the Suez isthmus, in order to concentrate naval and land forces in the Red Sea and so protect Aden and the Yemen from Portuguese, Spanish, and Dutch encroachments. This was almost exactly three hundred years before the Suez Canal Company went to work at Port Said.

In the century prior to the 'Age of Discovery'—that is, the fifteenth century—the Chinese Muslim admiral Zheng He (1371–1435) conducted a series of remarkable naval expeditions from China through the 'Spice Islands' and the Indian Ocean, as far as the Persian Gulf, the Red Sea, and the eastern coast of Africa.[24] With large fleets of ocean-going white ships displacing up to 1500 tons—making them an astonishing five times the size of the vessels used by da Gama or Columbus in their historic voyages—he made seven voyages and entered into Arabic and Persian folklore as 'Sinbad the Sailor', and so we inherited what was long regarded as an apocryphal legend, like that of Aladdin and his Wonderful Lamp. But, unlike Aladdin, he was an historical figure.

His voyages were ended by the Ming emperor Zhengtong, in order to concentrate the resources of an inward-looking realm on defence against the Mongols of Esen Khan to the north.[25]

Islam was certainly outflanked by the West in the sixteenth century, but it was also trumped by the vast acquisition of wealth by the West in the Americas; by the rise of systematic capitalism and technological inventiveness in the West; and, more subtly, by the rise of mercantilism in the West which, as Bernard Lewis has observed:

> helped European states and companies to achieve a level of commercial organization and concentration unknown in the Islamic world. The extraterritorial immunities bestowed on them—as an act of condescension—by Muslim rulers, made it easier for them to exploit and, in time, to dominate the open markets of the Islamic world.[26]

And this, of course, is the fourth reason why the parallel between China (or East Asia more broadly) and the Islamic antecedent is useful. During the decade before Huntington wrote his book, the issue of mercantilism and open markets, 'bestowed ... as an act of condescension' by the United States after World War II, was precisely the issue that was seen to be at stake in the debate over the strengths of the 'East Asian model' from the early 1980s on.

The Asian financial meltdown of 1997–98 and the long stagnation of the Japanese economy in the 1990s, coupled with the revitalisation of the American economy, put a major question mark against the 'East Asian model'. But its proponents have turned as nimbly from Japan as 'number one' to China as 'number one'—rather as the global Left has turned from Marxism to all manner of other anti-Western causes, even Islamism, since the collapse of the communist cause. In the case of the Europeans in the Islamic realm four or five centuries ago, however, the mercantilist boot was on the other foot.

In the sixteenth century, at the very time the Europeans were outflanking Islam and conquering the Americas, the Ming emperors in China were labouring to complete the Great Wall of China in an effort to shut out the Mongols. They apprehended no danger to their realm from the sea. And why should they have? After all, throughout its long history China had only ever been threatened from the north; never had it been assailed by a maritime power. Indeed, it had no reason to imagine, in the fifteenth century, that maritime powers of a kind that might conceivably threaten its sovereignty even existed.

The Great Wall, completed by the Ming emperors, is still widely believed to have been constructed by the first great emperor, Qin Shih Huangdi, in the third century BCE. It is also believed to be visible from the moon. In fact, the Great Wall was not completed as a continuous defensive work until the seventeenth century, is not visible from the moon at all, and was no sooner completed than it was opened to the Manchus by Chinese generals rebelling against a corrupt imperial court. As Arthur Waldron has pointed out, the irony deepens when we consider that the Great Wall has been turned into a sort of icon of China's enduring civilisation—not least by the Communist Party itself, during Deng Xiaoping's reform and opening era. It would be better seen as a mournful symbol of the futility and failure of Ming introversion.[27]

Such reflections were the theme of the famous and trenchant Chinese television series *River Elegy*, screened in China in 1988 which, in Merle Goldman's words:

> condemned China's traditional civilization, represented by the Yellow River, the Great Wall, the dragon, and other symbols, as hindering the nation's modernization. Visually, the series conveyed the sense that the once flowing Yellow River civilization had dried up because of China's emphasis since the seventeenth century on stability, isolation and conservatism. With vivid cinematography, it compared China's civilization with the extinct cultures of the Middle East, South America and Africa, warning that if China did not open itself to the outside world, symbolized by the blue ocean leading to the West, it too might become extinct ...[28]

In other words, the sort of civilisational conservatism and defensive unity advocated by Huntington for the West were just what led China into stagnation centuries ago, and which continue to bedevil it, because of the Communist Party's obsession with maintaining a monopoly on political power and ideological authority.

Instead of such conservatism and uniformity, what is needed is a certain amount of disunity and dissonance of the sort that, in market economies, is called competition. The Ottoman, the Ming, and the Qing empires suppressed such dissonance to the best of their ability until it was too late for them to compete or adapt. The Europeans, conversely, were animated by a fierce spirit of competition, and this was the source of their vitality—though, as the terrible wars of both the seventeenth and twentieth centuries showed, it brought with it the risk of mutual destruction.

Huntington's prescription for what he went so far as to call the 'survival of the West' consists in a call for circling the wagons:

> The survival of the West depends on Americans reaffirming their Western identity and Westerners accepting their civilization as unique, not universal, and uniting to renew and preserve it against challenges from non-Western societies.[29]

Now, this begs some very basic questions. First of all, it was rather dramatic to write of the

West's 'survival' being in the balance when, by Huntington's own account, 'The West is and will remain for years to come the most powerful civilisation.'[30] Second, he asserted that the West must, at once, recover a sense of its uniqueness and give up its universalist aspirations. Yet he also claimed that Western Christianity is, 'historically the single most important source of Western civilisation'[31]; and, as Bernard Lewis has pointed out:

> The idea that there is a single truth for all mankind and that it is the duty of those who possess it to share it with others begins with the advent of Christianity ...[32]

Huntington was trying to have it both ways. Would he have had us reaffirm the uniqueness of our strife-torn heritage on a Catholic basis without universalist theological claims; on a Protestant basis without universalist evangelical aspirations; or on an Enlightenment one without universalist natural law and critical reason? If any one of these, he was founding his whole argument on a contradiction in terms. If none of them, what Western civilisation could he have been talking about?

Of course, Huntington's real problem—or rather ours, he would want to suggest—was that what the Chinese did not do in the sixteenth century they are beginning to do in the twenty-first: looking outward and actively engaging with the world. And this brings us back to the prospect of confronting his behemoth: a China disposing of a wealth and weight that might enable it at last to overpower the West. In his own words: 'By 2020, the age of Western dominance will be over.'[33] If by this he meant that Western political leaders will not, by 2019, be able to decide the fate of the world as Woodrow Wilson, David Lloyd George, and Georges Clemenceau did at the Versailles Conference in 1919, he was clearly right. This is especially, and rightly, so in regard to the treatment of China at Versailles, compared with the way it is already treated—never mind how things may stand in a decade or two. What threat need this represent to the West, though? Much depends on just how emphatic one anticipates the end of Western dominance to be.

Huntington was not very helpful on this point. He declared, on the one hand, that, 'The West is overwhelmingly dominant now and will remain number one in terms of power and influence well into the twenty-first century.'[34] On the other hand, 'by the middle of the twenty-first century, if not before, the distribution of economic product and manufacturing output among leading civilisations is likely to resemble that of 1800. The two hundred year "Western blip" on the world economy will be over.'[35] It is not clear that these two statements are reconcilable. In 1800, the United States was an economically marginal state of several million citizens. By 2050 it is likely to be a gigantic economic powerhouse with up to 500 million people. The idea that China's economy will overshadow it in the manner that it did, in bulk if not in mercantile dynamism in 1800, is fatuous.

Since Huntington was, and is, by no means alone in imagining that China is looming up as a twenty-first-century colossus, it's important to ponder the sort of 'displacement of the world', in Lee's phrase, that this scenario would entail. Consider that, in the century between the end of the Napoleonic Wars in Europe (1815) and the Versailles Conference (1919), some 55 million people emigrated from Europe, out of a total population in 1815 of approximately 150 million, and in 1919 around 400 million. They emigrated overwhelmingly to the Americas, but some also went to Australasia and Africa. The ability to emigrate and colonise these lands was a huge source of political and social relief and economic expansion for the European peoples generally—but especially the British, who got the lion's share of the available territory.

As it happens, the number of 'overseas Chinese' (including the 23 million in Taiwan) is currently just under 55 million (being reduced by some six million with the return of Hong Kong to China, in 1997). Suppose, however, that between now and, say, 2100, the same proportion of Asia's (not just China's) population emigrated as they did from Europe's much smaller population pool in the nineteenth century. Very roughly, this would mean an outpouring of about 500 million people. Where would they go, in a world without vast territories vulnerable to conquest and settlement?

What of military power in the perspective of Huntington's half millennium? If we allow our imaginations to run along the lines he sketched out, it is conceivable that China will, in the first quarter—or, more realistically, the second quarter—of the present century acquire state-of-the-art military power on a scale that it has not had, in relative terms, since the far-off days of the Song Dynasty. Might it not, well within this time frame, become too powerful for the United States to directly challenge, without serious risk of a global conflagration? There seem to be grounds for believing that this is the grand strategic aim of China's more ambitious military planners and political leaders.

How far off are the days when Chinese naval flotillas of impressive size pass the Malacca Strait on their way to the Straits of Hormuz? There were unconfirmed reports in the early to mid-1990s of China building naval tracking stations and a naval base on the Andaman Sea, in the Bay of Bengal, and on the coast of Burma. Already a decade ago the grand vision of Admiral Liu Huaqing of the Chinese Central Military Commission was that, over the next half century, China would build up its blue water naval power, to the point where it would be the dominant power in the Pacific, as far east as what was designated 'the second island chain'.

The second island chain is a line which runs east of Japan, Guam, and the eastern coast of Australia. Liu Huaqing's vision was one of sharing naval primacy with the United States in the Pacific Ocean by 2050—some thirty years further out than Huntington's watershed date of 2019. No other power has even seriously aspired to this since the Battle of Midway, not even the Soviet Union at the height of its power. Nor does Japan appear willing to accept even the beginnings of China's ambition to dominate the East China Sea. Here again, unfortunately, Huntington let us down completely. He failed to so much as sketch out how such a vision might unfold in the decades out to 2050, even though he claimed to believe that, in those very years, China's rise would 'dwarf' both the rise of the United States and the expansion of Japan in the first half of the twentieth century.

Despite the fact that he failed to develop a halfway serious or systematic scenario for the rise of Chinese economic and military power, Huntington nonetheless declared that the United States 'cannot tolerate a powerful adversary in East Asia', and is already engaged in an effort to 'divide China territorially, subvert it politically, contain it strategically and frustrate it economically'.[36] These were remarkable claims to make during the early Clinton years (and highly likely to feed Chinese paranoia), but they are rather difficult to sustain. A good case could be made, to the contrary, that the United States has been trying with great patience and circumspection for many years to draw China into the world beyond its borders, and to engage it in trade and economic agreements.

In any case, it is not the United States but China which, by Huntington's own account, is the problematic power in the equation, since every earlier great modern power, he says:

> has engaged in outward expansion, assertion and imperialism coincidental with or immediately following the years in which it went through rapid industrialization and economic growth. No reason exists to think that the acquisition of economic and military power will not have comparable effects in China.[37]

Really? Is this, then, a matter of fate or of geopolitics? And where, precisely, did he anticipate China's outward expansion taking place? Unfortunately, he again stopped short at just the point where one would expect a serious scenario to be put forward. China, he said, will probably not engage in very much territorial acquisition beyond the South China Sea and perhaps Mongolia.

This hardly seems comparable with the imperialism even of sixteenth-century Portugal, to say nothing of more substantial powers over the second half of the second millennium. Yet he went on to assert that the United States had to either take a firm decision to contain China or resign itself to accepting Chinese hegemony in Asia. The biggest danger ahead of us all, he suggested, was that the United States will fail to make a clear strategic choice in this regard, leading it to 'stumble into a war with China without considering carefully whether it is in its national interest and without being prepared to wage such a war effectively'.[38]

Characteristically, he made no attempt to outline what waging such a war 'effectively' might entail, should it occur at any point in the next few decades. What he did, instead, was conclude with a scenario for a war of China against the West, set in 2010, which ends with NATO and Russian combined forces assembling in Siberia, and undertaking what he, astonishingly, described as a 'final' offensive across Manchuria and through the Great Wall to Beijing.[39] His future-war scenario would have been more intriguing had it consisted of a limited war, in which the United States was defeated by China in Asian waters (much as Russia was defeated by Japan in 1905), or else a major war which went disastrously wrong for the West, precipitating a drastic mutation in the balance of global power. The first is at least conceivable. The second remains hard to imagine for some considerable time yet.

What Huntington gave us, instead, was little more than a thinly veiled reprise of the Western expedition of 1900 to put down the Boxer Rebellion. This is neither interesting nor plausible. As it happens, it is highly likely that, well beyond 2010, 'raw' American military power will remain overwhelmingly greater than China's. It is also likely that any conflict between the two powers for the foreseeable future would be an offshore affair, in which US naval and air power and the US nuclear arsenal would present insuperable obstacles to China acting much beyond its own coastlands. Inserting American ground forces into China, on the other hand, would be inconceivable in any but the most apocalyptic of scenarios, and altogether unnecessary for the purposes of checking Chinese aggression, should it eventuate.

It is conceivable that China might score a tactical victory of considerable importance over an irresolute United States—such as the capitulation of Taiwan should the US back away from defending or resupplying it—but something far more dramatic than this would be required to justify Huntington's forecast for the rise of China. In fact, there are constraints on the growth of Chinese power, independent of any notional American effort to contain it, that should lead us to more sober estimates of how big this 'biggest player' will become. These constraints are such that China's continued growth will be caught between the imperative of unity (for the sake of stability and market coherence) and the pressures of fragmentation and evolution (for the sake of flexibility and vitality).

It was Deng Xiaoping himself who, during a visit to Singapore in the early 1980s, was overheard to remark, 'Ah! If only I had just Shanghai!' The very uniformity of language and ideology that are entailed in an empire hamper the capacity of its subjects to manoeuvre, learn, and reinvent themselves. Even more decisive, however, is the consideration that China, so long turned in on itself, has finally turned outward into a world which has changed radically from the one in which earlier imperial powers carved out their spheres of hegemony.

In such a world, China is almost certainly at its maximum feasible territorial extent, and would find no cost-efficient rationale for even attempting significant further expansion. Indeed, China could disintegrate or disaggregate quite as readily as it may exert imperial sway over Asia. Even if it does not do so, the conditions of its continued economic growth are more likely to make it a cosmopolitan and commercial civilisation than an imperialist one—particularly if its civilisational influence gains a new lease on life in central, north, and southeast Asia, in the manner of the great Tang dynasty of the eighth and ninth centuries CE.

All this will be especially evident, one way or another, in China's impact on Australia—America's chief ally in Asia and the only truly Western state in China's 'natural' sphere of influence. If we conceive of late-twentieth-century 'Western civilisation' by drawing an analogy with the Grecian world of the third century BCE, Australia may be likened to Sicily. Already settled by the Greeks for centuries, the great Mediterranean island became a bone of contention between the contending empires of the Carthaginians and the Romans in the third century BCE and could not avoid being drawn into their huge wars. Like Sicily, Australia is a meeting point between east and west, north and south. It must increasingly and energetically seek its prosperity—and possibly contend for its very survival, if Huntington was even half right—by exploiting the opportunities and thriving on the stimulating dangers that this situation affords.

It was something along these lines that Ross Garnaut surely had in mind when he remarked that China's rise is 'immeasurably' to Australia's benefit. He may have been too sanguine, but plainly he had a very different view of the matter to that of Huntington, who saw Australia's efforts to enmesh itself more fully in Asia as self-defeating. Seeing only a clash of civilisations in the future, he urged Australia to draw in under the shelter of the American mantle and affirm its Western identity, as its last best hope to avoid being swept away in the rising tide. Conversely, there are those who have begun to suggest that Australia should, in fact, pre-emptively acquiesce in Chinese hegemony, well in advance of such hegemony becoming a reality.

The choice thus presented is, however, a false one. Huntington's version of it—a choice between defecting guilelessly and fatefully from the West or huddling under the Western banner as it retreats—is neither as simple nor as craven as he suggests. It is in the changing and expansion of Asia, not in a siege mentality about the West, that the future lies—not for Australia alone, but for the world at large. China is simply part of this picture, not something that transcends it. By Huntington's own account, Asia is a vast geographic region filled with extremely diverse civilisations: Sinic or Confucian, Japanese, Buddhist, Hindu, Muslim, Russian.

There is not, therefore, any incongruity in a Western polity and culture enduring in Australia. In any case, where is the enticement in doing what he counselled us to do: withdraw into a conservative, defensive, culturally diffident bastion of 'Western civilisation' to fend off the strange and the challenging? Through history, this has not been the Western way. It is less than ever so in the early twenty-first century. Ever since the Greeks explored the Mediterranean and planted their colonies on its then wild Western shores, the approach of the Greek natural scientists and sceptical philosophers, and of the West more generally, has been to inquire, contradict, experiment, trade, and negotiate.

A similar spirit arose after the downfall of the Roman empire, giving rise slowly to what Huntington described as Western civilisation—Western Christendom. Through many centuries, the post-Roman Western barbarians learned from the Arabic Muslims, even as they fought them; developed various state forms; invented the politics of popular representation and civil liberties; invented modern capitalism and experimental science; and fought their way free of theological orthodoxy to a civilisation of which one could truly say *e pluribus unum*—out of plurality unity. This stands in significant contrast with the fate of those other civilisations, especially after 1500, which looked inward rather than outward, to the past rather than to the future, and to dogmatic creeds rather than to critical reason. That Huntington should have counselled us to emulate failed civilisations in the twenty-first century was poor counsel indeed, and should on no account be heeded.

Chapter 2

Chinese Grand Strategy and American Hegemony

The structural constraints imposed by competitive international politics will interact with the chaotic domestic processes in both the United States and China to most likely produce an antagonistic interaction between these entities at the core of the global system.

—Michael D. Swaine & Ashley J. Tellis, *Interpreting China's Grand Strategy: Past, Present and Future.*

Does the United States—and, with it, the whole Western world—stand at the end of its era of global dominance, as Samuel Huntington asserted a decade ago? Does it suffer from what Paul Kennedy, even before the end of the Cold War and the beginning of the 'unipolar moment', called 'imperial overstretch'? If so, could China rise to challenge the United States and bring about a dramatic shift in the global balance of power—a 'hegemonic transition'? In the previous chapter, I argued that Huntington's prognosis suffered from numerous internal inconsistencies and his policy prescription was, in any case, not only incoherent but dangerous. But Huntington is far from being the only China specialist or strategic analyst to foresee such large-scale change.

There has been a school of thought for some years now which has held that the United States has unsustainably large commitments around the world and that many of those commitments involve unjustified intervention in the affairs of others. The time has come, they contend, for the U.S. to abjure such interventions and withdraw from its unsustainable commitments. The argument heated up considerably in 2003–2004, following the decision of the United States to invade Iraq and overthrow Saddam Hussein. It will remain important for some considerable time to come.

Kennedy is the doyen of those who have argued for withdrawal from allegedly unsustainable commitments. But he is far from alone, and the more recent literature is, in some respects, even more thoughtful than his 1988 magnum opus. Michael Mann's *Incoherent Empire* (2003) and Niall Ferguson's *Colossus: The Rise and Fall of the American Empire* (2004)[1] are especially impressive among the most recent offerings. But it was Kennedy, alarmed by the massive accumulation of American indebtedness in the 1980s, who set something of a trend when he pointed out that maps of U.S. force deployments around the world had come to 'look extraordinarily similar to the chain of fleet bases and garrisons possessed by that former world power, Great Britain, at the height of its strategic overstretch'.

It was the inability of an overstretched Britain to defend Australia in 1941–42 that led it to turn to the United States, and the withdrawal of Britain from its Asian empire has been the background to Australian strategic thinking for the past half century. Suppose, then, that the U.S. was to gradually withdraw from its Asian bases over the coming half century, beginning (as it has) with Subic Bay and Clark Field in the Philippines and including, over time, South Korea (from which it seems to be at the beginning of a gradual withdrawal), Yokosuka, Okinawa, and Guam. Suppose that all this took place, as Lee Kuan Yew expected even in the early 1990s, under the shadow of the massive rise of Chinese power?

Suppose, further, that the long-term vision of Chinese naval strategists, which I referred to in chapter one, gradually starts coming into being: that by 2050 China will have a blue-water navy sharing primacy in the Pacific with the U.S. and exercising effective control over the Pacific out to the 'second island chain', running from just west of the Aleutians, down through the Marianas, and along the eastern coast of Australia. What would be the implications for the global balance of power, let alone for the United States and for its current set of alliances in the Asia Pacific—with South Korea, Japan, and Australia? Conversely, what would it take to head off such a possibility? After all, if Kennedy and Huntington were anywhere near correct in their forecasts, such a shift in the balance of power in the Pacific Ocean is, indeed, a long-term possibility.

Others argue that not only is the United States overstretched, but it is also unjustified in its interventions and its attempts to extend its economic and political principles around the world. They, too, argue that it is time for the U.S. to start pulling back, if only in order to be able to defend itself against the storm that they see brewing. Chalmers Johnson, head of the Japan Policy Research Institute and emeritus professor at the University of California, San Diego, has added his voice to those of Kennedy and Huntington in calling for the U.S. to withdraw and scale down its commitments. He did this well before September 11 or the war in Iraq, re-emphasising his argument with *The Sorrows of Empire* in 2004.[2]

Johnson built his reputation with work on the social roots of the communist revolution in China and the organisational roots of the Japanese economic 'miracle' since 1945. In *Blowback: The Costs and Consequences of American Empire* (2000), he argued that 'awareness of an impending crisis of empire' needs to be generated 'among American citizens and their leaders' so that the United States can brace itself for a century of 'blowback'—angry retribution—and moderate the consequences of having too long maintained an 'imperial course' after the end of the Cold War.

'Instead of demobilising after the end of the Cold War,' he stated:

> the U.S. imprudently committed itself to maintaining a global empire. This [his book] is an account of the resentments our policies have built up and of the kinds of economic and political retribution that, particularly in Asia, may be their harvest in the twenty-first century.[3]

He believes it is time for a discussion about how the Cold War served to conceal what was, all along, an imperial American project.[4] He asserts that such a discussion should lead the U.S. to get out of South Korea, give up its military bases in Japan, unilaterally cut back its nuclear arsenal to basic deterrence levels, and declare a no-first-use policy. It should also embrace global economic diversity, instead of pressing for globalisation of the Washington Consensus, pay its dues to the United Nations, ratify the treaty banning land mines, and sign and ratify the treaty establishing an international criminal court.[5]

There are a number of different issues here that need to be distinguished if we are to avoid getting into a hopeless muddle about the U.S. and its prospects. First, there is the contention that the Cold War strategic policy of the U.S. was an 'imperial project', rather than a defence of freedom against totalitarianism. Whether or not that is the case, it need not entail the conclusion that that project was 'concealed' by the Cold War and now, having been revealed, should be renounced.[6] There is, secondly, the issue of the arrogance and intrusiveness of the U.S. What Johnson did not allow is that, even if all his specific charges were true, the democratic 'imperial project'—or some version of it—might still be preferable to the alternatives, and decidedly preferable to his prescription of retreat and abnegation.

Third, there is the assertion that the U.S should retreat and disarm, lest the resentments of its allies and enemies blow up in it face in the twenty-first century. But Johnson failed to reflect on the possible dangers of such a policy. As Pericles warned Athenians disposed to such a policy of abnegation in 430 BCE: 'What you hold is, to speak somewhat plainly, a tyranny; to take it, perhaps, was wrong, but to let it go is unsafe. And men of these retiring views, making converts of others, would quickly ruin a state.'[7]

While he and his kind may retort that Athens ended up losing the war, in part because it insisted on retaining its empire, the reality was that it lost because of the specific ways in which it sought to do so. Had it retreated from its empire there is little reason to believe that it would have enhanced its security.

There is, of course, a great deal of scope for debating how best to exercise and defend the primacy that the United States has achieved through its victories over fascism and communism in the twentieth century. In this regard, the concerns of Johnson and others are congruent, to some extent, with the judgment of Thucydides that, after the death of Pericles, the Athenians pursued an increasingly unwise and ultimately self-destructive strategy, contrary to everything he had counseled while he lived. In doing so, they brought about their own defeat and the loss of both their empire and their glory.

The words of the great ancient historian are, perhaps, worth pondering in the present climate:

> For as long as he was at the head of the state during the peace, he pursued a moderate and conservative policy; and in his time its greatness was at its height. When the war broke out here, also, he seems to have rightly gauged the power of his country ... and the correctness of his foresight concerning the war became better known after his death. He told them to wait quietly, to pay attention to their marine, to attempt no new conquests, and to expose the city to no hazards during the war and, doing this, promised them a favourable result. What they did was the very contrary, allowing private ambitions and private interests, in matters apparently quite foreign to the war, to lead them into projects unjust both to themselves and to their allies—projects whose success would only conduce to the honour and advantage of private persons and whose failure entailed certain disaster on the country in the war.[8]

This has a certain hair-raising resonance against the background of controversies over the invasion of Iraq in 2003 and the widespread view, both in America itself and around the world, that American foreign policy is to too great an extent shaped by private interests rather than the public interest or the greater good—a view which, on both the Left and the Right, already held considerable sway in the 1910s in regard to Woodrow Wilson's decision to take the United States into World War I.[9]

The most fundamental requirement of responsible analysis is to think through the consequences of one's policy proposals. In alleging that American leaders since the end of the Cold War have not done this adequately, Johnson may have many a telling debating point. The problem with his own prescription is that he then fails to think through at all adequately what its consequences would very likely be. This is the third objection to his line of argument: that he fails to differentiate between the nature and implications of his various policy proposals.

For example, it would surely be possible for the U.S. to pay its dues to the United Nations (assuming this to be desirable, given the parlous condition of the organisation) without, at the same time, retreating strategically in the manner Johnson demands. Similarly, it is plainly possible for the U.S. to maintain its primacy by various means, adjusting basing and alliance relationships, without retreating to the Western hemisphere as Johnson urges. This is why there has been such a lively debate among both policy practitioners and academic specialists about the nature and exercise of American power. One thinks, for example, of Joseph Nye's *The Paradox of American Power* (2002) or Ivo Daalder and James Lindsay's *America Unbound* (2003).[10]

In the present context, it is Johnson's prescription for strategic policy that merits the most careful reflection. The U.S. should, he wrote in 2000, 'adjust to and support the emergence of China on the world stage.'[11] This is the context in which he urged that his country withdraw from South Korea and Japan as 'staging areas for the projection of power into Asia'. But if, indeed, China is emerging onto the world stage in anything like the form Lee Kuan Yew fondly imagined, the dangers are considerable, and could be exacerbated—not alleviated—by a hasty and self-effacing American retreat. Certainly, such a withdrawal would not guarantee the emergence of China in a benign form. From a regional point of view—whether one sits in Tokyo, Taipei, Hanoi, Manila, Jakarta, or Canberra—prudence might well call for a quite different policy, including proactive measures to ensure that China emerges as a state we can all work with, and not simply as a resurgent power displacing the United States in Asia as if by some natural right.

Kennedy, Huntington, and Johnson are among many people who see the problem of world order largely in terms of American grand strategy. But if the rise of China is our concern, clear-headed examination of its grand strategy is just as important. Our collective capacity to engage in this demanding exercise was considerably enhanced by the publication, in 2000, of two seminal RAND monographs: *Interpreting China's Grand Strategy: Past, Present and Future*, by Michael Swaine and Ashley Tellis, and *Patterns in China's Use of Force: Evidence From History and Doctrinal Writings*, by Mark Burles and Abram Shulsky. Both monographs extend the analysis by Alastair Iain Johnston in his path-breaking book, *Cultural Realism*.[12]

Swaine and Tellis concluded that, while there are severe constraints on China's prospects for successfully challenging the United States, it could still seek to mount such a challenge, because its interests and the flexing of its revitalised muscles will almost inevitably bring it into collision with America's desire to maintain its hegemony. They argue their case with far greater rigour and attention to counter argument than did Johnson. It is their findings, not his, I suggest, that should form the basis for a vigorous discussion of what lies ahead. They warn, sombrely, that:

> If the advocates of the democratic peace are correct, a U.S.-led international order of democratic states of which China is a part might be able to avoid the worst ravages of security competition. Yet … the structural constraints imposed by competitive international politics will intersect with chaotic domestic processes in both the U.S. and China to most likely produce pressures toward a antagonistic interaction between these entities at the core of the global system.[13]

How much more so might this be, given that China is not yet part of a democratic order of states, and is not in any meaningful sense a democratic state itself? Nowhere is the prospect of antagonistic interaction more evident than in the tensions over the status and fate of Taiwan, though Sino–Japanese rivalry has also shown signs of disturbing the peace of East Asia and the Pacific basin. But the struggle over Taiwan's future has all the classic signs of a *casus belli* between an aspiring and an existing hegemonic power. It is for this reason that the issue receives so much attention later in this book.

Swaine and Tellis are neither militarists nor fatalists, but they were acutely aware, at the turn of the century, of the grim lessons of the past three millennia of human history—notably, the countless wars fought by China during that long period of time. They set out trenchantly the reasons for being sceptical of the view that democratisation (if it occurs) and the rise of 'virtual' states will render traditional power competition obsolete. They insisted that they were not counselling the 'containment' of China, any more than they were recommending what they called 'pre-emptive appeasement'. Instead, they urged what they dubbed 'constructive engagement', which would seem to have considerable overlap with Chalmers Johnson's call for adjusting to and supporting China's emergence. However, what they recommended was surely an 'imperial project' in his sense, for they declared that 'the predicates of engagement should focus on eliciting Beijing's recognition that challenging U.S. leadership would be both arduous and costly and, hence, not in China's long term interest'.

Against this background, the appearance, also in 2000, of a slender monograph under the title *America's Asian Alliances* was rather timely. Co-edited by America's Robert Blackwill and Australia's Paul Dibb, it was the work of the Australian American Leadership Dialogue, a remarkable body which was set up in the early 1990s to facilitate deeper acquaintance and direct high-level conversation between Australian and American political leaders, policy makers, and security policy intellectuals. The central thrust of the monograph was that the challenges ahead 'can best be met by strengthening America's alliances with Japan, South Korea and Australia, and by retaining a strong U.S. military presence in the Asian region'. This, of course, would be directly contrary to the prescriptions touted by Johnson, Huntington, and Kennedy. In the years since the book appeared in print, South Korea appears to have drifted somewhat from its closeness to the United States, while Japan and Australia have strengthened their links with it.

The willingness of all three countries to commit troops to Iraq, despite the passionate international controversy about the war which overthrew Saddam Hussein, suggests that there is enduring vitality in the alliances. However, in all three countries, considerable popular opposition to these deployments raises questions about the future deepening of alliance commitments. There are real grounds for concern that the broad Left in all three countries is inclined toward detachment from the American alliance and even towards accepting Chinese primacy in Asia. We need to clearly bear in mind the wider and deeper strategic context of existing alliance commitments, and the popular opposition to them, if the significance of such a drift in public or Leftist sentiment is to be adequately gauged. Above all, this context centres on the extent of the rise of China, or a possible momentous mutation in the shape and nature of the Chinese polity, and the question of whether its aspirations are hegemonic and integrationist.

The Iraq campaign temporarily distracted attention from Sino–American relations, but there is an enduring need to ponder the central concern of the contributors to *America's Asian Alliances*: how to draw China into the new Washington-led system. Philip Zelikow, in his contribution, pointed out that the pre–World War II Washington system, devised in the 1920s to draw Japan into a stable regime in the Pacific, broke down in the 1930s because Japan felt unduly restricted by it and resorted to 'drastic measures to undermine it'. There are many indications that those shaping China's strategic policy are determined to avoid going down the path that led Japan to war with the Anglo–American powers in 1941; but Zelikow's argument was that we need to take all possible measures to reinforce this disposition.

In particular—and this sits uneasily with the Johnsonian abnegation line—Zelikow argued that the U.S. simply cannot afford to respond to security crises of the near future in the erratic way it did in 1948–50 to the communist revolution in China, and to North Korea's decision, in 1950, to seek to reunify the Korean peninsula by force. According to Zelikow, in 2000, the U.S. already faced 'a greater and more complex set of policy challenges in East Asia than at any time since the end of the Vietnam War'. For this reason, he suggested, the alliance structures needed to be overhauled in anticipation of possible crises, and not allowed to atrophy to the point that they would be incapable of rapid and effective coordination in the event of unforeseen or momentous developments.

Possibly the most interesting chapter in the book was Blackwill's 'An Action Agenda to Strengthen America's Alliances in the Asia Pacific Region'. However, it is notable that Paul Dibb—then at the tail end of his long role as the central figure in Australia's strategic-analysis community—pointedly dissented from many of his co-editor's recommendations, particularly Blackwill's pivotal call for a closely coordinated alliance between the four powers. 'Asia is an increasingly dangerous place', Blackwill warned. 'Big power competition in this huge arena is alive and well.' But Dibb was unconvinced that an explicit quadripartite alliance between America, Japan, South Korea, and Australia would ameliorate such competition. He might well have quoted Alastair Johnston's remark that we all need to find ways to unlearn the dubious maxim 'if you want peace, prepare for war.'[14]

The approach urged by Blackwill and Zelikow, with a view to containing China, became even more urgent as a means of containing anarchic terrorist forces in the wake of September 11 and the wave of Islamist terrorism throughout Europe, the Middle East, and South-East Asia that followed. Those events signified that there was a clear need to rethink and revitalise regional and global security alliances, regardless of what China might eventually do. In the process, it threw open the possibility that China itself might see the benefit of security cooperation and become part of the regional security framework, rather than the chief object of its concerns. This is precisely where the possibility of serious political reform—or regime breakdown—in China becomes pivotal.

Blackwill called for a enhanced role for Japan in Asian security affairs, and urged that Australia significantly increase its defence expenditure, in order to give itself both the military and analytical capacities to 'insert itself systematically into the Washington policy process ... to give frequent counsel, to point out opportunities and to warn of impending problems in various U.S. policy options regarding Asia.' The recommendation that Australia enhance its analytical capacity was only acted on after the Bali bombing and was strongly focused on counter-terrorism, but the level of dissent over the war in Iraq suggests that broader and more robust capacities are required. Indeed, given the importance of the global debate about the nature and uses of American power, greater analytical capacity in regard to the United States itself is clearly in demand. This is particularly true in regard to China.

No-one is any longer in doubt about the significance of China in Australia's future. Moreover, Australia itself is increasingly in the midst of the power shift that is occurring on the global scene, having been for almost its entire history remote from the centres of power and on the margins of the great tides of world affairs. This underscores the vital importance of deeper analytical capacity on China, including serious scenario-planning around possible variations in China's economic and political configuration and disposition. Such analysis must absorb Alastair Johnston's demonstration that Chinese strategic culture, far from being averse to the use of force, has historically been strongly realist.[15]

Thinking through China's possible futures requires deep critical analysis, grounded in first-class scholarship, and the testing of mental models and basic assumptions. It cannot be achieved through superficial extrapolation of barely understood statistical trends, or reactive briefing on moment-to-moment or year-to-year crises. Rethinking China will require strenuous analytical work and substantial cultural adjustment throughout the American alliance. It will demand sustained commitment, and freedom from the pressures commonly exerted by bureaucratic hierarchies, ministers jealous of their prerogatives, and governments defensive about their policies. Quite as much as any refashioning of military and diplomatic relations between America and its allies, this will require a far greater commitment to shared analysis of and dialogue about China in the years ahead.

Chapter 3

Variations on the LAM: plotting China's futures

The paradox of China's technological and economic power is that China must implement structural political reforms, not simply freer markets or greater investment, before it can unlock its potential as a global competitor ... Unfortunately, the burden of a long history of fragmentation and authoritarian rule weighs heavily against China's successfully completing this final modernization.

—George Gilboy (2004)[1]

The foundation stone of all geopolitical estimates regarding the rise of China has been its economic growth since it began doing away with the economic follies of Maoist communism. The reform and opening initiated by Deng Xiaoping and his circle of advisers in 1979 triggered economic rejuvenation at a rate, and on a scale, exceeding the most optimistic expectations. After faltering briefly in the wake of the political crisis of 1989, growth resumed in 1992–93—spurred, once again, by Deng's determination to give economic reform its head. Even his death in 1997 did not bring the process to a halt, chiefly because he had done all he could to ensure that those who succeeded him were committed to carrying it forward.

Consequently, more than twenty years of rapid economic growth have generated the widespread view that China is destined to become the economic superpower of the twenty-first century and, in consequence, a strategic rival to the United States. This view did not really gain currency until the 1990s, but by 2000 it had achieved a status close to unquestioned orthodoxy in much public discourse. Given that even in the early 1990s there were those who still assigned such a role to Japan, the re-evaluation of China's potential has occurred with a rapidity quite as remarkable as the growth of its GDP. This is especially so given that, even by 2004, China's GDP, at $US1.3 trillion, was less than 12 per cent the gross size of America's; and its GDP per capita, at $US1,200, was well under 5 per cent of America's.[2]

The problem with much of the conventional wisdom on the subject is that it is based on little more than linear extrapolations, decades into the future, of raw and unexamined recent growth rates. It assumes benign outcomes across a large number of variables crucial to China's possible futures, without critically examining any of them. As the best research has recently shown, China's unreformed political system has directly obstructed the development of sound market practices and commitment to serious research and development within its domestic economy; has left its rapidly growing export industries overwhelmingly dominated by foreign firms and dependent on foreign capital and technology; and has generated problems of debt and structural dysfunction which could yet result in a serious systemic crisis.[3]

There are, in addition, demographic, social, and environmental problems of an increasingly grave nature which are seldom discounted against the superficially impressive gross growth rates in making judgments about China's future power and cohesion. For the purposes of argument, I shall refer to the simplistic and overawed linear way of thinking involved here as the Linear Ascent Model (LAM).

Among the more egregious instances of LAM forecasting, of course, was Huntington's poorly thought-through and overblown vision of the rise of China, as discussed in Chapter 1. How someone responds to Huntington might be considered almost a litmus test of the degree to which they subscribe to LAM-like thinking about China. It is true that China's impressive geographic size, enormous population, long history, imperial demeanour, and recent posturing as a restless state anxious to be seen as the central power in Asia all add an aura of plausibility to this sort of rhetoric. Yet tough questions need to be asked of those who conjure up extravagant pictures of the future of China. In fact, any one of a number of very different Chinas, and very different international strategic environments, are possible later in this century, perhaps even within a decade, given the underlying dynamics of China's economy and polity in 2005.

My concern, here, is not to assert the falsity of the claim that China will become the 'biggest player in the history of man'; but simply to suggest that we restrain our more lurid imaginings and balance them with the complex realities of China and the world around it. Since, even by Lee's estimate, we would have between 20 and 40 years to come to terms with the rise of China, there does not seem to be any urgent reason for leaping to conclusions. To the contrary, since so much is clearly at stake, we would be well advised to make a thorough appraisal of the LAM and what even its most plausible variations appear to entail. This would equip us to make more judicious assessments of how big and powerful, in both relative and absolute terms, China is likely to become.

It is all too common that people charged with forecasting do so by simply extrapolating the trends they observe in the present, envisaging the future as a repetition of past historical patterns, and not even subjecting those patterns themselves to serious critical examination. To set LAM-think in critical perspective, it is worth pondering the fate of various forecasts of this nature made in the late 1980s about the Soviet Union—because it is all too clear now how linear and lacking in critical insight many were.

For example, writing in a 1986 study, notably, on the *weaknesses* of the Soviet Union, Australian strategic analyst Paul Dibb declared confidently:

> The Soviet Union's internal political system is not considered here, because no fundamental changes are to be expected ... What has been built so painstakingly over the generations, with much sacrifice, ruthlessness and conviction will not be allowed to disintegrate or radically change. The USSR has enormous unused reserves of political and social stability on which to draw and in all probability it will not, in the next decade, face a systemic crisis that endangers its existence.[4]

He was merely part of a chorus who were saying much the same thing at that time. Almost no-one in the Soviet studies fraternity predicted in the mid-1980s that the Soviet Union might collapse within the decade. Yet Dibb's book, one of the more sceptical assessments of Soviet strength, was written and published just three years before the collapse of the Warsaw Pact and five years before the collapse of the Soviet Union itself. How could he have had absolutely no presentiment of impending events?

An even more striking example of lack of foresight is this declaration by Paul Kennedy in 1988:

> ... the blunt fact is that East Germany serves as a strategical barrier for Soviet control over the buffer states of Eastern Europe ... and since the men in the Kremlin still think in terms of imperialist Realpolitik, letting the German Democratic Republic gravitate toward (and into) the Federal Republic would be regarded as a major blow ... what is also clear is that Moscow has a congenital dislike of withdrawing from anywhere.[5]

It is surely remarkable to consider that the very year after this was published the vision of Europe's future offered by Kennedy—an expert on the rise and decline of great powers—was turned upside down. What was Kennedy missing? There is a lesson to be learned here about linear projections, and for them to be applied to LAM-like prognostications about the future of China.

Most people would probably accept a more modest variation of the LAM than those proffered by Huntington or Lee Kuan Yew: a scenario in which China becomes wealthy and powerful enough to shift the balance of power across the Pacific Ocean and so unsettle the state of affairs to which the West has long been accustomed. They would drop the portentous words of those prophets and their explicit references to scale, but keep the basic projection and its central claims about China displacing the long-established balance of economic and military power in the world. There are, in fact, many variations on the LAM which do this. The problem is that, rather than becoming more specific and verifiable than the Huntington or Lee variants such projections tend to become even more vague and simplistic. The question of how rapidly China is likely to continue growing, and to what dimensions, tends to disappear over the horizon of about 2030 on a simple and unbounded curve of astounding economic growth.

The lurch into LAM-think occurred in the early 1990s, when recalculations of the size of China's GDP, using a variety of purchasing-power-parity measures, indicated that it was significantly larger than long-established estimates had allowed. Throughout the 1980s, while it became increasingly clear that China's economic reforms had led to rapid growth in the country's gross output, traditional exchange rate–based estimates of the overall size of the economy still indicated a deeply impoverished and backward country. Deng Xiaoping himself viewed things in this light, declaring more than once that China would need fifty years of peace and stability to 'modernise' its economy. However, a small numbers of close observers noted in 1990 that the accepted way of estimating the size of China's economy did not square with observable evidence of the material standard of living in the country.

The exchange-rate–based method yielded an estimate of China's GDP at around $US370 per capita in 1990, even though it had reportedly been growing at an estimated 10 per cent per annum for a decade. This put China at a miserable one-third of what was then estimated to be North Korea's per capita GDP; yet North Korea's economy was a train wreck and deeply impoverished. Something had to be wrong with the accounting. Evidence in regard to food consumption, access to consumer durables and housing, as well as general standards of health and longevity, led some analysts to recalculate China's GDP. They did so using rough estimates of what China's 'real' GDP would have to be, in order to explain the spot evidence of the standard of living.

Because such recalculations depended on trying to gauge what ordinary Chinese were really spending or consuming, the estimates of GDP per capita varied markedly, from around US$900 to US$2500 or more. The revised figures, of course, entailed vastly different estimates of the size of China's economy, but all of them were much higher than previous estimates. Since everyone agreed that this much larger economy was also growing rapidly, there suddenly appeared on the horizon the image of a Chinese economy of massive proportions. And, from that image—inflated statistically to varying dimensions, in varying proximate time-frames—the idea emerged that China would be the dominant power of the twenty-first century.

It is striking what a little elementary arithmetic can do to alter people's perceptions of reality. Consider that the earlier method of estimating the size of China's economy indicated, as recently as 1990 and despite having doubled in size in a decade, that it was still only about the same size, in terms of gross output, as Australia's economy. Then a basic reality check was done, some rudimentary figures were punched into a few calculators and, *mirabile dictu*, China's economy was found to be as large as Japan's and set to overtake that of the United States itself. In fact, as of 2005, it remains a very long way from overtaking the United States even in terms of gross measures of output, to say nothing of more critical and subtle indicators of strength and dynamism.

Taking various purchasing-power-parity estimates of China's GDP per capita as a starting point, and assuming GDP growth rates of anywhere from 6 per cent to 10 per cent per annum for the indefinite future, variations on the LAM produced extraordinary predictions of the size of the Chinese economy by the end of the 50-year modernising period stipulated by Deng Xiaoping. If, for example, one extrapolated the growth of China's economy at an average of 8 per cent from 1981 simply using the formula for calculating compound interest accumulation, the figures are rather startling. Over the 23 years to 2004, it would mean the economy grew 5.87-fold. Over the fifty years from 1981 to 2031, it would grow 46.9-fold. Over the hundred years to 2081, 2199-fold. At what point does this become a *reductio ad absurdum*?

Has China's economy actually grown six-fold since the reforms began? It is extraordinarily difficult to tell. The statistics available are problematic for several fundamental reasons, not the least being that the material evidence for growth on this scale is largely confined to the more prosperous, urbanised areas of the country. In the countryside there has certainly been growth, but it is not at all clear that it has been on anything like the scale that six-fold growth implies. Moreover, the decline in the production of public goods has been palpable, and the enormous stress placed on the environment must, realistically, be discounted against growth—perhaps by as much as two to three GDP percentage points per annum, according to specialists on China's environmental problems, such as Canada's Vaclav Smil.[6]

Yet even if we allowed that China's economy as a whole—rather than simply the economic well-being of the top 200 million Chinese—had grown six-fold since 1981, the further extrapolations surely belong in the realm of statistical fantasy. Does anyone seriously believe that China's economy will have expanded to almost 50 times its 1981 size by 2030? To imagine the indefinite extension of such growth, for another fifty years beyond 2030, demonstrates just how fatuous the LAM use of linear projections can become. Chimerical projections of this nature conjure up a sort of spectre, which haunts Sino–US relations, feeding misconceptions and triggering ill-conceived prescriptions for how to deal with the rising power of China. We need, therefore, to reckon seriously with how we think statistically about China's future.

The use of the LAM in relation to China involves a number of related assumptions: that China's economy is already very big, and growing rapidly; that this growth rate will be sustained indefinitely; that the serious challenges facing China in pursuit of such growth will be overcome; and that the state will be able to exert sufficient coordinating control over this hypertrophic process to emerge a superpower. As Tom Fingar, then head of China analysis for the US State Department's Bureau of Intelligence and Research, put it in 1996, 'If the assumed conditions ensue—and that is a very big if—China in 2010 would look and behave like a better functioning, more prosperous, militarily stronger and somewhat less repressive version of China in 1996.' And in 2005, that is pretty much what we have. The question is, what happens next?

Over the past nine years, China has continued to grow at a rapid clip, while showing various signs of stress and strain. Some profound problems emerged in the institutional structures under-girding the entire economy—the financial institutions—to the extent that, in 2001, Gordon Chang, a 20-year veteran of business analysis in Shanghai, wrote of the coming 'collapse' of China. By this he appears to have meant, at the very least, a crash which would trigger fundamental political and institutional restructuring, but perhaps after considerable turmoil. Directly contesting LAM-think as lame thinking, Chang argued that the apparently formidable China of the first years of the twenty-first century is 'a paper dragon. Peer beneath the surface and there is a weak China, one that is in long-term decline and even on the verge of collapse.'[7]

Chang's prognosis was seconded in 2002 by Joe Studwell, editor of the *China Economic Quarterly*, in a book greeted by financial analysts of China as an antidote to 'the stuff and nonsense', the 'hype and lashings of snake oil' that have fuelled exaggerated expectations of China's future economic prospects.[8] Studwell observed that, from the mid-1990s, the Chinese economy was facing decelerating rates of even notional growth and that this assessment was, in any case, based on China's official statistics,'which became more opaque the closer analysts looked'. The data simply did not add up, wherever one looked, he argued:

> The most inquisitive observers began to wrestle with an unspeakable prospect: that

the world might have fundamentally misread the market ... There began a slow, and often reluctant, re-examination of the assumptions that had been made about the Chinese market place. It turned out to be the opening of a statistical Pandora's Box.[9]

If the statistics for the past decade or two are a Pandora's box, the foundation for extrapolations into the future, even the relatively near-term future, collapses.

This is especially so if the projections go much beyond 2010—say, out to 2020 or 2040. The broad scale LAMs certainly involve such projections, but seldom are they plotted on graphs with any precision or supporting argumentation. The Australian government's East Asia analytical unit, in the Department of Foreign Affairs and Trade, made an attempt at plotting at least GDP growth as the backbone of the LAM in 1996, just as the Pandora's box was being opened. Entitled *China Embraces the Market: Achievements, Constraints and Opportunities*, it included a table headed 'When Will China's Economy Be Bigger than the USA's?' The outcome was viewed as inevitable. It is just this sort of table that seizes the imagination of the unwary and uncritical, so it is worth analysing more closely.

The table showed three graphs, depicting projections of China's GDP compared with that of the USA, from 1994 to 2038, with the US economy growing at an average of 2.7 per cent per annum, and China's at 6 to 8 per cent. What varied between the three graphs was the starting point for China's GDP per capita: US$1500, US$2000 and US$2500, respectively, each in purchasing-power-parity terms. Starting at US$1500 per capita in 1994, and growing at an average of 6 per cent per annum, China's economy would become larger than that of the US by 2036. But, of course, if started at US$2500 and allowed to grow at 8 per cent, by 2036 it would become almost triple the size of the US economy, with an aggregate output equivalent to $US70 trillion (in 1994 terms).

Now consider a few things that the report's authors did not factor in. First, the starting figures used were purchasing-power-parity estimates, not exchange rate–based ones. Such estimates are anomalous for an economy becoming more and more integrated into the international market and are likely to be revised downward, not upward, as that integration proceeds. Second, no economy has ever grown for more than 15 years at the rates here assumed for China over a 50-year period. Third, the US lifted its growth rate in the late 1990s to around 5 per cent and, with the emerging new wave of technological innovations, may well surge ahead of manufacturing China in the early twenty-first century.[10] Fourth, even as it is, China's export-led economic surge is enormously dependent on foreign capital and technology, and is not developing the institutional strengths to take over from foreign firms in the next decade or two.[11]

There are, also, very real problems of congestion and stress in the Chinese economy that could retard and even derail its growth in the foreseeable future. China's already burdensome and demographically lopsided population seems certain to increase by some hundreds of millions between now and the middle of the twenty-first century. Yet at the same time it is rapidly aging, which will bring challenges that even mature economies are already seeing as serious. Such basic considerations should lead to some caution about the robustness of the LAM. And these are only a few of the more obvious considerations that impinge on the subject the moment one's thought turns from mere arithmetic to the substance of economic history, demography, economic geography, political sociology, and environmental science.

Take economic history, for example. One of the tropes that surfaces in LAM-think is the observation that China had the largest economy in the world in the early modern era, so the anticipated resumption of that status has the character of a more-or-less 'natural' global balance to it. Huntington is one of those who have made this facile observation. By the middle of the twenty-first century, he asserted in 1996, the West's share of global economic product would have shrunk back to the very modest share it had around 1800, and China's would again be the largest. An OECD study completed in 1995 reached the conclusion, in fact, that China's economy remained the largest in the world until the late-nineteenth century. This finding was cited by the Australian government study referred to earlier, as if to buttress its variation on the LAM.

Such raw estimates, however, fail to take account of the nature of the Chinese economy in the late-nineteenth century, the problems it faced, and the reasons for its decline in the twentieth century. The reality is that, after two millennia of imperial rule, the Chinese economy of the late-nineteenth century was not nationally integrated, and bore no structural resemblance to the dynamic Western economies of that time, however large it may have been in gross terms. Even by comparison with Japan it was quite unimpressive in terms of its internal dynamics. A nascent commercial capitalism and the first seedlings of industrial capitalism were in evidence along the coasts of China, but tea still formed the overwhelming bulk of its exports, and such capitalism as did exist depended heavily on the Western enclaves in the treaty ports.[12]

As it turned out, there was no straight line—no royal road, as it were—from the Chinese economy of 1879–80 to a robust economic future. To the contrary, a cluster of what the

Marxists used like to call 'contradictions' skewed its development, starting with the financial and banking collapse of 1883, and leading to decades of upheaval, foreign invasion, and introversion—from which it emerged only in 1979–80. There are profound 'contradictions' at work in the present, too. There are, therefore, profoundly serious reasons for being cautious about projecting straight lines or smooth curves from the present day to ten, twenty, or forty years hence.

As Hao Yenping observed, two decades ago:

> by the 19th century, there were two Chinas: a maritime China, caught up in the economic growth of modern times, and looking beyond her frontiers; and a continental China, agrarian, bureaucratic, conservative accustomed to her local horizons and unaware of the economic advantages of international capitalism. It was this second China that consistently controlled political power.[13]

Even now, we can see that the economic growth of the late-twentieth century has been heavily concentrated in maritime China, and the vast interior hinterland remains very unevenly integrated into either the national economy or the international trading order. Moreover, many of the same instabilities affect contemporary capitalism in China as plagued it in the 1870s and 1880s, not least in regard to banking and financial institutions. The challenges now, though, are of quite a different order of magnitude, and the pressures producing them are volcanic in their intensity. The process initiated by Deng Xiaoping a generation ago has turned into a roller-coaster ride of reforms, as efforts alternate between sustaining momentum and maintaining tolerable equilibrium. It is far from over, and it is not at all certain where it will lead. The LAM is seriously inadequate for dealing with such unpredictability.

Even those who engage in LAM-think generally allow that China faces serious challenges. What is notable, however, is that they tend to prefer extrapolations of dubious growth curves to more serious, multi-dimensional assessments of China's futures. Even a cursory survey of the complexities involved suggests that, if a sustained ascent is to occur at all, it is most unlikely to be linear. Rather, China faces a number of critical problems, and to be able to deal with them will require a change of character which the Communist Party under Jiang Zemin was quite unwilling to countenance. The new leadership, under Hu Jintao and Wen Jiabao, is feeling its way, but has yet to show a capacity to tackle the challenges head-on. The most immediate of these is macro-economic management. The greater challenge of fundamental political reform remains to be negotiated.

It would be irresponsible to rule out the possibility that China will fail to negotiate some critical thresholds in the early decades of the twenty-first century. Instead of being awed by simple statistical extrapolations, we would do better to make more complex calculations about the impediments to China's continued growth and political cohesion, and think seriously about the mutations that both China's polity and economy must undergo if its growth is to be sustained and managed. And, let there be no mistake about this: if it *cannot* sustain rapid growth for a long time to come, it faces very serious political and social problems. Even a serious downturn could have dramatic repercussions.

In place of the LAM, we should think of four models for change in China over the next generation. These might be labelled *mutation*, *maturation*, *metastasis*, and *militarisation*. None is linear and none entails uninterrupted ascent or a Chinese-dominated twenty-first century. Mutation would involve a fundamental reshaping of the polity to cope with internationalisation and a complex economy. Maturation would involve a flattening of the growth curve, but only to a level enabling China to cope with the enormous demands of a population that is unlikely to stabilise short of 1.7 billion by mid century. Metastasis would occur if the multiple and formidable challenges facing the Chinese polity prove overwhelming, and result in a collapse of the undertaking to modernise a unified China—as predicted by Chang and Studwell. The fourth model, Militarisation, would involve a nationalist effort to cope with the stresses of rapid change and uncertainty through a massive increase in military power, much as Germany undertook before 1914 and Japan before 1941.

The mutation model is the one the rest of the world should be seeking to support and encourage. It has been foreshadowed, in part, by the mutation of polities elsewhere in East Asia over the past half century—notably in Japan, South Korea, and Taiwan. It would entail a substantial furthering of the withdrawal from power by the Communist Party and substitution in its place of more democratic norms and, even more crucially, a far more sound and reliable rule of law. That this is possible has already been demonstrated not simply in other parts of East (and South-East) Asia, but in China itself. The leadership of the Communist Party saw and acknowledged, even while Mao Zedong was still alive, that a general move in this direction was necessary. Deng Xiaoping took the first, vitally important steps. There is much further to go, and there are many watchful eyes trained on Hu Jintao, Wen Jiabao, and their colleagues, looking for signs that they will be able to lead such a process—neither resisting it nor blundering in carrying it out.

The maturation model would be relatively benign. It could, however, leave China somewhat stranded, keeping its head above water, but failing to realise the deeper promises of both economic transformation and political democratisation. In many respects, save for the fact that a foreign dominated, export-led economic surge continues for the present, and social problems continue to mount rather than diminish, this is where China appears to be heading under Hu Jintao. It is struggling to find a way up to the next level of transformation, overwhelmingly because the political system obstructs such a development. The leadership show every sign of having responsible intentions and aspirations, but seem unable or unwilling to embark on the measures that would enable their gigantic country to finally and irrevocably reinvent itself and leave behind its history of sclerotic, excessively centralised, and economically stultifying governance. When George Gilboy counsels that we be less alarmed than some are about the rise of a huge, mercantilist China, he is thinking in the terms of the maturation model.

The metastasis model is that implicit in the work of Gordon Chang, Joe Studwell, and others. It is also what lurks in the minds of quite a few neo-authoritarians in China itself, who fear that things could fall apart unless a 'strong' government holds them together. The problem with such neo-authoritarian thinking is that it risks bringing on the very crash it seeks to avert, because it encourages a corrupt and repressive Communist Party to cling to its power rather than provide legitimacy and security to all those who are most energetically trying to bring about institutional change in China. The danger, conversely, in metastasis-model thinking outside China is that it risks curtailing whatever support might otherwise be provided for reform and mutation in China, either because of hostility to the regime or pessimism about the sustainability of growth.

The militarisation model gains in credibility with each annual double-digit increment in China's official defence budget, and with each exercise in *Machtpolitik*, in which it threatens to go to war to retake Taiwan and browbeats Japan or demands of regional states that they acknowledge its 'natural' role as the hegemonic power in Asia. Entrenchment of militarisation and a disastrous drift to war are not inevitable, whether China mutates and takes its economic transformation to new levels, or matures and struggles, or metastasises and explodes in frustration. They could occur, however, with grave consequences for China and the world at large. There are indications that serious policy planners in China are well aware of the disastrous consequences for Germany and Japan when they embarked on a military challenge to the Anglo–American ascendancy in the first half of the twentieth century. Appreciative of the fact that embarking on a similar course this century would bring substantial, possibly self-defeating, difficulties, they are anxious to avoid such an outcome.

Which of these models turns out to be the best guide to how China evolves between now and 2020 is not predetermined, and certainly cannot be determined merely by tracking a few sets of gross statistical measures such as GDP, foreign exchange reserves, exports, or percentages of total world trade. Nor is mere prediction the business those outside China should be in. Rather, they should be—in so far as they are government or corporate strategists and leaders—energetically engaged in scenario planning, and simultaneously hedging against metastasis or militarisation, while seeking by all imaginable means to bring about maturation at worst and, preferably, mutation. One thing is pretty certain, however: those caught 'on the LAM' are likely to be put out of their reckoning.

Part Two

China and Taiwan

Chapter 4

Kinmen and Kinship

The great majority of Chinese who crossed to the Taiwanese frontier before 1875 were 'outlaws' and 'renegades' in the eyes of imperial Beijing and this must be understood as the background for much of contemporary Taiwan's unhappy relationship with the continent ... Taiwan was an open frontier poorly and lightly governed.

—Peng Mingmin, *A Taste of Freedom*

Taiwan stands at the centre of any debate about China's twenty-first-century power and its strategic ambitions. How China behaves towards the prosperous and democratic island state of 23 million people tells us a good deal about how it is likely to exercise its power if that power increases. A rough parallel between the cases of China and Taiwan, on the one hand, and the United States and Cuba, on the other, can help us retain a sense of proportion in this matter, but it does not enable us to view it with complacency or indifference. It is important that the matter be resolved creatively, rather than destructively—and that will not be easy.

The presentation of an 'anti-secession law' to its rubber-stamp legislature in late March 2005 was a sobering reminder, to all those keeping a watchful eye on the Taiwan question, that China's position remains inflexible. The law was designed to inhibit anyone in China from so much as raising the idea of allowing Taiwan formal independence. It imposes on the Chinese government the duty to launch a military attack on Taiwan should it declare independence, or even if it fails to accept unification within a certain time frame. This position leaves China dangerously little room to manoeuvre, and risks bringing matters to the brink of war in the foreseeable future.

Such rigidity makes no sense if China's priority is to engineer a peaceful solution to the stand-off across the Taiwan Strait. As a leading Taiwanese newspaper commented when the law was first formulated in late 2004:

> Taiwan has been willing to talk for a long time. It simply wants to do so without preposterous preconditions which nobody could possibly find acceptable. This leaves

the ball in Beijing's court to soften its stance and allow talks to take place. Actually Beijing needs an internal debate about how best to woo Taiwan. But all the regime understands is pressure. It thinks pressure works and it is about to go some way toward criminalizing the suggestion that pressure should be abandoned. This is a great and dangerous leap backwards.[1]

What remains unclear is whether or not China is genuinely seeking a peaceful solution to the situation—unless by 'peaceful' one means the capitulation of Taiwan without a shot being fired. Conceivably, its determination to regain sovereignty over Taiwan is rooted in a determination 'to be master of the Western Pacific, something it cannot be while it does not control Taiwan.'[2] From this perspective, China in 2005 bears disturbing similarities to Germany and Japan in the early twentieth century. Rather than accommodating China, our efforts should be directed at shifting its priorities and steering it away from a collision course with the United States and Japan.

While unease at the very idea of confronting China is widespread, it would be naïve to turn a blind eye to the implications of China's obdurate behaviour. As one clear-eyed commentator expressed it in late 2004:

> Those with strategic interests in the region, the U.S. and Japan, need to wake up to the fact that China's intention to take over Taiwan is not based on some nonsense about the inalienability of historically Chinese-controlled territory—note that China has made no claim to Outer Mongolia. China wants Taiwan because it wants regional dominance, for which the 'unsinkable aircraft carrier' is the key. There is a lot more at stake here than questions of Taiwanese identity.[3]

There are, of course, plenty of diplomats and businessmen who agree that 'there is a lot more at stake here than questions of Taiwanese identity'—but who, for that very reason, think it prudent to bow to China over Taiwan. This would almost certainly be a grave error. We need to think harder and deeper than superficial expediency might suggest, and we can start by getting the matter in some historical perspective. The little island of Kinmen is as good a place as any from which to begin.

Visiting Kinmen (formerly known as Quemoy) is like visiting Checkpoint Charlie before the Berlin Wall came down, or Panmunjom, up on the militarised border between North and South Korea. It is a tiny island of 150 square kilometres set right inside a major inlet in the Chinese coast, just two kilometres from the old port city of Amoy, which is now the thriving special economic zone of Xiamen. Through the powerful binoculars at the Mashan Hill Broadcasting and Observation Station, on the northernmost tip of the island, you can clearly see the Xiamen skyline and across to the coastal hills of Fujian. Across there, hundreds of

Chinese missiles are targeted at Taiwan. To look through the lenses at Mashan Hill is to see alternate possible futures magnified.

The communists routed Chiang Kaishek's armies on the mainland in 1948-49, but the Nationalist dictator held onto Kinmen. In late October 1949, the communist Tenth Army tried to overrun the island, by sending 10,000 soldiers in fishing boats in the dead of night to the beaches of Houchiang Bay, on Kinmen's north shore. For days the battle raged on the beaches and in the coastal villages of Nanshan, Peishan, and Kuningtou. For once, however, the rampant People's Liberation Army (PLA) was defeated. It found itself unable to re-supply its landing force by air or sea and, as a result, had to watch while it was ground to pieces. All of the attacking force were killed, or wounded and captured.[4]

At the Kuningtou War Museum, just above the beach where the PLA landed, you can now see extraordinary dioramas, huge paintings, and dramatic photographic displays commemorating the victory. The photographs include pictures of Generalissimo and Madame Chiang Kaishek inspecting Nationalist troops on the beaches after the battle had been won. And in the village of Peishan, now peaceful and prosperous, you can still see the battle-scarred remains of an old villa that the PLA commander turned into his command post at the height of the fighting. Outside the museum stands a massive sculpture of a soldier with a fixed bayonet, and a single character inscribed on the plinth: 'loyalty'. Capitulation would have been easy, but the Nationalist troops stood, fought, and won. Their loyalty to an apparently hopeless cause has not been forgotten.

It is easy now, given the long survival and eventual flourishing of the Republic of China on Taiwan, to forget just how hopeless the cause of holding Kinmen against the communists must have seemed in October 1949. Mao Zedong had proclaimed the People's Republic of China from the Gate of Heavenly Peace in Tiananmen Square, Beijing, on 1 October. The United States had virtually written off the Nationalists. U.S. secretary of state Dean Acheson was looking for ways to 'sell' recognition of the communist regime, and the abandonment of Chiang Kaishek, to the American Congress and public. Indeed, as far back as November 1948 U.S. military observers in Nanjing, the Nationalist capital, cabled Washington that 'Communist forces will eventually overwhelm the government wherever it locates itself. This will occur before the government, even with United States assistance, can train, equip and put into the field sufficient forces to stem the tide.'[5]

Yet, against all the odds, the Nationalists stemmed the tide at Kinmen. The communist armies did not choose to halt short of it; they were defeated in their attempt to seize it. Chiang

Kaishek had prepared Taiwan as a place of retreat and refuge in the previous few years. When his governors took over from the Japanese in 1945, they ruled so corruptly and incompetently as to spark an uprising in February 1947. His lieutenants quelled the uprising, massacring many thousands of Taiwanese. As his power crumbled on the mainland, several million Nationalist soldiers and civilian supporters scrambled across the Strait, seeking safety from the communist juggernaut. Directly in its path, and shielded only by the narrowest stretch of coastal water, stood Kinmen. Yet it stood up to the juggernaut and halted it.

The defeat of the communist assault on Kinmen was remarkable enough in the prevailing strategic circumstances of the time. But what seems truly remarkable is that it has, ever since, remained in Nationalist or Taiwanese hands. That Mao's forces did not surge across the Taiwan Strait in 1949–50 is rather more astonishing than the fact that Hitler's forces did not surge across the English Channel, in the summer of 1940. For Britain was a powerful, imperial state defended by the Royal Navy, whereas Taiwan was a largely defenceless island, much of whose population deeply resented the imposition of a corrupt dictatorship from the mainland in the immediately preceding few years. The reason Taiwan stood was simply that the Taiwan Strait is wider and harder to cross than the English Channel, and Mao Zedong had no naval or amphibious forces. Kinmen, on the other hand, is so very close to the Chinese mainland that it is as if Hitler's forces had not, for some reason, been able to seize an island just two kilometres off the coast of Dunkirk, or Brest.

Kinmen's survival needs to be understood in the wider context of Taiwan's own successful consolidation as an anti-communist bastion, since it played a major role in the story. Chiang Kaishek had forfeited American confidence since 1945 and, had the U.S. recognised the communist regime in 1950, he may well have been defeated soon thereafter. The refusal of the U.S. to recognise the communist regime has had geopolitical consequences from the Korean War right down to present-day concerns about a twenty-first century Sino–American trans-Pacific power struggle. Even in 1949, the U.S. joint chiefs of staff and other leading military figures wanted to defend Taiwan against the Chinese communists. Dean Acheson, a far-sighted and level-headed statesman, preferred to let it fall so as to speed rapprochement between China and the West, and he had President Truman's ear.

On 5 January 1950, Truman declared publicly that America 'would neither intervene militarily in the Taiwan Strait nor provide military assistance to combatants in the Chinese Civil War.'[6] Since his government had been providing a great deal of assistance to one side in that civil war until 1949, this was tantamount to saying that the United States was abandoning Chiang Kaishek and the Nationalists to their fate. On 12 January, Acheson himself went further, in a fateful address to the Press Club in San Francisco, in which he outlined America's grand strategy and pointedly excluded Taiwan and South Korea from American protection[7]. What followed should be a sombre lesson for those who believe that the best course of action in the Taiwan Strait now would be for the United States to substitute 'strategic clarity' for its longstanding policy of 'strategic ambiguity', by declaring that it would not intervene in any conflict between China and Taiwan.

Taking Acheson at his word, the Chinese communists began to prepare for an assault across the Taiwan Straits in early 1950, while Kim Il-Sung, in North Korea, launched a massive attack on South Korea on 25 June 1950, in a bid to unify the country under communist rule. It was all very well for the United States to declare neutrality, but no one else was neutral—least of all the Soviet-led communist bloc. During the five years from the end of World War II, the communists had overrun Eastern Europe and the whole of China, and gained a firm grip on the northern half of Korea. Under intense pressure regarding his overall grand strategy, Truman felt compelled to respond. He authorised U.S. forces based in Japan to counter-attack in Korea, and sent the Seventh Fleet into the Taiwan Strait. At this point, in Julius Caesar's famous phrase, the die was cast. Taiwan was, ironically, to be defended not because the United States was committed to keeping it from China, but because North Korea had invaded South Korea, thus suggesting that there was a strategic threat throughout East Asia.

Why did Truman place the Seventh Fleet in the Taiwan Strait in the summer of 1950, when he had clearly stated that he would not intervene in the outcome of the Chinese Civil War and that he wanted to be quit of Chiang Kaishek? Even Douglas MacArthur had said, in March 1949, 'There is no earthly military reason why we should need Formosa (Taiwan) as a base.'[8] And Acheson had asked rhetorically, as late as March 1950, 'Why should we reverse our entire objectives as regards China, in order to fight the Chinese for an island that is not vital?' The conventional wisdom has long been that, when the Korean War broke out, the U.S. simply changed its mind about Taiwan. In late May, MacArthur had already started describing it as 'an unsinkable aircraft carrier and submarine tender' of crucial strategic significance—phrases with an eerie ring to them half a century later. John Foster Dulles, Dean Rusk, and secretary of defence Louis Johnson began a major pro-Taiwan push in April and May 1950. The outbreak of the Korean War, so the story goes, simply convinced Truman and Acheson that this line was correct.

In fact, it was not as simple as that.[9] The Seventh Fleet was not sent in to protect the Republic of China on Taiwan so much as to ensure that Chiang Kaishek would not seize the opportunity afforded by the war in Korea to launch a counter-attack against the communist forces on the mainland and thereby embroil the United States in a war with China. Truman and Acheson still hoped to strike some sort of understanding with Mao Zedong. The Seventh Fleet manoeuvre was a holding operation. Indeed, the White House was irritated by pro-Taiwan lobbying in Washington. George F. Kennan, who shared the irritation, wrote in his diary, 'I hope that some day history will record ... the irresponsible and bigoted interference of the China Lobby and its friends in Congress.'[10] However, despite Truman's and Acheson's efforts, the Korean War did lead the U.S. to become embroiled in a war with China, due largely to the aggressive strategy pursued in North Korea by General MacArthur in late 1950. This situation scotched the White House's plans for rapprochement with China. It also, paradoxically, made Taiwan impossible to abandon and, with it, the Republic of China, which had imposed its rule on Taiwan.

This brings us back to the little island of Kinmen, which remained in Nationalist hands throughout the Korean War, even as the communists conducted a large-scale campaign of terror to consolidate their grip on power in China.[11] Following the 1953 armistice in the Korean War, China turned its attention once more to the question of Taiwan. In 1954, it launched an artillery attack on Kinmen and on Mazu, another little island close to the mainland that the Nationalists had hung onto. The objective of the attack appears to have been to demonstrate to the United States that it had best not formalise any security understanding with the Republic of China on Taiwan, if it wanted to avoid another Sino–American war.

As its military gestures in the mid-1990s were later to do, this move backfired and had precisely the opposite of its intended effect. It triggered closer security ties between the U.S. and Taiwan, in the form of the Mutual Security Treaty of 1955, which was to last for a generation. Chiang Kaishek strengthened the garrisons on Kinmen and Mazu to 110,000 soldiers, while building formidable defences against possible communist amphibious assault. The United States installed nuclear Matador missiles in Taiwan, and began building an airstrip there capable of servicing B-52 nuclear bombers. Taiwan truly had become an 'unsinkable aircraft carrier' in the American 'containment' of China.

Having failed in its initial objective of deterring the United States from developing security ties with the Chinese nationalists on Taiwan, the communists tried again four years later. On 23 August 1958, they launched a massive bombardment of the little islands, which was seen in Washington not only as a reckless provocation but as the prelude to an attempt to seize them, and even to carry the war to Taiwan.[12] Once again, the United States responded by increasing its assistance to Chiang Kaishek. Within a fortnight, it had reinforced the Seventh

Fleet to include an astonishing six aircraft carriers; had expedited the shipment of artillery, aircraft, and Sidewinder air-to-air missiles to Taiwan;[13] and had rehearsed contingency plans for nuclear strikes deep into the Chinese heartland. Indeed, such contingency plans pre-dated the Chinese shelling of the islands.[14] Had these plans been acted upon, they would, according to the estimates of the U.S. joint chiefs of staff, have entailed millions of Chinese civilian casualties.

Contemplating such strikes was, surely, an extraordinary response to the shelling of two small islands. In this respect, the crisis seems comparable to the Cuban missile crisis, just over four years later—except that, unlike the Soviet Union, China had no nuclear weapons. After this experience, China resolved to develop them as rapidly and as independently as possible. However, the episode is even more interesting when we consider recent research indicating that, contrary to the long-held prevalent view, Mao Zedong had no intention of seizing the islands and certainly did not want a war with the United States. Chinese sources show that 'Mao strongly desired tensions with the West in order to mobilize the [Chinese] public', but 'was clearly afraid of American reprisals, even before the initial attacks.' Lin Biao even proposed warning Washington in advance of the shelling, so that no American advisers would be killed, but Mao rejected the idea.[15]

So what was Mao's game plan? According to Thomas Christensen, one of the most perceptive contemporary analysts of Sino–American strategic confrontation, 'Mao was not trying to determine just how much land the United States would allow China to seize, but was probing for the best and safest way to create tensions short of war to further his [domestic] political goals.' Paradoxically, Mao wanted Chiang to hang tough on the islands, since seizure of them by the mainland 'would have only assisted Taiwanese separatism'. Zhou Enlai reportedly told the Soviet military attaché in Beijing on 5 October 1958 that the Chinese communists wanted Chiang Kaishek 'to remain on Quemoy (Kinmen) [and] Matsu (Mazu) ... In this way, when we want to create a period of tension, we can attack Quemoy and Matsu a bit.'[16]

Had the American side been more cool-headed at that time, they might have surmised this instead of preparing apocalyptic and wholly unnecessary plans for nuclear war with China. They might also have reflected, as Christensen points out, that 'even in the best of weather, the PLA lacked landing equipment sophisticated enough to ensure easy breach of the formidable [Nationalist] defences on the offshore islands'. And late August was the height of the typhoon season, making an amphibious assault even less plausible. The possibility that Mao and his communist strategic planners might have wanted to ensure that Chiang held onto the offshore islands is not a thought that appears to have crossed the minds of strategists in Washington. This is well worth pondering in present circumstances, as a striking example of how completely major powers can misread one another's intentions during a crisis.

It was not as if Taiwan's retention of the islands served American interests, however much it may have served the political interests of the Chinese communist regime. In late September 1958, once the crisis had passed, the Americans even urged Chiang Kaishek to pull his forces off the islands. Not surprisingly, he rejected the idea. The Nationalist dictator wanted to retain the islands as a cause of tension to keep the Americans on edge. Paradoxically, the communist dictator also wanted Nationalist troops on the islands, so that he could use tension with the Americans domestically with minimum risk of escalation to actual war, and also as a way to encumber any American move toward a 'two Chinas' policy. Both sides manipulated American uncertainties for their own strategic ends. The entire saga is rich in instructive ironies for those charged with handling the matter in the twenty-first century, under changed circumstances.

The 23 August Bombardment Memorial Hall, by the shore of Lake Tai in the centre of Kinmen, provides no indication that the memorialists understood either the irony of the 1958 events or their implications for the future. There are dioramas showing the trajectories of the shelling from the Fujian shore. There are photographs and shell fragments and even tables indicating variations in intensity of the bombardment. What is notably absent is any documentation to show that Mao had not intended to seize the islands unless the Nationalist forces fled; that he had dangerously underestimated the level at which the United States would respond; and that the United States itself had badly misread the significance of the shelling, in late August and early September 1958. These geopolitical considerations are incomparably more important than the little drama of the bombardment trajectories or the 'defeat' of the communist attack, as depicted by the memorial.

This is an important point because the greatest risk of conflict in the Taiwan Straits in the years ahead is through miscalculation rather than deliberate aggression. The Chinese White Paper on Taiwan of February 2000 trumpeted Chinese determination to recover sovereignty over Taiwan. It fetched a stern response from the United States, to the effect that use of force against Taiwan would bring down 'incalculable consequences' on China.[17] President Bush later reiterated this stance, with his statement that the U.S. would do 'whatever it takes' to defend Taiwan in such an eventuality. So the rhetoric and mindsets of the 1950s were still largely in place, though real intentions remain shifting and uncertain. Five years later, the mind-set implicit in China's declaratory policy appears unchanged, as its anti-secession law indicates. The visits to China in late April and early May 2005 by Taiwanese opposition leaders Lien Chan and James Soong gave some indications that a crisis can be postponed, but the underlying tensions remain serious and are far from being resolved.

Against this background, there are several fundamental lessons to draw from the 1958 crisis. First, we should learn that relatively minor confrontations can be used by political leaders (Mao being only one example) as exercises in stirring up ideological fervour, or justifying particular domestic policies. Therefore, the rhetoric or even military actions involved should not necessarily be taken at face value. Second, we have seen that American threats of force in 1958 were not only excessive in the circumstances but did not have the effect of forcing China to back down, as most people have assumed. The false assumption that coercion worked in 1958 could lead American strategists to believe that it would also work in coercing China to abandon its sovereignty claims over Taiwan.[18]

The third lesson is, I think, the most important. What happened in 1958 over Kinmen and Mazu shows that great powers do not collide simply because it is their tragic destiny.[19] On the contrary, they often blunder into one another in a fog of mutual misperception, driven in considerable measure by the inscrutable complexities of their respective domestic political commitments. Modern wars, in other words, are not inevitable. They are more often than not catastrophes that no one wants, or even expects. It was not the intention of the Truman administration in 1948–1950 to embroil itself in war with China or to defend the Republic of China on Taiwan, yet it found itself doing both. It was not the intention of Mao Zedong in the late 1940s or the late 1950s to embroil himself in a war with the United States. Yet he ended up in a brutal and costly conflict in Korea, in which hundreds of thousands of Chinese soldiers were killed (including one of his own sons), and he very nearly brought on a cataclysmic U.S. nuclear strike against China in 1958.

In these circumstances, Kinmen embodies what we may hope for in the future, just as it embodies the complexities of the past. The garrison has been drastically reduced in the past decade, despite recurrent tensions across the Strait, because the democratic government in Taiwan has not the slightest intention of using the island in the manner that Chiang Kaishek long intended. The Taiwanese government, no longer having any strategic designs on China, is uncertain what to do with Kinmen and Mazu. Its ambivalence might add another uncertainty to the strategic equation. It might be tempted to withdraw from the little islands by 2008, as the United States urged Chiang Kaishek to do in 1958. The problem is that, in present circumstances, this move might be seen as conceding China's claim to the islands and, by implication, to Taiwan itself. Alternatively, the move might be resisted by China because it could be seen as Taiwan distancing itself from geographic contiguity with the mainland.

That geographic contiguity is, in a sense, the umbilical cord which still ties the Republic of China on Taiwan to the larger polity on the mainland. Yet a great deal has changed since the 1950s. To look across the water now from the Mashan Hill Broadcasting and Observation Station is to look less at a strategic moat than at a bridge between provincial communities. Although it is a strategic frontier, trade now crosses it quite freely. Wu Chengtien, the only New Party (pro-unification) member of the Taiwanese legislature since 2001, represents Kinmen. He is a relaxed, articulate, and charming individual who has excellent relations with the mayor of Xiamen. The two of them are politicians whose commitments embody the old saying that 'all politics is local politics'. Together they are doing all they can to ensure that broader geopolitical considerations do not intrude on the mundane reconciliation that has been reached across the water over the past decade or so.[20]

In May 2002, Taiwan's president, Chen Shui-bian, visited Kinmen. The island used be a watchtower of war, he told a small audience at the Shen Tuan Teahouse on nearby Tatan (Boldness) Island,[21] but now it had become "a lighthouse of peace". According to President Chen, this was an even more important historic role than its earlier one: it should become known as the frontline for peace across the Taiwan Straits in the twenty-first century. Its monuments should serve as:

> witnesses to the Cold War, reminding the world, as well as the two sides of the Taiwan Strait, of the importance of seeking peace and avoiding the disastrous roads of both war and cold war … Soon, the mainland will undergo a leadership transition … I would like to invite them to come here to the Shen Tuan Teahouse for a friendly chat over a cup of tea.[22]

The transition was completed in 2004 when Jiang Zemin stepped down from the Central Military Commission and handed clear national leadership to the new president, Hu Jintao. Hu has showed no sign of accepting President Chen's invitation to tea, but the whole Asian and Pacific region has a stake in encouraging their dialogue, in some form. Such encouragement could start by recognising Kinmen as the profound symbol that it is—a watch tower become a lighthouse—and could be extended through a shared understanding of the mutual misperceptions in Sino–American relations which made Kinmen a strategic frontier for decades.

If war should come in the years ahead, Kinmen would be strategically inconsequential, but would very likely be devastated all the same. If, however, peace can be expanded and the sovereignty issue resolved intelligently, the lighthouse may well enjoy a serene future. In such a future, the hundreds of ballistic missiles that China has assembled in Fujian would cease to have meaning or purpose, for amity would prevail across the Strait. The landmines that clutter Kinmen's foreshores could be removed. Above all, the fifty-year-old danger of Sino–American war could be appreciably reduced. This is what everyone should be seeking to ensure. The only question is whether a means to that end can be found which accommodates both the aspirations of the Chinese and the freedom of the people of Taiwan.

What will it take? Symbolically, a cup of tea on Boldness Island would be an extraordinary gesture by the two presidents. It would be especially so for President Hu, because it would mean stepping down from the imperial pedestal in Beijing and coming down to the Taiwan Strait to talk with the president of Taiwan. It need not be a visit to Tatan; it could be elsewhere, but it should consist of demonstrating that he seeks kinship with the Taiwanese and not lordship over them. Hu's domestic political rhetoric in his first years in office about being a man of the people might have encouraged a belief that he was capable of a far-reaching and charismatic gesture of this kind. His actions, however, have belied his rhetoric. He has not eased the pressure on dissent within China at all, and for as long as he declines to do so he cannot realistically expect much progress in relations with Taiwan.

Hu's standing in the world of international politics, and his freedom to lead his country in new directions, may be measured by his capacity to take progressive steps in regard to Taiwan. In this regard, China's anti-secession law looks like a regressive step, even if some of its architects may have seen it as an attempt to maintain what they see as stability in the situation. Kinmen, if not Tatan, because it is like a bridge across the Taiwan Strait, could be the meeting ground on which to proclaim kinship and amity across the Taiwan Strait, and to resolve the sovereignty issue without war. More plausibly, for the present, it could be referred to as a symbolic bridge, even if the leaders of the two polities do not meet there. It could be used as a point of reference in which both Hu and Chen made speeches appealing for the understanding, trust, and friendship of the other side. On such a basis, better bridges might in time be built.

Chapter 5

Conceiving a Paradigm Shift

Since beliefs about opportunities are crucial to human choice, a better understanding of belief formation and belief change is therefore vital to the social sciences.

—Dali Yang, *Calamity and Reform in China*

A paradigm shift is required in order to deal with the Taiwan problem. Paradigms are ways of construing reality rooted in certain fundamental assumptions. A shift occurs when it is found or decided that one or more of those assumptions is at best questionable. Most analysis of the Taiwan problem proceeds from a small number of largely unexamined assumptions. Chief among these is that China will never resile from its claim to sovereignty over Taiwan—but also, and crucially, that it has a right to such sovereignty, and that it would be humiliated or would suffer a loss of prestige should it fail to insist on recovering this sovereignty. If the present impasse is ever to be intelligently resolved without the people of Taiwan being forced to accept a Chinese sovereignty they do not want, these assumptions need rethinking. There seems to be a very widespread assumption that rethinking them is either impossible or pointless, because they are simply the unalterable realities of the case. *That* assumption is false.

To provide a simple demonstration of how easily we can see things back to front, or take our perspective on things completely for granted, consider the geometric phenomenon known as the 'Necker cube'. The Necker cube is the two-dimensional rendering of a transparent cube with a large dot in one corner. The question is, where does the dot sit? Most people looking at the cube for the first time spontaneously see the dot as being in the lower-left rear corner. But the longer they look, challenged as to the certainty of their perception, the more uncertain they become, and the more ambiguous the cube seems. The dot begins to appear as though it could be in the lower-left *front* corner, depending on how you look at the cube. It is, of course, an optical illusion: the 'facts' do not change, but the observer's interpretation shifts—and there is no single, true answer.

This curious phenomenon is one example of how human beings suffer from cognitive blind spots and biases that invisibly shape how we perceive and think about the world. It is not a matter of our being 'stupid', but of the universal hardwiring of our perceptual and cognitive systems. In recent decades, cognitive science has gradually been exploring these peculiar characteristics of the evolved brain and their consequences for human perception and judgment. A central finding of such science is that human beings are prone not only to certain kinds of optical illusion, but to certain kinds of gross error in judgment, due to misperception or to the ways in which they see reality. This occurs, often spectacularly, again and again in world politics, confounding statesmen and whole nations.

While we are all aware of dramatic misjudgments in history, it is more difficult to understand precisely how they occur. They tend to be seen simply as cases of stupidity, or of serious people being ambushed by the treacherous complexities of reality. It's actually more interesting than that. Consider Stalin's failure, in the first half of 1941, to accept that Hitler would invade the Soviet Union in June of that year. In the months before Barbarossa—the gigantic Nazi invasion that began on 22 June 1941—Stalin flatly refused to believe his top generals, Zhukov and Timoshenko, as well as spies in Berlin and Tokyo, when they told him that Hitler was preparing to invade.

He called them all fools, thinking that he was being shrewd. Hitler would never attack the U.S.S.R. before he had settled accounts with the British Empire, he told them; and if they did anything to provoke the Nazi war machine, heads would roll. His view was fixed, even as the Wehrmacht massed along his borders. And even after they launched their staggering blitzkrieg, he remained in denial for hours. He believed the attacks to be the work of a few German generals who were orchestrating a provocation in order to start a war Hitler himself did not want. 'Hitler surely does not know', he told his generals and his politburo in the Kremlin.[1]

This example is not unique. In a splendid re-examination of the fall of France to Hitler's forces in May to June 1940, published in 2000, Ernest May showed a similar fixed idea at work in the Allied high command. They never considered the possibility that the Germans would attack France through the Ardennes. Indeed, they were confident that Hitler would not dare to attack France at all, so powerful were its defences. Excessively confident in their strategic assumptions, they failed to detect the plain evidence of German intelligence, logistics, and deployment preparations for a massive thrust across Luxembourg, through the Ardennes, over the Meuse, and straight to the English Channel. When the German offensive began, the Allied generals refused for four days to accept the reality of what the Germans were doing, and by the time they did reassess it was too late to close the gap the Wehrmacht had opened up in the Allied defences. France was overrun in six weeks.[2]

A third notorious example of complacent assumptions leading to grave strategic error was the failure of the Israeli political and strategic leadership to accept that the Arab powers were about to attack them in the lead-up to the Yom Kippur War. Abraham Rabinovich's account of the war begins with the observation that '[a] military satellite beaming images of the Middle East to Earth late on the afternoon of 5 October 1973 would have confronted analysts with a perplexing picture.' Egypt had amassed 100,000 troops, 1,350 tanks and 2,000 artillery pieces and heavy mortars along the west bank of the Suez Canal. On the other side, the Israelis had only 450 troops and 44 artillery pieces and only 290 tanks in the whole of Sinai. Along the Golan Heights, where there was no canal to protect Israeli positions, 100,000 Syrian troops confronted only small Israeli forces, enjoying an advantage of eight-to-one in tanks, and even more in artillery. Yet the Israeli intelligence and military high command did not raise an alarm. They were convinced the Arabs would not attack. The stage was set for the near catastrophe of the Yom Kippur War.[3]

My concern here, however, is not with France in 1940, the Soviet Union in 1941, or Israel in 1973. It is with the broader cognitive implications of those case studies. Specifically, I am concerned with the combination of unexamined assumptions and over-confidence in generating gross military error, and in disabling defensive strategic planning. This is something that should be reflected on in the specific context of Taiwan. What I am suggesting is that we should re-examine the assumptions which structure the Taiwan question, both in China and around the world. Unless they are brought out into the open and unsparingly examined, there is reason to fear they could trap China itself and the states of the region in a confrontation and even a war which would serve no-one's interests.

I suggest that three fixed ideas govern strategic thinking on the Taiwan question. First, that Taiwan is, as a matter of historical and international legal reality, an inalienable part of China. Second, that China will not under any circumstances accept the independence of Taiwan. Third, that China is a rising strategic competitor of the United States in Eurasia. All three of these ideas need to be re-examined if the matter is to be handled intelligently, justly, and constructively. The key assumption is the first: that Taiwan is an inalienable part of China. The chief grounds for this claim are that it was part of the Qing empire until ceded to Japan in 1895, and that it was handed back by Japan to the Republic of China in 1945, so that the legitimate government of China must be deemed the legitimate government of Taiwan—and the legitimate government of China is the regime in Beijing.

These grounds are endlessly repeated, so that the inference from them comes to seem not only reasonable but, to many people, especially in China itself, compelling. Yet the claims themselves are more tenuous than repetition contrives to make them appear. Taiwan had a Chinese governor for only ten years before it was ceded to Japan in 1895, and was never a significant part of the Qing Empire. It had never been part of the Chinese empire before the Qing, and they were an alien dynasty imposed on China itself from outside its classical borders. When the island was ceded to Japan, albeit as the result of a war, it was ceded 'in perpetuity', giving Japan every bit as good a claim to the island now as the Beijing regime has. Unlike the Qing emperors, who neglected Taiwan completely, even when they sent a governor there in the late-nineteenth century, the Japanese vigorously developed the island during the half century they ruled it. In 1945 it was handed back to the Republic of China, which has never accepted rule from Beijing and still does not do so. Finally, the people of Taiwan resented and resisted the imposition of undemocratic rule from China in the late 1940s and, in the past twenty years, have won back their freedom and their identity.

Yet even if these many considerations were judged to be outweighed by an argument that Taiwan truly was part of the Republic of China from 1945 and that the Republic of China is, in some sense or other, part of China, there is an overarching consideration which needs to be brought into play. It is this: empires and nation states do change both their boundaries and the nature of their sovereignty over time. There is, therefore, no self-evident reason why China, whether or not it was governed by the Communist Party, should insist that it must re-establish formal sovereignty over Taiwan. Such a claim can stand only for as long as Beijing insists on it and demands that everyone else agree. Therefore, it is neither necessary to accept as 'true' the proposition that Taiwan is an inalienable part of China, nor sufficient to argue against it. What is needed, rather, is to work from inside the mind-set of those (chiefly in China) who hold to this proposition, and see if it is possible to induce a shift in that mind-set. It is in this sense that the example of the Necker cube metaphor is conceptually useful.

Only when we come at the first fixed idea from this angle can we reach a point where the second idea—that China will not under any circumstances accept the independence of Taiwan—can also be flipped around. While the idea that Taiwan is a part of China remains entrenched, the alienation of Taiwan will naturally be seen as an offence, a loss of face, a threat to China's territorial integrity, or a key part of American and Japanese containment strategy directed at keeping China weak—and not only by Chinese nationalists. China's revitalised nationalism in recent years feeds the emotional sense of many Chinese that their dignity is at stake in this matter.[4] The danger in this is that the emotion, stirred by Communist Party propaganda, will prevent anyone from inside or outside China critically rethinking the fixed ideas in question.

This is a crucial point, because both the first and second fixed ideas are fatefully linked to the third. Taiwan is seen as a crucial front-line pawn in the chess game that has opened between strategic 'realists' in both China and the United States. For that reason and through those sets of lenses, everything each side does to buttress its position will be viewed with suspicion by the other—in China, as clear evidence that the U.S. intends to contain it and even weaken it; in the U.S., as evidence that China is, indeed, an aspiring strategic competitor. The three fixed ideas, therefore, form a sort of vicious circle, which could become a downward spiral to war. The standard approaches to trying to 'manage' the matter tend to entail obeisance to the first two ideas and tacit acknowledgment that the third is the looming danger. They have floundered thus far because they depend on papering over the real problem: that the claim to sovereignty by the People's Republic of China, especially given that it remains a one-party dictatorship, is rejected by almost the entire people of Taiwan.

This problem cannot be papered over in the end. It is the root cause of the tension that has been building up in cross-Strait relations for over a decade. Although war is not inevitable, it is a possibility. It is a possibility, however, only because of China's threats to use force in pursuit of its sovereignty claim. The time when both sides of the Taiwan Strait claimed to be the government of the whole of 'one China' is long gone. Even if war does not come, the above three fixed ideas and the vicious circle they form stand in the way of the constructive evolution of Asia–Pacific affairs. There are those who believe that the whole problem will be peacefully resolved so long as the people of Taiwan are given no encouragement to believe that they can ever have their *de facto* independence legitimised. They believe China will simply absorb Taiwan economically, and the U.S. will gradually recede from the picture, as Britain has from Hong Kong. While this may be one possibility, there are reasons for being sceptical of this scenario.

There are clearly many people in Taiwan, arguably a majority, who do not desire unification with China—at least not on the terms that the current regime on the mainland is disposed to offer. The results of the legislative elections in Taiwan in December 2004 were not conclusive as regards the desire for a move to independence, but only because no serious political candidate campaigned for reunification and Taiwan was already, for practical purposes, independent; that is to say, wholly self-governing. The Taiwan Solidarity Union, the most outspoken pro-independence party, failed to gain the extra seats predicted in pre-election polls. Yet the Democratic Progressive Party, campaigning on a strong Taiwanese identity platform, gained two extra seats. Even more significantly, the Guomindang and the People First Party did not campaign on a pro-unification policy—only a policy of responsibility that would avoid provoking the ire of China.

Meanwhile, there are senior American figures questioning whether it would be in the American national interest to see Taiwan unified with China, even if such unification was voluntary. The United States has sought to restrain Taiwan's behaviour, but has urged it to buy more arms, established a *de facto* embassy in Taipei for the first time since 1979 and, in 2004, increased its military advisory commitment to the island state. Japan has also begun to quietly strengthen itself and, under Prime Minister Koizumi, has shown signs of growing resistance to what it perceives as China's hegemonic ambitions in East Asia and the Western Pacific. When former Taiwanese president Lee Tenghui requested a visa to visit Japan in late 2004, the Japanese government granted the visa, over China's strenuous objections. The heated exchanges between Beijing and Tokyo in early 2005 served to underscore the simmering tensions between the two East Asian giants.

Then there is the question of where China itself is heading, both economically and politically. In both respects, it faces major challenges in the next decade or two. It is by no means self-evident that reabsorbing Taiwan politically—especially if force and conflict were involved—would help it deal with those challenges. To the contrary, a case could be made that it would be better served by avoiding the re-absorption of Taiwan, even if it could readily do so, for the foreseeable future. One reason for this is the slyly pragmatic one that the issue—rather like Kinmen and Mazu in the 1950s—provides the barely legitimate regime in Beijing with a means to bolster its nationalist credentials; something which would cease to be the case were it to resume sovereignty over a recalcitrant Taiwan. In any case, it cannot readily do so, which complicates the matter considerably, both for its own declaratory policy and for the strategic calculations of other states. Yet the mounting nationalist fervour in China could carry its leaders into a confrontational stance from which they would find it difficult to back down and which could bring them very serious trouble.

Under present circumstances, China has a great deal to lose if it resorts to force; but it is afraid to renounce its use, lest this make it seem weak and lead to a straightforward Taiwanese declaration of independence. Equally, Taiwan is afraid to declare formal independence, lest China resort to force. Taiwan is actually independent in every respect, except that neither China nor the majority of the nations of the world acknowledge this reality, preferring instead the legal fiction that it is part of China (where 'China' is tacitly construed as meaning the People's Republic of China). The U.S. continues to insist that it has a 'one China' policy, but also that it will defend Taiwan with whatever it takes if China uses force to try to turn a legal fiction into a political reality.

This puts it in a highly ambiguous position, since it officially does not recognise the Republic of China on Taiwan as a state and is, therefore, technically interfering in the internal affairs of the People's Republic of China, just as Beijing claims. Meanwhile, President Chen has openly stated that Taiwan will declare independence if China uses force against it. Thus, all three circle around and around in a deadlock, which could break down into a disastrous conflict for all concerned.

Is there any way out of this vicious circle? Is there any way, in the terms of the conceptual metaphor I have suggested, to see the Necker cube differently? When I gave a paper on this subject in Taipei in 2000, China scholar Ed Friedman said to me, 'It's a great idea, what you're suggesting, but it'll never happen.' We cannot, however, be certain of that. What is far more likely, if we proceed down the path into the future in thrall to the fixed ideas I have identified, is that we will fail to find a solution to the Taiwan problem. The key to the whole conundrum, as in many complex matters, is that a counter-intuitive wisdom can advance the common good in ways that are simply not possible so long as received ideas determine policy.

The idea that Taiwan is an inalienable part of China needs rethinking and reframing, if a solution is to be found that does not involve war or lasting confrontation. All such rethinking requires is recognition, both in China and in the wider world, that *empires have no irrevocable claim to their provinces or territories*. If they did, China would have had no basis for reclaiming Hong Kong Island from the British empire after having ceded it in perpetuity. Nor would the Republic of Ireland have had any claim to independence from the British crown in the 1920s, having been ruled from London for longer than Taiwan was ever part of the Chinese empire. Such examples could very easily be multiplied. The northern part of Vietnam, for example, might be deemed part of China on the basis that it was occupied by the Chinese for 1,000 years—once again, a period of time incomparably longer than that in which Taiwan was in any sense at all part of the Chinese empire. Yet no-one makes any such claim now.

However, it is the notion that China will, under no circumstances, accept the independence of Taiwan that is the main shibboleth inhibiting clear and critical thinking about the issue, both in China and the rest of the world. Doubtless there are many who sincerely and firmly believe this proposition. It is based, however, on at least one largely unexamined assumption: that China's national interest and dignity as a nation state would be harmed if it was to accept the independence of Taiwan. There is a case that can be made that this is so, but that case is only plausible so long as one does not cross examine it and put the alternative case: that China's national interest and dignity would be better served by coming to terms with Taiwan's independence and developing a new, non-sovereign relationship with it. This ought to be relatively easy, for the simple reason that it already has a more or less viable non-sovereign relationship with it.

A case can be made, I suggest, that China's advantage would, in fact, lie in doing precisely the opposite of what the Chinese government currently declares, in law, as its sacred duty: that is, retaking Taiwan by force, if necessary, regardless of the cost in blood and treasure. In this case, the most rational answer to the question of Taiwan's future is a Chinese offer of *de jure* independence to Taiwan. Leave aside, for the moment, the consideration that this seems improbable and that many Chinese tempers flare when the mere idea is raised. The argument is that, if such an offer could be arranged, it would turn out to be to China's benefit. Whether it would be to the Communist Party's benefit is not quite so clear. What would shift the whole question onto another plane, however, would be a declaration from Beijing that the civil war is over, and that Chinese civilisation—rather than one political regime or ideology—has won.

Within 'one China' understood as Chinese civilisation or a broad Chinese commonwealth, there would be no need for Taiwan to bow to Beijing's sovereignty. Rather, it would be embraced warmly as a little brother and off-shoot state, and praised for its extraordinary achievements. A new relationship would then become possible. In such a relationship, cross-Strait trade could thrive, unfettered by political fears or historical animosities. China could benefit from Taiwan's freedom, instead of seeking to stifle it. The revitalisation and modernisation of Chinese civilisation, and the rejuvenation of its worn and despoiled natural environment, could then become the joint project of the mainland state together with its truly liberated scion. Let me emphasise that I am not making a *prediction* here that this is about to happen, or that it would be easy to bring about. I am simply spelling out the possibility of an alternative and peaceful resolution to the present impasse, and arguing that it need not be harmful to China's national interests or dignity.

The intuitive response to this proposal is likely to similar to Friedman's. He was right, up to a point. It is entirely possible that it will not come to fruition; but given that neither threats of force nor economic integration have shown much promise of achieving China's goal, and that resort to force would be enormously destructive, there is a need to put such a proposal on the table. Friedman and most others doubt that China could be induced to make this kind of offer to Taiwan because of a combination of pessimism about China and a deeply ingrained assumption that it would not be in China's interests. This is an attitude of mind redolent of Bill Jenner's *The Tyranny of History*.[5] To gain a different perspective, we need to turn that basic assumption around.

Turning it around entails making a sound case that Taiwanese independence is perfectly consistent with China's national dignity, and that avoiding hostilities over the matter is vitally important to China's enduring national interests. Such a case is readily available. There are four major *advantages* which China would gain from offering Taiwan *de jure* independence:

1. Taiwan could be converted from an enemy, or, at best, a wary neighbour, into a friend;
2. A serious cause of tension and misunderstanding with the United States could be removed;
3. All over Asia, other countries would feel significantly less apprehensive about the rise and territorial ambitions of China and be impressed by its vision and self-confidence; and
4. A constructive dialogue could begin with Taiwan about how to carefully bring about political reform in China.

To the first of these it is, of course, possible to retort that the Communist Party, or a post-communist military dictatorship in China, might find it useful to have Taiwan as an enemy and the United States wrong-footed, much as Mao Zedong calculated in regard to Kinmen in the 1950s. Tension with the United States might play well with a restive domestic population in need of a diversion from their own discontents and anxieties. The third point might fetch the retort that the Communist Party believes it is making quite an impression all over Asia as it is, and that a 'firm' line on Taiwan is all to the good in this respect. And the likely rejoinder to the fourth point is that the last thing the Communist Party seeks is dialogue with its democratic nemesis about political reform in China.

But all these objections surely entail the corollary that the Communist Party's ulterior motives and hidden agenda, not China's best interests as a nation, are what stand in the way of a constructive, imaginative, and truly liberating solution to the Taiwan question. Moreover, even the Communist Party is likely to be more or less aware of certain *disadvantages* which China would suffer should it use force in an attempt to compel Taiwan to kowtow:

1. It might suffer a humiliating military rebuff, with serious political consequences;
2. It could find itself at war with the United States—at a point when the U.S. is its biggest market—over Taiwan, which is its biggest foreign investor;
3. It would cause very serious alarm in Japan, Vietnam, and the Philippines, probably precipitating Japanese rearmament, and leading the smaller states to seek closer security relations with the U.S. and,
4. Even if Taiwan was defeated and the U.S. retreated, the resentment and anger in Taiwan and the economic damage done would be grave and long lasting.

In all probability, the Communist Party's preferred strategy is not to use force, but to prevail through a combination of coercive diplomacy and economic inducements. This is likely, at least in part, because the architects of Chinese strategic policy are rational enough to perceive the negative side of the equation just drawn. The creative task at hand is to make clear the positive side and to develop the case for a vital Chinese commonwealth in the twenty-first century, which includes a prospering and gradually democratising republic in China alongside a dynamic island democracy on Taiwan motivated by affinity with the mainland, not fear of it.

If this state of affairs could be brought into being, the third fixed idea—that China is a rising strategic competitor of the United States—might also more convincingly be challenged. The debate over this proposition in the United States is increasingly strenuous, and analytically very interesting. America's leading regional allies, Japan and Australia, have a very great stake in how it turns out. It is often remarked that regional states in general and Australia, in particular, would prefer, on practical grounds, not to have to choose sides between the two great powers should they collide in conflict. What is less seldom observed is that it would not be in China's interests to force such choices on the countries around it. On the contrary, just to the extent that it would prefer not to have its neighbours look to the United States for protection against its rising power, it would do well not to give them cause to fear that power.

The scenario of China freely and generously acknowledging the existing independence of Taiwan might be dubbed 'the Singapore gambit', in order to distinguish it from 'the Hong Kong gambit', which would entail the 'handing back' of Taiwan to China—just as Hong Kong was handed back in 1997. A number of facts make the Hong Kong gambit deeply problematic in the case of Taiwan. In the first place, Taiwan is not a colony of the United States, whereas Hong Kong was a colony of Great Britain. Second, the United States has no treaty with China comparable to the 1898 treaty under which Britain took a 99-year lease on the New Territories in Hong Kong, so there is no pre-set deadline against which negotiations might be initiated. Third, Taiwan, unlike Hong Kong, is eminently defensible in purely military terms, is well-armed, and has a substantial population long accustomed to self-government, who hold indelible historical memories of massacre and oppression by Chinese forces. All these facts greatly complicate the Hong Kong gambit as a solution to the Taiwan problem.

The Singapore gambit, while superficially less plausible, has the promise of being vastly more practical and easy to achieve if the authorities in Beijing could be induced to attempt it. It is modeled, of course, on the manner in which little Singapore withdrew from Malaysia exactly forty years ago in order to minimise communal strife within the unitary state.[6] For the purpose of this discussion, I am calling the probable, beneficial consequences of the

Singapore gambit 'the Australian outcome'. By this I mean that by offering Taiwan its *de jure* independence, China could, with good will, achieve a future relationship comparable to that which has existed between Britain and Australia for just over one hundred years, since Britain offered the Australian colonies full self-government. One might be sceptical of Chinese willingness to attempt such a future, but once contemplated it must surely exercise a certain attraction.

The immense changes that have come about in China since 1900, and even more since Deng Xiaoping repudiated Maoism and began to open China up to market reform and foreign trade, demonstrate beyond rational dispute the possibility of a conceptual breakthrough along these lines. That there are other possibilities is not in dispute. But I have put forward the Singapore gambit as the best possibility because it springs from the most generous assessment of the Chinese future. Instead of the parties to this complex matter succumbing to fatality by drifting into conflict, it would have them transform the situation to their mutual benefit. Those who think that the only future is one rooted in the fixed ideas previously mentioned will insist that some version of the Hong Kong gambit is the only way to avert a Sino–American war. That is more a fatalist than a rationalist position, however, and adopting it would suggest a refusal to learn from the numerous unanticipated breakthroughs in world affairs in recent decades (especially since 1989, the year of the Tiananmen Square repression in China). The future is not foreordained; it is waiting to be created.

Espousal of the Singapore gambit and the Australian outcome may seem a little ingenuous, but both are wholly consistent with a sombre world view. In the manner of Thucydides—whose history of the Peloponnesian War has been the primer of Western strategic and geopolitical thinking almost since the age of Sun Tzu—such a world view would hold that tragedies arise because of human blindness and obsession. Cognitive science is primarily about identifying human blind spots and biases, and making greater insight possible. Yet these blind spots and biases are, themselves, hardwired into our brains. They cannot be removed by any art currently known to us, only compensated for. So, if we are talking of mere prediction about the course of events, we should expect fixed ideas to govern it—and to lead to tragic conflict. What is required is not optimistic prediction, but profound insight into, and strenuous transformation of, the springs of geopolitical action in the historic encounter across the Taiwan Strait.

In his study of tragic drama, forty years ago, George Steiner remarked:

> The wars recorded in the Old Testament are bloody and grievous, but not tragic. They are just or unjust. The armies of Israel shall carry the day if they have observed God's will and ordinance. They shall be routed if they have broken the divine covenant, or

if their kings have fallen into idolatry. The Peloponnesian Wars, on the contrary, are tragic. Behind them lie obscure fatalities and misjudgments. Enmeshed in false rhetoric and driven by political compulsions of which they can give no clear account, men go out to destroy one another in a kind of fury without hatred.[7]

It is this sort of situation that threatens to confront us in the Taiwan Strait. It is entirely possible that both sides (or all sides, if we differentiate between Taiwan and its informal allies) are convinced of the rightness of their cause and would go to war in the Biblical manner.

This would not help them when, in reality, they would find themselves plunged into the tragedy of a 'Peloponnesian war', sprung from obscure fatalities and misjudgments, and enmeshed in false rhetoric. If such a war is to be averted, the false rhetoric that is rooted in fixed ideas must be supplanted by a different conception of what is possible. Steiner's grim summation of the tragic world view was, 'to put it in the terms of the tragic design drawn by Thucydides: our fleets shall always sail toward Sicily although everyone is more or less aware that they go to their ruin.' There are no prizes for guessing that, in this present-day scenario, our 'Sicily' is a potential war over Taiwan. Yet war need not come. Better outcomes are possible if we can imagine a paradigm shift and have the courage to implement it.

Chapter 6

Looking at the Taiwan Strait from 'Down Under'

Our objective should be ultimately to hold a plebiscite to determine whether the Formosans [Taiwanese] wished to become independent or to effect a union with the mainland of China. When we consider Formosa's chequered political history it is by no means certain that they would freely elect for union.

—Percy Spender, Minister for External Affairs, in a top-secret cablegram to Prime Minister Robert Menzies, 8 September 1950

The Singapore gambit and the Australian outcome require further elucidation. Are they merely chimerical notions, or are they serious suggestions? And even as serious suggestions, what chance is there of the great powers, especially China itself, paying them any heed? How could a middle power, such as Australia, make such proposals without causing ructions between itself and China—or even between itself and the United States, given the latter's stakes in East Asia and its delicately balanced China policy? The answer is deceptively simple: both the gambit and the outcome would be in the mutual interest of China and the U.S. Therefore it would be very much in Australia's interest to see something like them come about.

Three things will be required to bring about such a major development. First, a strong grasp of the dynamics of the strategic chess game of East Asia, in which Taiwan is such a significant pawn. Second, a deeply informed understanding of China's genuine interests and concerns in regard to Taiwan. 'Genuine' interests, here, should not be confused with declared or traditional interests—much effort must go into carefully disentangling the two. Third, the tact and patience to stay the course, given that the transformation is unlikely to be rapid and will involve developments as significant as the ending of apartheid in South Africa or the bringing of democracy to Eastern Europe.

Australia has a great stake in seeing the matter resolved peacefully and intelligently because of its huge economic relationships with China, Japan, Taiwan, and the United States.

Australia is the oldest and most credible democracy in Asia and the closest ally of the U.S. in the Asia Pacific. It also has much in common with Taiwan; and, as a former colony (or group of colonies) of the British empire that still acknowledges the British monarch as its nominal head of state, it is well placed to understand the ways in which empires and their colonies or dependencies can agree to the peaceful and intelligent renovation of their political relationship. Not only is the Australian outcome something that could serve China very well in regard to Taiwan, it is also something that Australia could do a good deal to encourage.

In the first instance, however, it will require a revitalisation of the debate within Australia itself over what it is committed to in Asia, and where it stands in relation to China and Taiwan. For a number of years, three views have been in circulation. The first is the *official* policy. It states that there is one China, of which Taiwan is a part that is apart. Reunification should occur by peaceful means, but is expected to occur in due course. This is a bipartisan view and has been articulated by both the major parties. The second is Australia's *tacit* policy. It is that Taiwan may well not accept reunification and that China may use force, in which case Australia would side with the United States in defending Taiwan, albeit with serious misgivings. This has been stated on the record by a number of senior figures, but now seems to be wavering, out of fear of offending China.

The third view is the *neutralist* position. This view holds that reunification is inevitable and China's position is completely justified. The United States, in this view, is wrong to prolong what has become a dangerous situation. It should make it clear to Taiwan that it needs to negotiate seriously about reunification, and soon. If Taiwan goes down the path to independence, we should not support it, nor should we join the U.S. if it supports Taiwan. We should make it clear to both Taiwan and the U.S. now that this is how we see the matter. This view has been forcefully articulated by former prime minister Malcolm Fraser. It seems also to be the view of a number of senior Australian diplomats and defence officials.

None of these options is imaginative enough, and none is likely to serve Australia, Taiwan, or China well, for reasons outlined in the previous chapter. Their proponents are likely to retort, plausibly, that these positions are simply a matter of geopolitical realism, dictated by the constraints of great power politics. Yet, plainly, this cannot be true for all three. The mere fact that three possibilities are conceived and debated demonstrates that no single one of them is dictated by geopolitical circumstances. Rather, each is generated by geopolitical anxieties and dependent on assumptions that, while appearing robust, are not any more unimpeachable than assumptions, in the mid-1980s, that the Soviet Union would endure indefinitely.

Consider, first, the official Australian policy. Sober and responsible though it may seem, it exhibits notable and alarming similarities to the official policy adopted by the Whitlam government in regard to East Timor in 1974–75.[1] That policy consisted of informing the Indonesian government in September 1974 that Australia regarded East Timor as a natural part of Indonesia and, while it could not condone the use of force to achieve incorporation, saw such incorporation as inevitable. The policy, communicated to the Indonesian president by Prime Minister Whitlam against the explicit advice of the Department of Foreign Affairs, was seriously flawed. It left Australia no means for inhibiting Indonesian resort to force in 1975.

The parallel lies in assuring a large power (Indonesia in the case of East Timor; China in the case of Taiwan) that we support its incorporation of a small island territory, though we would prefer to see this done by peaceful means. It should alarm all those concerned with the future of Asia that the East Timor scenario might be played out again, on a larger scale, in the case of Taiwan. China's disposition is strictly comparable to that of Indonesia a generation ago, although Taiwan's capacity to resist, in 2005, is much greater than was that of the East Timorese in 1975. The greatest uncertainty lies in the disinclination of surrounding states, led by the United States, to do anything to resolve the impasse between the two states.

If it seemed probable that the majority of Taiwanese desired reunification, the danger would be only moderate. This is not the case, though. Just as in East Timor in 1974–75 a clear majority of the people did not desire incorporation into Indonesia, so too in Taiwan today a clear majority do not desire to be part of China on any terms that the current regime in China has so far seen fit to offer. They might acquiesce if they had confidence that their rights and freedoms would be fully respected in a democratic China. But now, and for the foreseeable future, China is a dictatorship, not a democracy, and there is no basis for such confidence.

This makes the situation in regard to China and Taiwan inherently unsustainable. In consequence, Australia's official policy, in common with the declared policy of almost all the world, is adrift. Its tacit policy, on the other hand, in common with that of the United States, runs an increasing risk of miscalculation or Chinese frustration precipitating war. The neutralist line, apart from being morally dubious, is out of touch with realities in Taiwan. The status quo might be maintained for some time to come, but sooner or later something has to give. We should apply our minds to thinking the matter through before things get out of hand.

Anyone who has some acquaintance with the history of the matter will, naturally, be inclined to think that the realities of the situation are intractable and that past efforts to induce China to reconsider its position have been fruitless. These are understandable claims yet, regardless of past endeavours, present circumstances require that we be thoughtful and creative, rather than fatalistic or opportunistic. The context in which the matter has to be worked out has changed demonstrably, in several ways, since the end of the Cold War. That alone should prompt deeper reflection than fatalism affords. But, it is not only this change of context that is cause for reflection. We need, also, to remember and reflect on the history of decision-making on the Taiwan question going back at least three decades.

Ever since the recognition of the People's Republic of China as the sole government of China in December 1972, Australian policy in regard to Taiwan has been circumspect. This cautious approach was always concerned with the territorial status of Taiwan and a reluctance to concede China's claim to sovereignty, and was played out in tantalising detail in foreign policy debates within Australia over recognition of the communist regime, from late 1949 through until late 1972. Perhaps no statement on the record has greater contemporary resonance than that made in September 1950 by the then minister for external (foreign) affairs, Percy Spender:

> In my view, we should oppose the immediate handing over of Formosa [the old Portuguese name for Taiwan] to China, either as a matter of right or as a solution to the present position ... What we should aim at is neutralisation by political means ... I think, also, that our objective should be ultimately to hold a plebiscite to determine whether the Formosans wished to become independent or to effect a union with the mainland of China. When we consider Formosa's chequered political history, it is by no means certain that they would freely elect for union.[2]

This was at a time when there was much distaste for the regime of Chiang Kaishek[3] and no clear agreement on the strategic significance of Taiwan itself.[4] Over the following twenty-two years, but especially during 1970–72, considerable efforts were expended to explore the possibility of a 'two Chinas' or 'one China, one Taiwan' solution. Those efforts were in vain. However, the agreed communiqué with China in December 1972 included, at the insistence of the Australian government, a central ambiguity regarding the territorial status of Taiwan.

This is more than usually important in present circumstances, and worth revisiting for that reason. The ambiguity lay in the wording of the fourth paragraph of the communiqué, which addressed the question of Taiwan. It read:

> The Australian Government recognises the Government of the People's Republic of China as the sole legal government of China, acknowledges the position of the Chinese Government that Taiwan is a province of the People's Republic of China and has decided to remove its official representation from Taiwan ...[5]

To *acknowledge* China's position was not to endorse it, but to settle for a formula that made diplomatic recognition possible without requiring the outright abandonment of Taiwan.[6] With difficulty, but great persistence, that position has been maintained ever since. This stance means is that there is no need for Australia's declaratory policy to change in order for a new initiative to be accommodated. What needs to change is the mind-set in China.

That said, it is clear that Australia's policy has always been largely hostage to the policy of the United States, from 1949 up to the present. Australian thinking has not always coincided with that of American policy-makers, but it has consistently had to come to terms with it. This was certainly the case in the 1950s. It was embarrassingly so in July 1971, when the Australian government was not kept closely informed by Washington of the Nixon administration's decision to recognise the People's Republic of China and 'derecognise' the Republic of China, after refusing to do so for twenty years.

While the Australian government was already engaged in patient efforts to negotiate recognition of the PRC itself at that time, it felt stung by the American failure to keep Canberra informed. The Australian prime minister, William McMahon, wrote directly to President Nixon, complaining that:

> we were placed in a quandary by our lack of any foreknowledge of what is certainly a very dramatic step in the foreign policy of the United States: the more so because we have attempted in all circumstances to coordinate our policies and cooperate in what you are doing.[7]

The quandary had as much to do with domestic politics as with international affairs, for the leader of the opposition, Gough Whitlam, had visited China and met with Premier Zhou Enlai on 5 July, declaring very publicly that an Australian Labor government would immediately recognise Beijing as the sole capital of China.[8]

The McMahon government responded forcefully, declaring on 12 July that Whitlam's announced position was 'dangerous' and should be disavowed by the Australian Labor Party.[9] Unfortunately for McMahon, Henry Kissinger had been in Beijing between 9 and 11 July, and had arranged for Nixon to visit China and basically enact what Whitlam had openly declared he would do. The forthcoming visit by Nixon was announced on 16 July, leaving McMahon in the lurch—hence his letter to the American president.

The response from Washington came in the form of an observation by American secretary of state William Rogers to Australian ambassador James Plimsoll that arrangements for Nixon's visit to China had been an 'exceptional' matter, 'on which it had just not been possible to let many know. Inside the United States Government itself it had been a closely guarded secret, known to very, very few.'[10] An annoyed McMahon wrote on his copy of the Plimsoll cable, 'But they trusted the Pakistanis [through whom Kissinger had set up his own secret visit to Beijing]!! Not us!! Or Japan!!'[11] The Japanese government certainly felt similarly slighted by Nixon. Guomindang officials in Taiwan tersely informed the American government that such secret and abrupt initiatives were not the way to treat friends and allies.

McMahon's letter stated explicitly that Australia's dialogue with China on the question of recognition had been going on quietly for some months, during which Canberra had kept Washington informed of the proceedings. The matter, he said, 'basically boiled down to an insistence [by China] that we abandon the Republic of China on Taiwan.'[12] This was not something that Canberra was prepared to do. What it did not know at the time was that Henry Kissinger had assured Zhou Enlai on 11 July that the United States did not propose a 'two Chinas' or 'one China, one Taiwan' solution, and that his own prediction was that Taiwan's political evolution would naturally trend toward reunification with China.[13]

These events upended Australia's cautious diplomacy. Australia's ambassador in Paris, Alan Renouf, had been conducting negotiations with Chinese diplomats on the recognition issue. On 20 July 1971, Renouf cabled Canberra, '... our present policy will not lead to anything and requires urgent re-examination in the light of what the United States has done.'[14] He was not referring to Kissinger's remarks, of which no one in Australia was as yet aware, but simply to Nixon's announced intention to switch recognition to the People's Republic of China.

Renouf went on to make a resounding set of remarks that have considerable resonance in present circumstances:

> It seems to me that, leaving aside political considerations within Australia, the development of United States' policy represented by President Nixon's announcement opens up 'a whole new ball-game' and, in particular, affords us a greater degree of freedom of movement than we previously had. Moreover [Taiwan] is strategically less important to us than it is to the United States and Japan and, as distinct from the U.S., we have no treaty ties with [Taiwan]. Finally, it is desirable, I submit, that we should on this issue try to avoid any impression of awaiting patiently the development of United States' policy (without prior consultation) and then following along behind.[15]

Renouf's reflections implied that Australia might consider abandoning Taiwan altogether, simply by consulting its own strategic interests without waiting on developments in Sino-American relations. The constraint on Australia's China policy was seen as having been lifted. This has a double-edged significance in 2005, but in 1971 its significance was much simpler. The door was open to Australian recognition of China, provided it was prepared to accept China's insistence that Taiwan was part of the People's Republic of China. It is notable, nonetheless, that even the Whitlam government, late in 1972, hedged on this official acceptance.

Even though the tide of events seemed to make recognition of the communist regime in China unavoidable; even though the nationalist regime in Taiwan remained a dictatorship that claimed sovereignty over the mainland; and even though it was led by a Labor government and prime minister, Gough Whitlam, who prided themselves on asserting their visionary independence from American foreign policy, Australia did not agree to completely abandon Taiwan or describe it outright as a province of China. This created an anomaly, of course, with which many people are still uncomfortable. Yet it kept the door open to some resolution of the problem other than the overthrow of the nationalist regime by its communist rival.

What the resolution might be was closely explored at the time, and those now considering the matter would do well to acquaint themselves with the record. In a memorandum to then foreign minister Nigel Bowen on 25 August 1971, the Department of Foreign Affairs pointed out that, while both mainlanders and Taiwanese believed that they were better off under the Republic of China than they would be under the People's Republic, independence for Taiwan was ruled out because of nationalist Chinese control of the island. Yet even the nationalists, Bowen was advised, believed that they would be better off in an independent Taiwan than under the People's Republic. Reconciliation across the Strait 'might be possible, but only after a lapse of time and a change of present leadership.'[16]

Since 1971, consistent both with this Australian anticipation of reconciliation across the Taiwan Strait, and also with Henry Kissinger's prediction that Taiwan's political evolution would trend toward reunification, there has been a widespread expectation that these things would occur. Yet they plainly have not done so. Following the death of Chiang Kaishek on 5 April 1975,[17] which occurred amid the rapid collapse of South Vietnam before the final communist offensive, Taiwan began to move further away from China, not closer to it. This development did not become apparent for some time, but from 1987 it was unmistakable—to the close observer.

The real trend, as explored elsewhere in this book, has been the abandonment of Maoism in China, the democratisation of Taiwan, the downfall of communism as a global ideology, renunciation by the government of Taiwan of any claim to sovereignty over China, the peaceful departure from power of the Nationalist Party in Taiwan and its fracture into several political parties competing for Taiwanese electoral support, and the emergence of a strong Taiwanese independence movement which has resisted consistent Chinese pressure over the past decade. In 1971, geopolitical realism dictated transfer of recognition from Taipei to Beijing as the real government of China. In 2005, a good case could be made that similar realism would lead to a revision of longstanding expectations about Taiwan being reunified with China.

The present context gives new meaning to Percy Spender's advice of more than half a century ago about opposing the handing over of Taiwan to China 'either as a matter of right or as a solution to the present position', and to instead make a Taiwanese plebiscite Australia's objective. Now, more than ever, it is clear that Spender was correct when he wrote 'when we consider Formosa's (Taiwan's) chequered political history, it is by no means certain that they would freely elect for union.' Demonstrably, such a plebiscite is just what the Democratic Progressive Party and the Taiwan Solidarity Union would like to hold—and would do so unilaterally, were it not for consistent Chinese threats to go to war.

The very fact, however, that China has to make such threats indicates that it is fighting a losing battle. The cause would be less fragile had China visibly embarked on a process of democratisation itself—and especially if Taiwan had not done so. Indeed, it is worth pondering the implications if the Guomindang had clung to dictatorial power in Taiwan under Chiang Chingkuo and some imagined hard-line successor, while the democracy movement in China had been legitimised by Deng Xiaoping, from 1979 onwards. Under such a scenario, it seems highly probable that there would be growing global support for China to insist on resuming sovereignty over Taiwan and even mass support for this in Taiwan itself. That the opposite has occurred is the Communist Party's fault alone.

Meanwhile, the Communist Party itself is under relentless structural pressure, both domestically and internally, to transform itself from a Marxist–Leninist party into at least an authoritarian nationalist party and perhaps, in due course, to go the way of the nationalist Party in Taiwan by legitimising political opposition and bowing to the will of the people it claims to represent.[18] As explained earlier in this book, we cannot predict in any straightforward manner how this will play out. The forces at work could yet create a kind of National Socialism with Chinese characteristics, resulting in a warlike state that is bent on asserting itself in Asia and the Pacific. In such circumstances, the Taiwan question would be cause for acute concern.[19] What can be predicted with much more confidence is that if we do not do some hard thinking about a preferable scenario, and how to encourage it, we risk drifting into serious trouble.

In Australia's case, such hard thinking necessarily takes place not only against the background of our relations with China and the enormous increase in our trade with it, since Deng Xiaoping began to open China to the world market in 1979, but also in the context of our abiding strategic alignment with the United States of America. Neutralist thinking in Australia sees this alignment as problematic, and inclines toward distancing Australia from America's commitment to defend Taiwan in the event of Chinese attack. The official and tacit policies simply take that alignment as a given, and leave the outcome largely in the lap of the great powers. It is not surprising that thoughtful diplomats and defence analysts are uncomfortable with this fatalistic approach. Yet neutralism on Australia's part would not help solve the problem. It would merely turn Australia into a spectator of unfolding events, and weaken its position both in relation to China and to the United States.

Another aspect of the breakthrough events of 1971 deserves recollection. Following Prime Minister McMahon's letter to President Nixon, an internal study pondered the long-term implications for Australia of America's decision not only to seek rapprochement with Mao's China, but to do so without consulting or informing its major regional allies—Australia and Japan.[20] The core finding of the study was that the Nixon initiative 'served as dramatic confirmation of the speed with which the United States is prepared to move in pursuit of its own interests, without consulting even its closest allies'. Not only this but, despite the protests of McMahon and others affected by the initiative,

> the non-committal and reserved comments that have characterised American briefings to Australian officials in Washington have served notice that other interested parties cannot expect to be taken into American confidence any more [now] than they were before President Nixon's announcement.[21]

The United States had, the study argued, decided unilaterally to dismantle its policy of containment of China, having reached an agreement with it that China would not use force to further its interests in Asia. 'The Americans have clearly taken a bold approach, based on the view that peace in South East Asia is "a foremost immediate objective"' and that, to this end, it was prepared to make a compromise with China over Taiwan 'in return for a Chinese willingness to assist in a settlement of the Indo–China war which will permit the United States to extricate itself from the military and political morass in that area.'[22] The overall strategy of the United States was to solve the China problem, in order to free itself 'to deal with its chief adversary, the Soviet Union.'[23]

The study urged that Australia reassess 'our policy towards China on the basis of our national interest', because 'American apparent readiness to ride roughshod, not only over Australia and other Asian sensitivities, but most importantly over those of Japan, demonstrates final acceptance by the United States that the containment of China will not work and that neither Taiwan nor Japan will be allowed to stand in the way of the achievement of an American accommodation with China.'[24] It followed, the study concluded, that Australia 'shall need now more than ever to formulate independent policies, based on Australian national interests and those of our nearer neighbours, that will enable us to react quickly to developments in United States policy towards China ...'[25]

In present circumstances, the neutralists tend to play up these antecedents, urging that American support for Taiwan is dangerous and that Australia should not allow its alliance with the U.S. to drag it into a war with China. A corollary follows even more directly from the precedent of the American initiative of 1971: Australia should be wary of supporting Taiwan too closely, lest the United States decide to deepen its relationship with China at the expense of its longstanding commitment to defend Taiwan against aggression from the mainland. For the present, that does not appear to be in prospect, but it cannot be ruled out. The question is, other than drifting with the existing state of affairs or toying with impractical and unprincipled neutralism, what options does Australia have?

Certainly, Australia should consult its own interests in this matter. It is an illusion, however, to believe that its interests would be best served by acquiescing in the betrayal of Taiwan into the hands of China, which is what the neutralists effectively propose. Australian interests would be better served by dealing squarely with the problem, and seeking a fundamental and equitable solution. Before putting any solution on the table, though, we need to think it through, and work at persuading the major parties to the dispute—foremost among them China—that a breakthrough is required. The Singapore gambit, as briefly outlined in the previous chapter, would be the ideal form of such a breakthrough. It now requires amplification, fully allowing that understanding the logic of the case is only a preliminary step to the demanding task of seeking to persuade others of its merits.

There should be no confusion about the basic realities on which the Singapore gambit is premised, because there is bound to be plenty of conjecture about its viability. The most salient reality in question is the fact that Taiwan today is simply not the same political entity it was in 1949, or 1971. Had it not been for the Korean War, Taiwan might have been abandoned by the U.S. and overrun by the Red Army in 1950. Instead, it has survived, prospered, reformed, transformed, and rearmed. It is no longer merely the ROC in exile, but a changed political entity. It is, in reality and not merely by aspiration, the Republic of Taiwan, in all but name. Moreover, the U.S. shows a renewed disposition to support it, both because it is a democratised capitalist entity, and because China is seen as an aspiring peer competitor that many in the Pentagon and elsewhere in the U.S. see fit to constrain.

This last consideration is not a good argument in favour of denying Chinese sovereignty, of course. On the contrary, just to the extent that it is made, it serves to inflame Chinese nationalist sentiment against American plans to 'contain' China. Yet, in a replay of the debates of 1949–50, it is not clear precisely to what extent or under what circumstances the U.S. would fight to defend Taiwan against the Chinese use of force. As Thomas Christensen argued a few years ago, there are hidden dangers in this situation—particularly to do with Chinese political grievances or frustrations—which simple, realist analyses are prone to overlook. It has long been the case that China lacked the capability to invade Taiwan. Christensen's point, however, is that its frustration with this reality may lead it to take steps which will pose very awkward policy dilemmas for the United States and could result in a war across the Taiwan Strait. Very serious consequences are likely to flow from such a war, even if it was short and China was sharply rebuffed, as it well might be.

The second basic reality with which all parties must reckon is that Sino–American rivalry is concentrated on Taiwan, regardless of the intrinsic merits of arguments for Chinese sovereignty or Taiwanese independence. Even the most thoughtful security specialists, such as Christensen, seem disposed to simply managing this dangerous and ultimately unsustainable impasse. This is clearly the case with Malcolm Cook and Craig Meer, in their otherwise substantial and judicious 2005 monograph *Balancing Act: Taiwan's Cross Strait Challenge*[26]. They call for a major and multilateral effort to revitalise and 'modernise' the status quo. But this only postpones the day when a choice must be made. The problem is that China does not agree that there can be any choice, and Taiwan is drifting further away from accepting China's demand for reunification. No one is proposing a solution, unless it is the dubious one of pressuring Taiwan into accepting reunification on Beijing's terms, which I have previously outlined as 'the Hong Kong gambit'.

The third basic reality in the situation constitutes the major roadblock to the Hong Kong gambit: the reality that Taiwan is now a democratic state whose people have an established right to determine their own future. This reality has developed by stages ever since 1986, if not earlier, from the deliberate decision by President Chiang Chingkuo, even before Lee Tenghui was nominated as his heir apparent, to move down the path of democratisation and to enfranchise a legitimate opposition—the Democratic Progressive Party. That momentous decision has led to a flowering of civil society and democratic politics in Taiwan of a kind not seen in China since 1912–1913, when forty million voters elected a national constituent assembly, only to have it dispersed by anti-democratic reactionaries. This has been extremely difficult for the People's Republic of China to come to terms with, but it is a reality that cannot be ignored.

The democratisation process has brought to the surface long-suppressed Taiwanese aspirations to independence. These aspirations have their roots in the deep historical past, as well as in the effects of half a century of Japanese colonial rule and the abuses of nationalist Chinese rule between 1945 and 1986. The terror, famine, chaos, and repression in China between 1949 and 1979 made Chinese rule under communism look even less appealing than it was under the Guomindang. The only way the revulsion from China might have been overcome in the 1980s and 1990s would have been for Deng Xiaoping and his successors to have emulated Chiang Chingkuo, and started China on the path to genuine democratisation. When they refused to do so in 1989, they all but shut the gate on the possibility of reunification with Taiwan.

Ever since Deng Xiaoping's overtures to Chiang Chingkuo in 1984, China has stated that it seeks only nominal obeisance from Taiwan under the so-called 'one country, two systems' formula. But its conduct in governing Tibet and Xinjiang does not inspire confidence in its willingness to allow genuine autonomy. Indeed, the same might be said of its handling of Hong Kong since 1997, though its approach has certainly been less heavy-handed there. In less than ten years since it was taken back by China, Hong Kong has been steadily stripped of the freedom it was supposed to have for the following fifty years. For this reason, Taiwan has much to lose by conceding Chinese sovereignty. It can hardly be expected to feel much gratitude if Beijing is offering to let it keep most of what it already has. What it needs is something other than the doubtful and revocable promise of a dictatorship that its democratic freedoms will be protected.

The problem is two-fold. First, Taiwan has a substantially adequate system, especially if it is able to proceed unhindered with long-needed constitutional reforms; whereas China does not, so differences and frictions would likely arise within the proposed one country. Second, Taiwan has a manoeuvrability and flexibility as a relatively small, self-governing entity that the behemoth People's Republic of China conspicuously lacks. Deng Xiaoping was alluding to this unwieldiness when he remarked, wistfully, in 1982, 'Ah! If only I had just Shanghai!' For this reason, Taiwan has nothing to gain by buying into China's political difficulties and economic disorders. Indeed, China itself stands to lose what Taiwan currently has to offer it, should it take it over. In short, Beijing's formula is both suspect and problematic. A better solution is needed by all parties to the dispute.

Nonetheless, China's claim to Taiwan is passionate and obdurate. There is a story of historical grievance behind its claim that must be understood. It arises from the Chinese impulse to stand up again after the disintegration of the Qing Empire between the 1830s and the 1910s. Having been taken from the empire by Japan with the Treaty of Shimonoseki in 1895, the restoration of Taiwan remains a symbolic part of this nationalistic consciousness. The grievance-based interpretation of the past, projected into the future by Chinese nationalists, is that, psychologically and symbolically, this wrong can only be righted when the island is restored to the sovereignty of the Chinese state. This refrain is endlessly repeated by Chinese policy-makers, and such restoration is described as a 'sacred duty'.

There are two major problems, however, with the People's Republic of China's claim to Taiwan. First, Taiwan has long since ceased to be a Japanese colony or protectorate. In this respect, it is completely different from Hong Kong before the hand-back in 1997. Taiwan was returned to the Chinese state between 1945 (the end of World War II) and 1951 (the San Francisco Treaty, settling accounts between Japan and the Western powers), but not to the Chinese communist state. The Treaty of Shimonoseki, logically, therefore, has no real bearing on the case. The more substantive issue is whether the Chinese *communist* state has any grievance to settle in regard to the anti-communist state on Taiwan.

The servants and soldiers of the Republic of China took refuge from the tsunami of communism on Taiwan in 1949. Completing the defeat of the Republic of China has been an objective of the Communist Party ever since. But, in the course of half a century, the exiled Republic of China on Taiwan has transformed itself into a democratic republic. It now bears far more resemblance in this respect to the Republic of Mongolia, which was also part of the Qing Empire more than a hundred years ago, than it does to the nationalist Chinese government-in-exile of the 1950s. Yet Beijing does not insist that Mongolia accept reunification with China. It simply relates to it as a major power to a close and vastly less powerful neighbour. Why could it not do likewise in relation to Taiwan?

Beijing's real grievance is surely that the ROC claimed for decades to be the sole legitimate government of China and insisted that there was only one China; but, having plainly lost this argument, changed its tune and asserted that there were two Chinas and that it deserved to be treated as a state, not a rebellious province. This is a legitimate point. In the late 1980s, and even more in the late 1990s, the leaders of the Guomindang—chiefly the Taiwanese-born and Japanese-educated Lee Tenghui—did shift the goal posts. The question is, why should China not agree to do the same? In particular, why should they refuse to acknowledge that it was not only the Guomindang that shifted the goal posts, but the people of Taiwan themselves? That is the heart of the matter.

The standard counter-argument is that any government in China that agreed to Taiwanese independence would sign its own death warrant, and would be denounced by its own citizens as weak and traitorous. To use the phrase uttered by Deng Xiaoping in September 1982 when Margaret Thatcher suggested he leave Hong Kong in British hands, such a move would make him 'no better than Li Hong-zhang' (the Chinese diplomat who signed away various territories of the Manchu Empire in the late-nineteenth century). There is considerable sensitivity surrounding this issue, but the Communist Party has not made the situation any easier for itself by making regular pronouncements about its so-called 'sacred duty', and its determination to make any blood sacrifice necessary to reassert sovereignty over Taiwan. It has, in fact, worked up irrational and xenophobic feelings by denouncing 'splittists', 'criminals' and 'reactionaries' in Taiwan, in the traditional communist rhetorical manner.

Nonetheless, there is a genuine nationalist fervour about the matter in China. The problem for the Chinese Communist Party is that, if it makes a misconceived decision to go to war, it risks humiliation and downfall anyway (much in the manner of the Argentinean junta after the Falklands War). Nor can it expect anyone on Taiwan to be sympathetic to a plea that the party will be overthrown if it does not bring Taiwan back within the fold. The only reason the people of Taiwan would have to fear the downfall of the Communist Party would be if it was succeeded by a fascist junta which acted on the party's threats to use force against the island state. But it makes no sense to suggest that the state should capitulate in order to avoid a hypothetical attack that it might, in any case, reasonably hope to repel. There is no logical way forward along this path.

Realistic assessments of the military balance have indicated for more than a decade that China faces all but insuperable difficulties in trying to invade Taiwan, even if it was not directly opposed by the United States[27]. It is not clear that this will remain the case; but, to the extent that the balance shifts, the situation only becomes more dangerous as China's confidence rises, and Taiwan's, and even America's, uncertainties increase. Coercive diplomacy has not served China well over the past decade.[28] Plainly, in the Taiwanese elections of 1996, 2000, and 2001,

Chinese attempts to bully the electorate backfired, contributing to exactly the outcome they were intended to deter: victories at the polls for Lee Tenghui in 1996, Chen Shuibian in 2000, and the DPP in late 2001. They also demonstrably strengthened anti-Chinese feeling in the United States, and deepened the likelihood that Taiwan would be militarily supported by the U.S. in a crisis.

The consequence was the stalling of cross-Straits dialogue between 2000 and 2004, accompanied by frustrated rhetoric coming out of China about its determination to achieve reunification at any cost and its refusal to rule out the use of force. Since the use of force—which has so far been deterred—would probably be stoutly resisted, with seriously adverse and even disastrous consequences for China, this threat seems to leave Chinese policy in something very close to a dead end. The visits to China by Lien Chan and James Soong in late April and early May 2005, respectively, certainly make it possible to imagine confrontation being postponed and the status quo prolonged, but this is a far cry from reunification being effected in any foreseeable time frame.[29]

It is precisely this situation, however, that calls for a breakthrough solution rather than strategic complacency. As Christensen warned in 2001, the impasse contains hidden dangers of Chinese, Taiwanese, or American *miscalculation* leading to a war that could escalate perilously and unpredictably. His article was an excellent analysis of a complex and unstable situation, but even he offered no way out of the impasse. His concluding paragraph read:

> It would be folly for Taipei to believe itself safe for ten years because of PLA weakness in comparison to either ROC forces or US forces in the region. This is especially true if this conclusion is drawn for all projected political scenarios, including ones in which Taipei has taken diplomatic steps that aggravate Chinese nationalism, threaten CCP legitimacy, and augur near term or eventual Taiwanese independence if PRC action is not taken. For the same reasons it would also be folly for Washington elites to use balance of power analysis to draw similar conclusions about the low likelihood of war across the Taiwan Strait, the ability of Taiwan to prevail quickly and easily in such a war with or without American help, or the ability of the United States to avoid dangerous degrees of escalation in a military conflict with China over Taiwan. Washington should take seriously both China's political concerns and military modernisation, and attempt to find the best possible balance of deterrence and reassurance so that war can better be avoided and the likelihood and costs of escalation of any war that should occur can be limited.[30]

I want to draw attention to the last sentence, in particular, because it shows that although Christensen feared the situation could get out of hand more easily and more seriously than balance-of-power realists imagine, he did not offer any way out of the situation itself.

Both China and Taiwan are, as in Alexander Pope's immortal line, 'willing to wound, and yet afraid to strike'. China has a great deal to lose in any conflict, but is afraid to renounce the threat of force, lest this lead to a straightforward Taiwanese declaration of independence. Taiwan is afraid to declare independence for fear that China will use force. It does declare, however, in Chen Shuibian's phrase, that it does not need to declare independence, because it is already independent. What is this, if not a declaration of independence, by any other name? Chen has added, though, that Taiwan will openly declare independence if China does use force to try to suppress Taiwan's de facto independence. The United States continues to declare that it will defend Taiwan against such a use of force. China cannot for the present successfully invade Taiwan, and risks military humiliation if it tries. It is seeking asymmetric means of deterring the United States from succouring Taiwan, but this strategy risks serious escalation in an uneven off-shore clash with the superpower.

In short, China faces an intractable strategic conundrum. So long as it insists that Taiwan accede to reunification, it risks frustration, at best; humiliation, at worst. Every step it takes to try to shift the odds in its favour risks hardening both Taiwanese obduracy and American support for Taiwan. Indeed, the recent subtle hardening of Japanese attitudes suggests that China risks confronting three of its largest trading partners in armed conflict—the United States, Japan, and Taiwan. Its search for asymmetric advantage is ripe with the prospect of miscalculation. By the calculations of its own military strategists, China appears to be damned if it does act and damned if it doesn't. Meanwhile, no single issue is so likely to aggravate Sino–American tensions as a prolonged and escalated stand-off over Taiwan.

Under these circumstances, regional states look on with unease, and trying to find ways to avoid getting caught in the crossfire (which is why Australian elder statesmen, like Malcolm Fraser, argue that Australia should opt for a neutral or even pro-Chinese position in the matter). Current diplomatic strategies do not offer the promise of a much-needed breakthrough. The reason for the dangerous deadlock is that all parties are trapped in a zero-sum assessment of the stakes. China is the key actor. But the real need is to address China's *mind-set* from a new angle, in the search for a vision in which China would cease to see Taiwanese subordination as being to its advantage, much less a 'sacred duty'.

Is it conceivable that China could bring itself to do this? Yes, it is. It was conceivable in the 1980s that the Soviet Union would pull out of Eastern Europe; but as late as 1989, when it was happening, few believed it would do so. It was conceivable in the 1980s that the apartheid regime in South Africa would release Nelson Mandela and dismantle its own grip on power, but few believed it would do so. It was conceivable in the 1960s that China would opt for economic reform and opening, but few believed it would do so. As it transpires, the determination within China that reform was necessary crystallised in the wake of the Great Leap famine, in 1961–62.[31] Although it took almost two decades for reform to begin, ultimately it was not imposed but adopted by the Communist Party itself. This is a good example of the fundamental change of a mind-set that is again needed in China.

What so often happens historically is that fundamental commitments change only after catastrophes, such as the Great Leap famine. But great statesmanship is about foreseeing such catastrophes and changing course *before* they occur. In publicly speaking of the possibilities for China and Taiwan to work together for the revitalisation of the Chinese nation, Hu Jintao showed the first glimmerings of such statesmanship in early 2005. This is the insight that must be enlarged and the prospect that should be explored as creatively as possible, on all sides. There should be no misunderstanding about the psychological roots of the existing mind-set in China, especially among old generals and intellectuals with a grievance-based sense of their country's modern history. Nor can such deep-rooted feelings be easily changed.

What is required is a rethinking of the whole modern logic of Chinese nationalism, going back to the debates of the 1890s and 1910s, under the would-be reformist emperor Guangxu and his scheming dominatrix, the dowager empress. The Chinese revolutionaries of 1911 overthrew their Manchu rulers, the Qing dynasty, in the name of a modern republic. Territorially, however, the Chinese republicans then set about trying to reconstitute the entire Qing Empire as the Republic of China. The Communist Party was no different in this regard from the Guomindang. Chinese nationalism at the very beginning of the twentieth century was thus shaped by the boundaries established by the foreign Manchu conquerors of Ming China.

It is surely ironical that the shaping of twenty-first century Chinese nationalism should be played out as an unresolved civil war between Chinese communists and Chinese republicans over the territorial boundaries of a foreign-ruled nineteenth-century empire against which their founding fathers had rebelled. This is especially so, given that one side in the civil war has for practical purposes renounced communism, and the other has renounced its claims to be the government of China. Yet, so ingrained is the territorial nationalism in question that this aspect of it, in all likelihood, does not so much as occur to a majority of Chinese.

The time has come, however, to transcend the assumptions and grievances that constricted the Chinese revolution in the twentieth century. The time has come to complete the overthrow of the Manchus by acknowledging that they were the foreign rulers of an empire, not the founding fathers of a nation state; and that, before they conquered the Ming empire, considerable areas of what is now regarded as Chinese territory were not parts of the Chinese empire at all. One such area is Outer Mongolia; another is Tibet; a third is Taiwan. The old Chinese heartland included none of these territories—least of all Taiwan, which was a neglected island off China's coast until the very last years of the Manchu dynasty.

Even from the point of view of reclaiming the territories of the Manchu empire, it makes no sense to turn Taiwan into a cause of a twenty-first century war; since there are far more important things at stake than regaining an island long since estranged from China and never a truly integral part of it. In any case, as I have argued, empires have no everlasting jurisdiction over their provinces, and China is no more an exception to this principle than were Turkey, Britain, France, or Russia. Other empires have broken into more than one state. The Roman Empire did so long ago; and, in the process, it indirectly gave way to a multitude of independent and vigorous states which are now freely negotiating to form the European Union. China plainly has the possibility of rethinking its own future on similar lines.

Wang Hui, the former editor of the leading post-Deng journal of ideas in China, *Dushu*, said in interview for *New Left Review*, a few years ago, that what he looked for in China was neither a 'New Left' rebellion against liberalism nor an ideological Friedmanite liberalism, but 'an unprejudiced intellectual curiosity'. This is what will be needed in the matter of cross-Straits relations, if the current impasse is to be transcended. Such intellectual curiosity needs to be directed at the proposition I have put in this book: that it would be in China's *direct interest* to offer Taiwan de jure independence as a matter of goodwill, realistic strategy, and political imagination. The disposition in many quarters will be to dismiss this proposition out of hand. But those who would seek a genuine breakthrough in the matter of China and Taiwan should explore it openly, frankly, and critically. If there are disadvantages for China in this, they should be tabled and weighed against the advantages. The starting point for the exploratory process is simply the recognition that both China and the world around it have changed enormously since 1949, and that neither needs to be the prisoner of the historical past in shaping a workable future.

The Communist Party was founded in 1921 in the belief that China needed radical change in order to become a liberated, modern republic. Yet when Mao took Beijing, he self-consciously set himself up as a quasi-emperor, almost in the manner that Yuan Shikai had attempted between 1913 and 1916, after he had suppressed China's first democratically elected national assembly. Mao failed China by becoming a totalitarian emperor. In this respect, he became a monstrous political heir of the great early-twentieth-century republicans, Liang Qichao and Sun Yatsen, who had wanted a strong state but could not have imagined the disasters Mao was to inflict on their country.

We should all remind ourselves that, following the death of the communist emperor, the best surviving minds in the party acknowledged that China had been very badly served by Mao, and desperately needed market-oriented economic reform and opening to the outside world. It also needed political reform to substitute, in Deng Xiaoping's own expression, 'the rule of law for the rule of men'. Though Deng failed in this objective, he succeeded in stabilising party rule and institutionalising the momentum for economic reform. Dali Yang's brilliant account of how the calamity of the Great Leap famine persuaded many people in China that economic reform was necessary is key here, for such reform could not be implemented until Mao Zedong's death. It was brought to pass, literally, over his dead body. It is perfectly conceivable that it will take a disastrous war for Chinese strategists to see that anachronistic territorialism does not serve China any better than Mao Zedong's misconceived economics. But why allow this to occur? Why not rethink the territorialism now and avoid the calamity that lies in wait?

Doubtless those least inclined to challenge the longstanding Chinese posture on this matter will object that China's communist leaders do not seek a calamity. They will insist that they have been very patient, and have made many concessions to Taiwan.[32] All they ask is for Taiwan to acknowledge the 'one China' principle. According to this argument, it is Taiwanese intransigence and American hegemonism that threaten to bring about war. This is, surely, the view of a good many people in China—perhaps it was the view of Jiang Zemin and Zhu Rongji, and is now that of Hu Jintao and Wen Jiabao. The problem is that their 'patience' and their 'concessions' are simply not attractive to the people of Taiwan. This much should be evident by now, but their mind-set is such that the evidence produces only frustration and impatience, rather than insight or vision. What is worse is that it is very difficult for anyone inside China to develop a serious alternative policy proposal because of the way politics and strategic planning are done there.

There are, as I have suggested in the preceding chapter, a number of significant advantages that would accrue to China if it offered Taiwan de jure independence with good will. At a time when China has joined the World Trade Organisation, is set to host the 2008 Olympic Games in Bejing, aspires to some form of Asian leadership, and faces huge challenges in completing the reform and modernisation of its economy and polity, the gains would be immense. By comparison, even the peaceful yielding of Taiwan to Beijing's pressure would do nothing to allay American or regional misgivings about China. And, even in the best-case scenario, it would not engender any greater friendliness and trust towards China in Taiwan than currently exists in Hong Kong.

Plainly, what is required here is not prediction, but suasion. Unless policy-makers in China can be persuaded that this course of action is to their clear advantage, they will understandably cling to the view that it is simply an invitation to accept defeat and humiliation. As long as this mentality rules in China—and no one should underestimate its sincerity or tenacity—China will forego the Singapore gambit and could resort to irrational and dangerous escalation of the confrontation across the Straits, out of what Christensen astutely called 'political desperation'.

Only a few years ago it was said that there were some in the Pentagon who *want* a short, sharp war with China, to show it who is boss. One would imagine that they have been sobered by the recent experience in Iraq. Yet there must still be those who believe that, terrorism notwithstanding, China is the biggest long-term danger to American primacy. There are also plenty of people in both the U.S. and China who fully realise that any regional conflict would be a dreadful setback for the Asia Pacific. The problem is that they are not sure how to avoid it, save by balancing on the high wire over the Taiwan Strait. Here, then, is the policy challenge. A case needs to be developed which would make it possible for China to see the Singapore gambit as something other than a victory for American hegemonism.

It might be objected that, if Taiwan was given its de jure independence, Tibet, Xinjiang, and perhaps even other parts of the old Manchu empire would redouble their own demands for independence. That is possible, but those demands are primarily the result of the failure of the Chinese government to respect the autonomy of the Tibetans and Uighurs, not of any emulation of Taiwan in inner Asia. Besides, Taiwan is already an effective polity in its own right, as Beijing acknowledges—something that neither Tibet nor Xinjiang is likely to become within even the most generous estimate of foreseeable circumstances.

So the case might just as rationally be made that a de jure independent Taiwan could be of great assistance to China in handling the awkward problems it has created for itself in Tibet and central Asia. The completion of the overthrow of the Manchu empire might well entail finding a way to grant greater independence to Tibet and Xinjiang as well. This should not inhibit anyone in thinking through the problem of Taiwan. The focus of the matter should be on what will authentically contribute to the opening of a new, free, and prosperous China, in which all that is best and most humane in Chinese civilisation can flourish—even as it absorbs, in the words of Hu Yaobang, the great reformist of the early 1980s, 'the achievements of all humanity'.

There is no evident reason why the Singapore gambit should not prove even more successful in the case of Taiwan than it was in the case of Singapore itself. After all, Singapore was tiny and vulnerable, and the ethnic animosities between the Chinese Singaporeans and the Malays deeply rooted, whereas Taiwan is already a substantial and solidly established trading state which has vast investments in China, and close cultural and ethnic links with it. Achieving this great geopolitical success, however, will require a paradigm shift in Chinese perceptions. It will require looking at the matter from the point of view of China's future, rather than its past. More specifically, it will require a generous vision for China, as opposed to a grievance-based vision that projects historical resentments and pretensions onto the future.

The precedents for this kind of generous vision are not hard to find. Not much more than 100 years ago, the British Empire granted full self-government to its colonies in Australia. There was no war of independence; no revolution against the monarchy. The consequence has been a century of remarkable freedom, prosperity, and close relations between the former colony and the former colonial power. The British Empire fought unsuccessfully to retain its control over the American colonies in the late-eighteenth century. In the twentieth century, it built a powerful strategic partnership with those former colonies, and conducted an enlightened and remarkably successful retreat from its empire in Asia, the Middle East, and Africa as it substituted political amity and mutually profitable economic ties for the burden of imperial rule. Nowhere was this more successfully achieved than in the predominantly English-speaking settler colonies.

So impressive was its achievement in this regard that, on a visit to London in 1984, Mikhail Gorbachev asked British Prime Minister Margaret Thatcher, 'How did Britain dismantle its colonial empire?' It seems not to have occurred to Thatcher at the time that this question was prompted by an emerging Soviet desire to dismantle its own 'colonial empire' in Eastern Europe. It did so in 1989, to the astonishment of the whole world. In this case, also, the relative peacefulness of the upheaval has contributed enormously to the gradual emergence of a new order in Europe that has now extended all the way to the Ukraine.

I mention these precedents because I believe they have something to offer China in the search for a constructive solution to its problem with Taiwan. The British precedent is presumably more inspiring than the outcome for the Soviet Union, which fell apart after relinquishing its control of Eastern Europe. It is, in any case, more apposite—since Taiwan, in relation to China, is far more like a British dominion than an eastern European state occupied by the Soviet Union. It would also be easier for China to achieve what Britain did, and avoid what happened to the Soviet Union, because Taiwan is not occupied by Chinese forces, or seething with resentment against China. Finally, Taiwan is far better established as a polity than were the Australian colonies in the 1890s, so there is no doubt about its capacity to remain a fully effective state.

Examined from this point of view, the prospect is very promising—so much so that it could well be regarded as a future waiting to happen. All it requires is a transformation in the mind-set that has dominated cross-Straits politics since 1949. It is highly unlikely that anyone in Taiwan, even the residual New Party, would put any obstacles in the path of such an outcome. There is, to the contrary, very good reason to believe that it would be embraced across the political spectrum as an enormous relief from decades of tension, and an unparalleled opportunity for Taiwan to work with China and find its unique place in the world without fear of becoming the cockpit of a great-power war.

In raising this option with China, it will be crucial to bear three fundamental points in mind:

- In making so fundamental a shift, great care will have to be taken to avoid political panic in China that could precipitate military action;
- Although there is a clear difference between the interests of 'China' and those of the Chinese Communist Party, both interests will have to be acknowledged in the dialogue; and
- For profound historical reasons, both the United States and Japan are badly placed to make this approach to China.

There is a potentially important role to be played by Australia, and perhaps Singapore itself, in developing a dialogue between China and Taiwan.

Over the coming few years, in the lead-up to the Olympic Games in Beijing, there is both the need and the opportunity to develop the dialogue to the point where conflict would become extremely improbable. Who knows? Perhaps a breakthrough in cross-Straits civility can be achieved in time for the Olympics—bringing lustre to the Games both for China and the world. Optimistic as this must seem, it is not impossible. It will become probable just to the extent that the common goal becomes not simply to avoid the outbreak of war but to transform a once seemingly intractable situation.

Chapter 7

Can Rationality Save Us?

Incomplete rationality coupled with environmental constraints leads to inefficiencies in history, some of which we call tragedies.

—Dali Yang, *Calamity and Reform in China*

Over the past 20 years, China has endeavoured to draw Taiwan into some form of agreement on being reincorporated within a single state, ruled from Beijing. Its blandishments have been insufficient to woo the Taiwanese, while its recurrent efforts at coercion have alienated them. In the words of Richard Baum, the re-election of Chen Shuibian in March 2004 as president of the Republic of China on Taiwan 'dashed, perhaps forever, Beijing's "one China" dream'.[1]—unless, of course, China goes to war and crushes Taiwan.

There is plenty of fear in Taiwan that China might attempt to do just this. On 28 February 2004, during the lead-up to the presidential elections, an estimated one million demonstrators formed a human chain all the way across Taiwan under the slogans, 'We want peace, not missiles' and 'We want democracy, not to be annexed'.[2] The demonstration was modelled on those held in the Baltic states in 1989, calling for independence from the USSR. The date was highly significant. It was the anniversary of 2/28, as it is known in Taiwan—the massacre of Taiwanese, beginning on 28 February 1947, by military forces sent from the mainland by Chiang Kaishek to enforce Chinese rule on the island.

Public opinion polls showed that Chen took the lead as preferred president over the Guomindang's Lien Chan for the first time in the wake of the 28 February demonstrations.[3] Having won re-election, albeit by the narrowest of margins, he declared on 6 April: 'The situation won't develop in the way the Beijing authorities desire, if they cannot adjust their Taiwan policy.' He called for the concept of 'one peace' to replace that of 'one China'.[4] In short, Chen was telling China that its policy of coercion was folly, and that it had to come to terms with the realities of the situation. Instead, Beijing responded by escalating both the rhetoric of and active preparations for outright coercion.

Already, during 2003, the Communist Party's leading group on Taiwan affairs reportedly had begun drafting a statute that would obligate the Chinese leadership to use whatever means were necessary to achieve the reincorporation of Taiwan within a set time frame, possibly as early as 2008.[5] By May 2004, frustrated at the failure of its policies and unwilling to fundamentally reconsider them, Beijing had begun to prepare for war. Its anti-secession bill, tabled in the National People's Congress in March 2005, formalised this posture. China had started to contemplate, for the first time, what Li Jiaquan, the founder and longest-serving head of the Taiwan Research Institute in Beijing, called 'a first strike posture'.[6]

On 12 August 2004, Reuters reported that China was no longer deploying military forces opposite Taiwan simply as a psychological deterrent, but was preparing for war.[7] Analysts in the US and Taiwan differed in their assessments of China's propensity to go to war and Taiwan's ability to withstand a determined Chinese assault,[8] but all agreed that the developments of the northern summer were, as RAND's James Mulvenon expressed it, 'disturbing.'[9] Against this backdrop, Wendell Minnick, of *Jane's Defence Weekly*, identified 2006—the Year of the Dog—as the danger year for Taiwan.[10]

His reasoning was as follows. Chen Shubian had proposed to promulgate a new constitution for Taiwan in 2006—a step, it was feared, that could finally trigger Chinese aggression, because it would be seen as a point of no return in the political evolution of the Taiwanese polity. China's rapidly modernising military capabilities were about to give it the capacity to quickly overwhelm Taiwan—a capacity it has not had in all the decades since 1949. Finally, the war party in China had come to the opinion that the mess that would be caused by such a war could be 'cleaned up' in the two years between 2006 and the Beijing Olympics scheduled for 2008.

In a thoughtful and unsettling piece written in August 2004, the Atlantic Council's Martin Lasater speculated that the Chinese leadership may decide to use force pre-emptively in the near future because, whereas they no longer believe that a peaceful reincorporation of Taiwan is possible, they increasingly believe that reincorporation by violent means is. Lasater went on to say that the leadership believes that their military forces are now close to being able to both deter US intervention and decapitate Taiwan's military and political command structure within a week, which would open the way for occupation of the island and the imposition of a pro-Beijing regime in Taipei.[11]

Lasater's remarks were particularly unsettling when juxtaposed with Thomas Christensen's observation in 2001 that China could go to war out of 'political desperation', and miscalculate the odds in its favour. They were also of great interest in light of Robert Karniol's statement, also made in August 2004, that China probably would not pursue war in the near future because, 'If they act rationally, the only way they can go to war is if they know they are going to win and I don't think those circumstances exist [or] are going to exist in 2007 or 2008.'[12] Karniol's caveat, *'if they act rationally'*, takes us to the heart of international relations theory about so-called 'rational actors'. Both Christensen in 2001 and Lasater in 2004 offered more cautious approaches to the matter—not because they believed China was more than usually 'irrational', but because they understood that states, in general, do not behave in the way implied by Karniol and some theoreticians. Those thinking through the dangers of the developing situation must grapple with this conceptual distinction.

Errol Morris' acclaimed 2003 documentary *The Fog of War* questions the role 'rationality' plays in international security affairs. The film is an extended interview with Robert S. McNamara about his experiences of war during a long lifetime.[13] It begins with his experience of the Cuban missile crisis in October 1962, when he was US secretary of defence. Based on what McNamara has to say about the missile crisis, Morris offers two lessons: we need to empathise with our enemies, and rationality will not save us. The second of these lessons serves as a useful way of examining what is at stake in the remarks by Karniol, Christensen, and Lasater.

What can Morris have meant by saying that 'rationality will not save us'? That irrationality is a better option? That we should trust our intuitions, or follow a great leader, rather than try to rationally analyse security affairs? None of these seems likely. The film leaves us to draw our own conclusions. But the problem it raised is perfectly real. It has to do with the apparently universal human tendency to reason from a narrow set of premises, while assuming that one is sharing the same reality with one's antagonists.

In *The Fog of War*, McNamara exhibited awareness of this problem when he declared of the Cuban missile crisis, 'I want to say—and this is very important—at the end, we lucked out. It was luck that prevented nuclear war … Rational individuals—Kennedy was rational, Khrushchev was rational, Castro was rational—rational individuals came that close to total destruction of their societies.' Yet, for all his experience of the problem, and the time he had taken since retirement to rethink the crises of the 1960s, he did not define what he meant by the term 'rational individuals'. Consequently, he fails to get to the heart of the problem that so concerns him—and which should certainly concern us.

Both McNamara and Morris would have done well to refer to a classic study of the Cuban missile crisis, *Essence of Decision*. Originally written by Graham Allison, it has long been used as a core textbook on strategic thinking in both business and government.[14] In 1999, Allison co-authored an extensively revised edition of the book with Philip Zelikow, drawing on materials released from the US and Soviet archives since the end of the Cold War. These materials led them to conclude that 'a number of explanations in the original edition [had been] incorrect and others insufficient', but that the 'alternative conceptual lenses' developed in the original edition highlighted the significance of the new material.[15]

The reference to 'conceptual lenses' relates to three models of explanation for how governments, in reality, generate decisions. The first is the rational-actor model, which Karniol committed to, implicitly, when he wrote of the Chinese not invading Taiwan 'if they act rationally'. The second is the organisational-behaviour model. And the third is the governmental-politics model. Allison and Zelikow articulated each model in turn, using the Cuban missile crisis as a case study. The overall effect was a striking demonstration of the limits of rationality in making national security decisions. More precisely, it was a demonstration of the limited utility of the rational-actor model in explaining why wars occur, and how national security decisions are made and international crises created.[16]

'Understanding that ordinary explanations, predictions and evaluations are inescapably theory-based is fundamental to self-consciousness about knowledge,' Allison and Zelikow remarked.[17] One of the most notable illustrations of this point is that those responsible for intelligence analysis and policy-making in national security affairs think about the problems they confront 'in terms of largely implicit conceptual models that have significant consequences for the content of their thoughts.'[18] The single most pervasive of these is the rational-actor model. 'Most analysts and ordinary citizens attempt to understand happenings in foreign affairs as the more or less purposive acts of unified national governments', the authors state. 'Laymen personify actors and speak of their aims and choices. Theorists of international relations focus on problems between nations in accounting for the choices of unitary rational actors.' This 'rational-actor model' is implicit in the very idea of 'China' (or 'Taiwan, or 'the US') acting, deciding, or having volition.[19] What Allison and Zelikow do is make the model *explicit*.

As they remark, 'To articulate a largely implicit framework as an explicit paradigm is, of necessity, to caricature. But caricature can be instructive.'[20] When we see spelled out the logical implications of our thinking, we are better able to realise how we tend to oversimplify reality, and invite errors such as those discussed by Christensen and Lasater. So, what are the elements of the rational-actor model and what are its logical implications if we apply them to the case of the Taiwan Strait question? The model consists of six fundamental (implicit) assumptions. The challenge is to think through how such largely inexplicit assumptions shape our intuitive assessments of international affairs.

The assumptions are: that the basic unit of analysis is a unified national government, consciously seeking to maximise clearly conceived strategic goals and objectives; that the national government, being unitary, has a clear and consistent set of strategic preferences and perceived choices, and a coherent estimate of the consequences that follow from alternative choices; that its actions are chosen in response to a clearly perceived strategic situation; that any given action by a national government is based on its estimate that such an action will maximise its chances of realising its objectives; that an increase in the perceived costs of an action will reduce the likelihood of it being undertaken, while a decrease in the perceived costs will increase that likelihood; and that the probable behaviour of a national government can be predicted through 'vicarious problem solving'—that is, by putting oneself in the position of the said national government and forming a coherent picture of what would constitute value-maximising behaviour.[21]

It was vicarious problem-solving that led CIA analysts to judge, in 1990, that Saddam Hussein would not invade Kuwait and, in early 1998, that India and Pakistan would not complete the development of nuclear weapons. The Agency's analysts reasoned that, from a rational, value-maximising point of view, as seen from Langley, Virginia, such actions would not be 'in their interests'. Needless to say, the analysts were mistaken in both cases. It was presumably with such misjudgments in mind that the head of CIA intelligence analysis in the mid-1990s, Douglas McEachin, asked rhetorically in 1999, 'How many times have we encountered situations in which completely plausible premises, based on solid expertise, have been used to construct a logically valid forecast, with virtually unanimous agreement, that turned out to be dead wrong?'[22]

Estimates of whether or not China will resort to war reflect many of the assumptions of the rational-actor model. When Christensen warned that China might go to war out of political desperation, he was to some extent departing from the model, but he did not do so explicitly. What he would appear to have been suggesting is that the degree of rationality we attribute to a national governments should, at least, be qualified by an understanding of the fundamental sources of their world view—a perspective which might not be particularly evident to vicarious problem-solvers.

Herbert Simon long ago argued that we need to distinguish between 'comprehensive' and 'bounded' rationality. Comprehensive rationality is quite strongly implicit in the informal model of rational action. It assumes that national governments—regardless of their objectives—consider all alternatives, and accurately assess their consequences, before rationally choosing the course of action that will maximise the benefit to them.[23] This is not to suggest that analysts or decision-makers consciously believe these things—only that they reason *as if* they do.

Bounded rationality, by contrast, acknowledges the serious and intractable limitations on both the knowledge and computational ability of national governments (or any putative 'rational actor'). Christensen, for example, stresses that both the Taiwanese and American governments are at risk of miscalculating the probability of war because they assume that the decision-makers in Beijing will see the situation, as they themselves do, in terms of China's broader interests and the overall balance of power, and thus be deterred. The Chinese government, by comparison, is in danger of being impelled down the path to war by an overmastering sense of political and geo-strategic anxiety that cramps its ability to compute those same interests, and the balance of power.

Allison and Zelikow take us further into the thickets of decision-making based on the documented events of the Cuban missile crisis. They postulate that governments are, in important respects, not rational actors, and offer two other models for how decision processes in complex strategic situations work. Their first alternative is the organisational-behaviour model. Its central premise is that national governments are not rational actors, much less individuals in the value-maximising sense, at all. Rather, they consist of vast conglomerates of 'loosely allied organizations, each with a substantial life of its own'.

They remind us that governments

> define alternatives and estimate consequences as their component organizations process information; governments act as these organizations enact routines. Governmental behavior can therefore be understood ... less as deliberate choices [by a unitary rational actor] and more as the outputs of large organizations functioning according to standard patterns of behavior.[24]

Such 'outputs' follow the logic of established operating procedures, rather than the logic of strategic rationality. President Kennedy indicated some informal awareness of this during the Cuban missile crisis. In an episode dramatised in the film *Thirteen Days*, he is depicted remarking to Bobby Kennedy and Kenny O'Donnell that he had read Barbara Tuchman's *The Guns of August* (a classic study of the causes of World War I), and that it had made him realise the extent of organisational *automaticity* that can turn a crisis into mobilisation, and an incident into an unstoppable war. There are, in fact, quite a few examples from the Cuban missile crisis that illustrate the general principle—not least, the shooting down of a U-2 over Cuba at the height of the crisis by a Soviet SAM battery (following standard operating procedures, without direction from either the theatre commander or Moscow) that almost ignited war.

A dramatic example of the advantages of the organisational-behaviour model over the rational-actor model can be shown with an example from the Vietnam War. In early February 1965, President Johnson sent a team headed by McGeorge Bundy to South Vietnam to assess the war effort and decide whether he should commit greater US forces. Just as they were concluding their visit, communist forces attacked an air base at Pleiku. More than 100 Americans were killed or wounded. The Bundy team advised Johnson that this was clearly a deliberate act of defiance by Hanoi and that it gave him no choice but to hit back hard. The advice contributed directly to Johnson's decision to escalate the war in Vietnam.

The Pentagon Papers, a study completed for Robert McNamara in 1967 on how the United States had become bogged down in Vietnam, described the Pleiku incident as the 'trigger' for escalation by the United States. But on a visit to Vietnam in 1997, McNamara learned that the attack on Pleiku was planned not in Hanoi, but by a field commander who had had no awareness of Bundy's mission and didn't even know that US personnel were present at Pleiku at the time. The assumption that a rational actor ('Hanoi', or the North Vietnamese government) had weighed all the alternatives and decided to attack in order to achieve a clear objective *vis-a-vis* the United States was simply erroneous. The field organisation had proceeded with its planned attack unaware of the possible implications.

'In every case', comment Allison and Zelikow, 'analysts, managers and political leaders should be acutely aware of the gravitational pull exerted by organizational propensities.'[25] In the case of the Taiwan Strait, this applies in a number of ways. It should begin with a recognition that conditions of tension may lead to an unwarranted escalation of air-defence and naval-patrol procedures; and that the notion of pre-emption may appear attractive to those in China who believe that its missile capabilities make this possible, or that a shifting balance of power makes it advisable. The key concern is, in Allison and Zelikow's words, that

> 'security organisations or other components of government acting on "taken for granted assumptions, predispositions, scripts, conventions and classification schemes" produce decisions that cannot be comprehended in terms of the rational-actor model.'[26]

Like the rational-actor model, the organisational-behaviour model is grounded in a number of assumptions: that the decisions of government leaders trigger organisational routines, the nature and logic of which they can only imperfectly control; that the established organisational routines for action constitute the full range of options available to leaders—something that is not always appreciated by the leaders themselves, but which is crucial to understanding what actually gets done; that the organisational outputs actually set real constraints on what decisions leaders are free to make;[27] and that innovation is all but impossible at the time of a crisis. Established routines cannot be modified readily or effectively at a moment's notice.

For a national government to undertake any action of consequence it will, as a matter of course, rely on organisational practices that have been developed on a routinised basis. Moreover, within government, organisations 'will tend to emphasize in practice the objectives most congruent to their special capacities and to the hierarchies of beliefs in the organization's culture.'[28] This point has specific application to the organisational cultures of the Communist Party's various intelligence, policy, and propaganda arms, as well as the military cultures on both sides of the Taiwan Strait, the US Navy, and so on.

There is a third model to consider. Allison and Zelikow note that 'The leaders who sit atop organizations are no monolith. Rather, each individual in this group is, in his or her own right, a player in a central, competitive game.' Different leaders and organisations have differing agendas, interests, and objectives, as well as differing sources of power to effect actions. Consequently, they struggle with one another and engage in bargaining games over which objectives should be given priority, and what means should be used to pursue them. In other words, policy is set 'not by a single rational choice but by the pulling and hauling that is politics.'[29]

This set of lenses is called the governmental-politics model. There are many competing interest-groups within China, and the Communist Party's standard rhetoric about the united and unshakeable will of the entire Chinese people has to be understood in this light. Equally, the many divisions in Taiwan—between the blue and green camps, between pragmatists and maximalists within the green camp, between the armed forces' old culture of Chinese nationalism and the politics of Taiwanese identity, and between business interests with investments in China and independence activists wary of Taiwan being drawn into China's orbit—all come into play.

The governmental-politics model, like the other two models, consists of a core set of assumptions: that policies or measures taken are not chosen as rational solutions to problems, but result from bargaining among officials with differing interests and unequal influence; that the bargaining among these players is structured, and constrained by deadlines, competition for resources, hierarchies of power, and multiple, interacting uncertainties;[30] that competitors have 'parochial' priorities and perceptions, not a cool, objective analytical attitude to some specific, common problem;[31] that competitors have differential access to 'action channels' for getting things done, or pushing things in a preferred direction; that, in any given state, there are 'rules of the game' (laws and conventions) that constrain the freedom of action of the competitors;[32] and that 'the pace of the game'[33] puts pressure on decision-making processes that the rational-actor model does not account for.

This model makes explicit what the BBC comedy series *Yes, Minister* so delightfully 'dramatised'—that policy decisions are the results of elaborate gamesmanship, and energetic pulling and hauling, not the outcome of cool, value-maximising rational consideration by a single decision-maker. Against this background, we are better able to appreciate the argument advanced by Martin Lasater that China may opt to use force in the Taiwan Strait.

Clearly, he believed that things have reached a dangerous pass. He observed that China's previous declaratory policy had been that force would be used if there was a formal declaration of independence by Taiwan; foreign intervention in Taiwan's internal affairs; indefinite delays in resumption of dialogue by Taiwan about reunification; internal unrest in Taiwan; or acquisition by Taiwan of nuclear weapons. 'However', he commented, 'a greater near term danger to peace in the Taiwan Strait is the conclusion of Beijing's political and military leaders that there is no possibility of a peaceful solution to the Taiwan issue,' and that the condign use of force was a viable option for China.

Lasater identified a long list of conditions under which this might the case. The first three are already, apparently, in place. First, Taiwan continues to reject the 'one China' principle; second, the issue is so politicised on the mainland that a change of policy in this regard becomes impossible; third, 'the PRC concludes that ... Chen Shuibian is totally untrustworthy, so that ... any new proposals by the Chen government are viewed with suspicion.'[34] He then added a fourth condition which, arguably, is also already in place: 'the United States will not or cannot exert sufficient pressure on the Chen government to stop incremental independence, such as (in Beijing's view) revision of the ROC constitution (as anticipated by 2006).'[35]

Consistent locutions of the kind 'Beijing believes' or 'the PRC concludes' testified to Lasater's underlying tendency to view the matter through the lenses of the rational-actor model. Yet, by considering a range of factors that would impinge on even a notionally rational strategic calculation by China, he achieved two things. He drew attention to the complexity of the decision facing any 'rational actor' in China and, at the same time, he indirectly pointed out how many interests, both inside and outside China, will be involved in the pulling and hauling of government policy-making. He did not, however, differentiate between the different Chinese leaders or interest groups, or examine the machineries by means of which they are informed or constrained in decision-making.

Lasater conceded, somewhat obliquely, that the rationality of China's leaders is bounded rather than comprehensive when he remarked, 'Most of [the] conditions are actually perceptions on the part of Chinese political and military leaders; they may or may not be true.'[36] But he did not discuss whether there might be differentiated perceptions among various parts of the Chinese government, and what pulling and hauling this gives rise to. Nor did he discuss the possibility that, because of parochial interests and objectives such as budget share or nationalist legitimisation, elements of the PLA and the Communist Party are far more anxious to push for the use of force than are large sections of the business community, or the nascent political opposition.

There are indicators of 'pulling and hauling' in Taiwan, too. Recent developments include the formation by Hsu Hsin-liang and others of a new political movement in opposition to Chen Shuibian, on the grounds that he is an independence 'fundamentalist' who will lead the island to a disastrous war with China. Lee Tenghui has called for Taiwan to acquire nuclear weapons. Similar indicators are present in the United States, where powerful interests are in competition over China policy, and the outcome of their competition is by no means clear-cut. Chinese policy-makers have had to learn, over time, that American policies are the result of struggles between the White House and Congress, the Pentagon and the State Department.

Not only did Lasater not allow for the complexities of governmental politics, with the various forms of leverage they allow to constrain or advance agendas, he also made no allowance for the organisational dynamics of the PLA and the Communist Party in assessing how decisions are made in China: he blithely referred to 'leaders in Beijing' as if they formed a unitary rational actor likely to draw the same conclusions on the basis of a shared set of perceptions and priorities over the indefinite future, and certainly for the next few years. This is surely untrue, and importantly so. Recognition of the number of different agendas running in China will be a vital part of any strategy for heading off the ominous possibility of war across the Straits, whether in the Year of the Dog or thereafter.

With the possibility of war looming in the not-too-distant future, the question is: can rationality save us? What the excursion into *Essence of Decision* shows is that we cannot rely on comprehensive rationality characterising the deliberations of the various countries involved. Bounded rationality, not comprehensive rationality, will shape how policy thinking is done on all sides. Moreover, the nature of organisational behaviours and governmental politics, whether in China, Taiwan, or the United States, significantly complicates any calculus of national interests and intentions. While this can seem like a statement of the obvious, it is necessary to spell it out, because by default everyone tends to attribute 'rational actor' intentionality to what are, almost without exception, the results of bounded rationality, organisational behaviours, and governmental politics.

Under these circumstances, the first lesson highlighted by Morris in *The Fog of War* comes into play—we need to empathise with our enemies, or potential enemies, in order to understand how they see the world and make decisions, lest we mislead ourselves through prejudice, or through naïve, vicarious problem-solving. The widespread acknowledgement of the 'one China' principle extended by all those who are fastidious about not offending it is an example of such empathy. Some empathy has also been extended to the Taiwanese by those in China who, for twenty years or so, have advocated the 'one country, two systems' formula. On the balance of present evidence, however, the empathy exhibited so far has been insufficient to solve the problem.

If the problem is to be solved short of war, something has to give. There is no way to be certain that what does so will be the assumptions which drive present policies; therefore, war may come. It may come because a war party in China pulls hard enough to take the country over the brink; or it may come despite no one particularly wanting it, because organisational-behavioural routines generate incidents and responses that spin out of rational control. Or it may come because vicarious problem-solving in Beijing or Taipei or Washington convinces some critical mass of decision-makers that a blitzkrieg or a declaration of independence or the defence of Taiwan by American forces or the abandonment of Taiwan to Chinese aggression will best serve the putative national interest.

There is no way to exert overarching rational control of such a complex situation. Likewise, there is no sound basis for trusting that the human beings most directly involved in making critical decisions will understand one another, think matters through clearly, or be able to exert sufficient authority over their own machineries of government and military power to contain the situation without conflict. Consequently, the usual modes of behaviour will substitute for rationality: balance-of-power manoeuvres, secret intelligence-gathering, multilateral diplomacy, calls for confidence-building measures, arms races, and public demonstrations of anger and resolve.

Yet the stakes are such that it is neither possible nor acceptable to be fatalistic or cynical about this situation. Like McNamara, we surely hold, at some level, that we can and should do better than we have in the past. As I have argued, there is a strong case to be made that China's objective interests would be best served by reconsidering its passionate commitment to the reincorporation of Taiwan as radically and imaginatively in the present decade as it rethought its economic policies in the decade after the death of Mao Zedong. The question is simply whether this thought-experiment can be conducted with decisive effect within China.

Writing in the *Straits Times* in April 2004, Ching Cheong went so far as to declare that 'Beijing now realizes that there must be something fundamentally wrong in its approach towards Taiwan.'[37] It is notable that he used the standard rational-actor locution: 'Beijing' surely does not 'realise' anything. Although debate within the various organs of the Chinese state, its universities and think-tanks is subdued by the Communist Party's heavy, censoring hand, there are clear signs that it is quite intense. But the pulling and hauling are not leading to the conclusion Ching implied. On the contrary, the rhetoric emanating from Beijing suggests that governmental politics in China are dangerously close to locking its policy into a no-win, confrontational stance.

The crux of the matter is that Taiwan will not accept incorporation on the 'one country, two systems' model, and China has not so far offered anything else. In 1992, there was a brief informal consensus around the idea that 'one China' could be interpreted differently on either side of the Strait, but this idea has been allowed to lapse; subsequently, whether 'rationally' or otherwise, the Chinese government has since rejected all proposals from Taiwan, whether Guomindang or DPP, that were based on a demand for parity between the two polities. As Ching Cheong remarked, each time a proposal was rejected, it caused an intensified resentment of China's hegemonic presumption in Taiwan and a hardening of separatist feeling. 'Now', he commented, 'Beijing is reaping its own bitter harvest.'

'Ironically', he went on, 'while Beijing rejected the 1992 consensus proposed by the [Guomindang], it is now urging the DPP to return to that as the precondition for reopening dialogue. But it is too late now. The DPP denies the very existence at all of the so-called consensus.' In any case, he added, China's political system is such as to repel Taiwanese of both blue and green camps alike. Only a fundamental reform of the political system in China would be likely to make some form of reunification acceptable to them, and such reform is not something the Communist Party seems willing to contemplate. Yet, in the words of a Chinese, academic Lin Shangli, the 'one country, two systems' formula depended for its success on 'the construction of the political system in the "one country"'—that is, a breakthrough to more liberal governance in China.[38]

What this discussion makes plain is that, amid all the complexities, there are, finally, only two basic stumbling blocks to a rational resolution of the Taiwan question: the Communist Party's continuing dictatorial rule in China, and the insistence by Chinese revanchists that the country's national dignity is inconsistent with the formal recognition of Taiwan. Neither position is rationally tenable and, therefore, neither should be accepted as immovable, nor as a sound basis for resolution of the Taiwan question.

There is no justification for the Communist Party being permitted to maintain its hold over a country that has suffered so much under its rule, and that now has a burgeoning middle class capable of sustaining more responsible governance. The assertion that China's national dignity is inconsistent with Taiwan's independence is also unsustainable. On the contrary, China's national dignity will surely be diminished should it go to war to crush the aspirations of 23 million Taiwanese. The question to be insistently pressed upon those responsible for China's national security policy must be: what do you mean by 'dignity'? A new understanding with a free Taiwan that brought lasting amity and trust, redoubled trade, and the decreased possibility of a disastrous regional war would do far more good for China's national dignity than the subjugation of Taiwan. If reform and opening of the economy could bring such overwhelming and unexpected benefits to the country, why shouldn't a similarly radical rethinking of territorial claims do the same?

In so far as any collectively more or less 'rational actor' ponders the Taiwan question in China, amid the failures of twenty years of insistence on reincorporation of the island republic, it should be possible for it (or them) to weigh the benefits of embracing Taiwan against the costs of resorting to war in the attempt to take it back, and to look for ways to reframe the question constructively. The authorities in Taiwan could assist such a process by seeking to articulate the case for amity even more clearly than they have done to this point. Those in surrounding states with the courage and imagination to do something other than cling to the status quo would do well to advance this case, with quiet insistence, to Chinese officials and scholars.

Rationality *could* save us, if by rationality we mean critically thinking the matter through, and subjecting current policies, on all sides, to careful scrutiny. It will only fail us to the extent that such critical thinking is inhibited by the usual suspects: the fog of mutual incomprehension that pervades international affairs; the pursuit of parochial interests and objectives by various compartments of government within different states; and the unreflective persistence in established patterns of belief and behaviour within the instrumentalities of those states—particularly their armed forces.

Rationality does not, of course, occur in a vacuum. David Hume asserted that 'reason is the slave of the passions'. His aphorism might be reworded, 'merely formal rationality is the slave of fixed assumptions'. But critical rationality is another matter. How can critical rationality be brought to bear on fixed assumptions? Even in the most open society, this occurs only with considerable difficulty—and China is still far from being an open society. Even its policy-making institutions remain restricted in the exercise of critical rationality by the relentless efforts of the Communist Party to maintain and enforce its monopoly on political power. Yet China is the key in this matter. Change based on new insight must come from within China, if the Taiwan problem is to be resolved without war.

Part Three

Chinese Culture and the Modern World

Chapter 8

Ancient History, Modern Cinema and Political Allegory

Twenty six years after Cheng, the King of Qin, was enthroned (in 246 BCE), he unified the world for the first time, making it into thirty-six commanderies and called himself the First Emperor.

—Sima Qian, *The Grand Scribe's Records* (c. 100 BCE)[1]

Film can be a powerful medium of cultural and political education. Its great strength is its capacity to reach millions of people across a country, or across the world. For this reason, it has also been a tool favoured by political propagandists since at least the 1930s. No film is more notorious in this regard than Leni Riefenstahl's superbly crafted documentary celebration of the Nazi movement in Germany, *Triumph of the Will*, which played to packed houses throughout Germany in the mid-1930s.[2]

The new Chinese cinema of the past twenty years has produced some remarkable films: humane, beautifully crafted and, in several cases, politically daring. One thinks of films such as Zhang Yimou's *Red Sorghum* and Chen Kaige's *Farewell My Concubine*. One of the most audacious of recent years was Zhang Yimou's *Shanghai Triad* which, in the best tradition of Chinese theatre, held up the past as a mirror to the present, by implying that the Communist Party, under the aged Deng Xiaoping and his protégé Jiang Zemin, was comparable to the notorious Green Gang—the old criminal syndicate in pre-revolutionary Shanghai.

It was all the more interesting, therefore, that Zhang Yimou chose to write and direct *Hero* (2002)—a film that, for all its visual beauty and technical craftsmanship, has the air about it of a piece of Communist Party propaganda. It is possible that many viewers outside China will experience *Hero* as no more than a martial arts spectacular, in which Zhang Yimou attempts to out-choreograph Ang Lee's highly successful *Crouching Tiger, Hidden Dragon*. But, when directed at the mass audience in China, and the domestic and exiled political opposition to the Communist Party, it is much more than that. The film carries the unambiguous political message that the First Emperor, (read the Communist Party), should not be assassinated (overthrown), because he (it) has always had a grand vision of peace and unity for China. It concludes that China is 'our land' and the First Emperor its authentic hero, so that those assassins (dissidents) who renounce rebellion are, also, heroes—even if they remain nameless.

This is a hugely regressive step on the part of a supposedly visionary and humane filmmaker. For more than 2,000 years the denunciation of the First Emperor, Qin Shih-huangdi, for his cruelties and massacres, his burning of books and purging of scholars, has been a classic part of China's suppressed political culture. He has long been characterised as a self-satisfied and oppressive individual who was lacking in humanity (*ren*) and righteousness (*yi*), and was unwilling to admit fault.[3] All these criticisms could be directed, with at least equal justice, at the Communist Party.

Yet *Hero* portrays the First Emperor as handsome, brilliant, and humane. There is no evidence of his crimes, only of his overwhelming military power, steadfast courage, and unnerving insight into the thinking and machinations of those who plot against him. The film's obeisance to the memory of the founding tyrant of China's imperial past is all the more unsettling considering that Mao Zedong likened himself to the First Emperor—much as Stalin was inclined to liken himself to Ivan the Terrible or Peter the Great. If Zhang was not seeking to glorify the party, he must have been extraordinarily politically naïve. Even if his film was not intended as a propaganda stunt, he cannot escape the charge of having done for Chinese cinema and for the dictatorial regime in Beijing what Leni Riefenstahl did for Hitler—albeit with a little more subtlety.

There could hardly be a greater contrast, in this respect, than that between Zhang Yimou's *Hero* and Chen Kaige's *The Emperor and the Assassin* (released by Silkscreen Films in 2000). Both films tell of the First Emperor's brutal unification of China, and of attempts to assassinate him and put an end to his ruthless quest for dominance. But Zhang's propaganda is far less grounded in historical fact than is Chen's powerful political parable. Where Zhang makes the emperor a figure of wisdom and grave responsibility who seems wholly self-sufficient, Chen makes him a haunted and unstable character whose bloody quest to unify 'all under Heaven' is denounced by those closest to him. Zhang weaves a fictional and fanciful story around the emperor, whereas Chen takes a historical story and reworks it in a manner worthy of Shakespeare. This does not make Zhang's film uninteresting—on the contrary, it is quite fascinating, if a little alarming, that he should have given us, and his compatriots, such a film in the early twenty-first century. But Chen's film is altogether more free-spirited and challenging.

The Emperor and the Assassin is breathtaking in its scale, its cinematic grandeur, and its theatrical boldness. Chen and his collaborators have taken a classic Chinese story and, in a manner redolent of both Chinese and Western masters of theatre, breathed into it a subtle, but powerful, contemporary spirit. Where Zhang Yimou's *Shanghai Triad* threw a challenge to the Communist Party, *The Emperor and the Assassin* implies that the Communist Party's repression of dissent, suppression of Tibet, and threats to use force against Taiwan should be considered in the same light as the brutal imperialism of Qin Shih-huangdi in the third century BCE. This, I think, is the meaning of the film.

The story behind the screenplay is the famous tale of treachery and murder told by Sima Qian, and recorded around 100 BCE in the *Shiji* (*The Grand Scribe's Records*). According to this source, in 227 BCE, as the King of Qin moved relentlessly to crush the other six kingdoms left in the 'Chinese' world, the crown prince of Yan sent an assassin to kill him. Yan was a principality in the north-east of what is now China, around where Beijing now stands. Its crown prince had been a hostage in Qin, but had become angry with the King of Qin and fled back to Yan. Since Yan itself lacked the military power to attack Qin, he looked for other means to strike at the enemy, and eventually prevailed upon the wandering scholar and swordsman Jing Ke to attempt assassination. Jing Ke, we are told by the historian, was actually a man of peace; but an exiled Qin general, Fan Yuqi, persuaded him to attempt the assassination at the crown prince's behest by offering his own head as bait to win the trust of the tyrant of Qin. Awed by this sacrifice for a greater good, Jing Ke accepted the mission.

The success of the mission depended on gaining access to the presence of the King of Qin. General Fan's head was used to ensure access. The weapon for the assassination, a dagger, was to be concealed in a case containing a map of Yan, which would be opened in the king's presence—and then, before courtiers or guards could react, the king would be struck down. The plot almost succeeded, Sima Qian tells us. Jing Ke and his assistant, Qin Wuyang, gained admission to the king's presence with the dagger concealed in the map case, and the head of General Fan in a container. Then, however, Qin lost his nerve and nearly gave the game away.

But Jing Ke kept his cool. He smiled and asked the king to excuse his companion, who, being a simple man from a backward region, 'has never seen the Son of Heaven and therefore shakes with fear'. Qin was excused and Jing Ke gave General Fan's head to the king, unrolled the map and, at the psychological moment, seized the dagger and lunged at the king. The king, however, was able to get clear of the blow and fled around the pillars of the audience hall, pursued by the assassin, who finally hurled the dagger at him, but missed and hit a pillar. Jing Ke was then struck down, and the king killed him with his own sword.

The detail of Sima Qian's account is in the film,[4] but Chen Kaige and co-writer Wang Peigong gave a dramatic interpretation of the historical material that lends it altogether more depth and contemporary resonance. One is reminded of the way in which Shakespeare took stories from Plutarch or Holinshed, and created subtle variations on them, in order to throw into relief his explorations of politics and humanity. For example, in *The Emperor and the Assassin*, Chen and Wang created Lady Zhao, a character who does not appear in the history at all. Gong Li, the actor who plays Lady Zhao (and incidentally, is Zhang Yimou's former mistress), has had a wide range of stunning roles in many of the films mentioned, from *Red Sorghum* to *Shanghai Triad*.

The invention of Lady Zhao is a bold move, and one for which historical purists might criticise the film-makers. Yet it is a poetic masterstroke. She seems to have been created to represent the soul or conscience of the King of Qin and an emissary of the Goddess of Humanity—if not the Goddess of Democracy. She is a sort of anti-Lady Macbeth. Whereas, in Shakespeare's great tragic drama, Lady Macbeth urges her husband on to crime and usurpation, Lady Zhao urges her lover, the King of Qin, to promise that he will look after all the people of the warring states, and bring peace—not the sword—to the Chinese world. When he goes further and further down the path of ruthless conquest, she turns against him and becomes Jing Ke's lover and co-conspirator. This is not mere 'Hollywood' melodrama on the part of the scriptwriters. It is a very deliberate poetic and political gloss on Chinese history.

The relationship between Lady Zhao and the King of Qin in the film is an interesting construction in other respects, too. Historically, King Zheng is known to have had numerous concubines and to have treated women as cruelly as he treated everyone else. In the film there is no evidence of any woman in his life other than his great love, Lady Zhao, who talks to him as an equal, rebukes him and, after the death of Jing Ke, freely leaves him—something inconceivable in the historical reality on which the film is based.

Early in the film, Lady Zhao announces her intention to leave, because she feels their childhood intimacy has given way to the coldness of the power-oriented palace. She admonishes him that he wants someone who will simply keep quiet and be there when he deigns to visit, but she wants to be able to talk out loud and be herself. This is, surely intended to stand for the modern Chinese citizen rebuking the Communist Party for its suppression of the freedoms of civil society. Does King Zheng mock her, or confine her? No. With tears in his eyes, he goes down on his knees and begs her to stay, saying that he has been hoping to unify all under Heaven, then marry her and make her his queen. The Queen of all under Heaven? She is intrigued and awed by his promises, and so begins their dialogue concerning the terms on which she would consent to marry him.

The film begins, and ends, with King Zheng reflecting on the 'command of his Qin ancestors' to unite all under Heaven[5]. Surely, this is a message directed at the current leaders of the People's Republic of China who talk of the 'sacred duty' to reunify the 'motherland' without regard for possible bloodshed? Even the fairly level-headed Zhu Rongji, indulged in this sort of bellicose rhetoric during the very year the film was released, when he was premier. One can only wonder what the real hawks within the Chinese power elite are prepared to contemplate.

What is behind this chauvinistic fervour? *In The Emperor and the Assassin*, it is, at least ostensibly, a grand vision of peace and harmony, and an end to the centuries of warring. In one memorable scene, the hostage crown prince of Yan is led into the Imperial Map Hall by a dwarf in the service of the king and shown a map of the imagined unified empire. 'My master', declares the dwarf, 'will offer you high office in his service, if you will accept his rule'. The crown prince proudly declines, saying that Yan will never surrender its freedom. The same defiance meets the would-be 'Son of Heaven' throughout the six remaining kingdoms in the 'Chinese' world—Zhao, Yan, Qi, Wei, Han and Zhu—and, consequently, he finds that the realisation of his ambition creates not peace, but 'mountains of bodies and rivers of blood'.[6]

This confluence of ambition and blood is the central 'Shakespearean' theme of the film. Whenever the king quails before the human costs of his 'mission', he is confronted by a zombie-like figure, the Master of Rites, who challenges him, 'King Zheng, have you forgotten the command of your Qin ancestors to unite all under Heaven?'[7] In Chen and Wang's theatrical symbolism, I read the Master of Rites as standing for Chinese Communist Party dogma, or the jingoistic nationalism that it is gradually substituting for its decayed Marxism. He is the embodiment of the tyranny of history in the Chinese world, haunting and poisoning its efforts to break free from the oppressiveness of the past.

Perhaps the most interesting dramatic interpolation by Chen and Wang is the scene in the temple of the Qin ancestors, where the king is goaded into choosing between the Master of Rites and his own natural, but unacknowledged father and erstwhile prime minister, Lu Buwei. The Master of Rites challenges the King: kill either me or your own father. Lu Buwei makes the choice for him when he commits suicide by hanging himself in the temple, in his son's presence. He thereby ensures that no one will believe the King of Qin was his illegitimate son, rather than the heir to the previous ruler.

Given the controversial nature of the tale about First Emperor's real paternity, it is particularly interesting that Chen and his colleagues have chosen to portray the most derogatory version of it. The story that Lu Buwei had fathered Zheng before passing his mother over to the prince of Qin (and Zheng's 'legal' father) Zichu, is credited by Sima Qian. But modern historians suspect that the story was interpolated into the work of Sima Qian by a later Han scribe, 'in order to slander the First Emperor and indicate his political as well as natal illegitimacy'.[8] As Dirk Bodde wrote, 'The interpolation has been eminently successful ... for until recent times, the story of the First Emperor's bastard birth was doubted by almost no-one.'[9] Bodde's remarks show that a more conservative interpretation of the story was available to the screenplay writers, had they been interested.

It is important to understand, however, that the tale of Lu Buwei and the First Emperor is, by all accounts, complex and, in general, Chen and Wang adhere to it in detail. After the death of Zheng's father, in 246 BCE, when the future First Emperor was only thirteen years old, Lu resumed sexual relations with Zheng's mother, his former concubine, then passed her on to the lascivious Marquis Lao Ai. When the king came of age, in 238 BCE, he had Lao Ai and his whole family executed. He dismissed Lu the following year, and when he was banished by the king, in 235 BCE, Lu took his own life by swallowing poison.[10]

The use of the tale by Chen and Wang is surely quite deliberate and I want to suggest that their intention was to create a stunning political allegory. Their Lu Buwei may be seen as the real father of modern Chinese nationalism—Sun Yatsen. (An alternative reading would be that Lu stands instead for Liang Qichao (1873–1929), the constitutionalist and republican, and Sun Yatsen's intellectual rival, as the natural father of the Chinese revolution.) If we conflate Sun with Lu, though, we can still interpret this figure as the 'lover' of the Chinese revolution before there was a Communist Party. We can continue the analogy by suggesting that Sun fathered the one-party state, showing Mao Zedong the way to totalitarian power, but could not be acknowledged as Mao's political father without undermining the legitimacy of the communist state.

The allegory need not be complete and detailed for us to appreciate the underlying allusion: the real father of republican China must be repudiated and 'commit suicide' if the Chinese Communist Party's dogma is to have its way, and if the legitimacy of its tyranny is to remain unquestioned. The alternative, of course, is a more human and honest reckoning, and a retreat from the 'command of the Qin ancestors'—the tyranny of history. Why cannot King

Zheng repudiate the Master of Rites, and embrace his natural father? In the film, Chen has him agonise, out of filial emotion, until the decision is taken out of his hands.

The strength of this scene, and of many like it in *The Emperor and the Assassin*, is what makes Chen and Wang's screenplay remarkable. Even if they did not consciously intend so elaborate a political allegory, the film is richly suggestive. As I have remarked, the interpretations available to the viewer set it in marked contrast to Zhang Yimou's political propaganda, *Hero*. After all, had Chen Kaige wanted to give us political allegory of the conservative kind, he need only have retained the version of Lu Buwei's death by poison recounted by Sima Qian. Instead, he chose to make Lu's suicide central to the drama about Zheng's rule. Dramatists do not, as a rule, do such things for no reason.

The character of Jing Ke has also been reworked by Chen and Wang, but while this alters the historical story it does not introduce any confusion. On the contrary, it once again illustrates what the two scriptwriters were trying to communicate to us in making their film. Historically, Jing Ke was not a professional assassin. In the film, he is a repentant professional assassin who has become sick at heart and has renounced violence. It takes a great deal of persuasion and compelling evidence of the atrocities of the King of Qin for him to agree to attempt a final assassination.

Why have Chen and Wang chosen to portray the character in this way? Jing Ke may be seen as personifying the revolutionary youth of twentieth-century China. Having become sick of violence after the orgy of chaos and bloodshed under Mao Zedong, that youth has no wish to kill again. They could be persuaded to contemplate violence in one cause only: the ending of the ruthless tyranny of the 'King of Qin' (the Communist Party), with his insistence on dominating 'all under Heaven' (the whole Chinese world). Significantly, the choice by Jing Ke to attempt the assassination is sealed by the king's massacre of the children of Handan, capital of Zhao, whom he orders buried alive.

This seems to be an obvious allusion to the Tiananmen Square massacre of young students, and the imprisonment of thousands more, in June 1989. Certainly, it is impossible not to recall that incident when watching Lady Zhao weeping bitterly over the dead children. It is the massacre that finally induces her to break with the King of Qin and curse him bitterly for his savagery. When Wei Jingsheng, a former Red Guard who, since 1978 has been an outspoken advocate of democracy in China, declared from abroad in the late 1990s that the Communist Party should be overthrown—even at the risk of civil war—he was on the same moral plane as Jing Ke in *The Emperor and the Assassin*.

There is a further connection with Tiananmen Square that Western audiences are likely to miss, but which would surely not be lost on Chinese viewers. The detail is in a rebuke to the King of Qin by Lady Zhao, when she is trying to persuade him to relent in his ruthless use of force. 'Your name used to be Zhao Zheng', she reminds him, referring to the name he was given at birth, before he became King Zheng, never mind the First Emperor. It's hard not to see in Lady Zhao's question an echo of the name of Zhao Ziyang, who was opposed to the use of force in Tiananmen Square in 1989, and who was removed from office because this stance did not please Deng Xiaoping.[11] 'Your name used to be Zhao Zheng' can be heard here as 'Zhao Ziyang used to be the face the party presented to the people'—but now it is the face of bloody repression.

Another of the 'Shakespearean' variations on Sima Qian is the curious representation of the Marquis Lao Ai. According to the historical record, he was a lecherous courtier given by Lu Buwei to the queen mother to satisfy her sexual needs when Lu himself had to make prudence the better part of ardour and withdraw from his affair with her. These details are included in the film, as is Lao Ai's later, desperate attempt at a palace coup, when his own liaison with her threatens to bring him down. What Chen and Wang add, however, seems to have no source in the annals of Chinese history.

When brought before the monarch, Lao Ai gains immensely in dignity, and engages in a sharp exchange with King Zheng about his hypocrisy and ruthlessness, and the price of absolute power. The scene is quite unexpected because Lao Ai seems, to that point, to be a scheming and shifty character. Suddenly, when faced with death for high treason, he finds a voice that had been suppressed by the atmosphere of power and intrigue in the court. And when, at last, he is led away by the guards, he laughs at the king as a bastard and a pretender. We are spared the historically attested death of Lao Ai by dismemberment. As viewers, we are given one more dignified indictment of the tyranny of the King of Qin, and the nightmare of his grand dominion.

The Emperor and the Assassin has been compared to the great films of Sergei Eisenstein, David Lean, and Akira Kurosawa. Such comparisons are justified. The most interesting comparisons are with Eisenstein's *Ivan the Terrible* and David Lean's *Doctor Zhivago*. Both *Ivan the Terrible* and *The Emperor and the Assassin* are tragedies of power in the Shakespearean sense. In Eisenstein's film the struggle is between Ivan and Euphrosyne Staritsky, who jealously defends the feudal fragmentation of Russia against his vision of a unified and powerful state. By comparison, Lady Zhao opposes King Zheng not for the sake of the old, feudal fragmentation or because she seeks power herself, but out of humanity. She speaks with the voice of the present generation to the great historical tyrant of China, and her voice resonates against two millennia of rule by 'divine right' in the Middle Kingdom.

The parallel with *Doctor Zhivago* is less direct, but the message is again one of humanity versus an obsession with political power. Boris Pasternak wrote his Nobel Prize-winning novel as a plea for the beauty and self-creating freedom of life against the tyrannous pretensions of Marxism–Leninism. His poet—to the irritation of Isaac Deutscher and other Marxist critics—lived the symbolist freedom of the human spirit in defiance of the party, and died unreconciled to the cause of historical materialism.[12] Zhivago's life, in resistance to overbearing power, is beautifully captured in Robert Bolt's screenplay, but it is even more poignantly articulated in Pasternak's novel.

Like Lady Zhao, Yuri Zhivago sets the integrity of the personal life against the Marxist-Leninist quest to engineer the human soul. He scorns the pretensions of the 'engineers' that they can reshape life. In a famous passage from the novel, Zhivago exclaims to the communist partisan Liberius Mikulitsin:

> Reshaping life! People who can say that have never understood a thing about life—they have never felt its breath, its heart—however much they have seen or done. They look on it as a lump of raw material which needs to be processed by them, to be ennobled by their touch. But life is never a material, a substance to be moulded. If you want to know, life is the principle of self-renewal, it is constantly renewing and remaking and changing and transfiguring itself, it is infinitely beyond your or my inept theories about it.[13]

Chen's cinematography and the nature of Lady Zhao's revulsion from the emperor seem to me to suggest a similar sense of what life is really about.

That the sublime Gong Li should be chosen to represent and enact this message is wholly appropriate. Her sheer beauty of both body and person—like that of Julie Christie as Lara in *Doctor Zhivago*—embodies the poetry of humanity and puts to shame the ugliness of the will to power. These parallels serve to underscore just how distinguished and classical a piece of cinema *The Emperor and the Assassin* is. For all its visual effects, *Hero* can make no such claim. Given the political realities of China, it is more akin to *Triumph of the Will* than it is to *Doctor Zhivago*. By using the same, pivotal period in China's ancient history but framing it in radically different ways, *Hero* and *The Emperor and the Assassin* set the terms of debate about China's future political evolution. We should be in no doubt as to which is both the better film and the better future.

Chapter 9

Overcoming the Confucian: rethinking Chinese tradition

> *China has lost two major worldviews since encountering the modern West in the course of the nineteenth century. Scriptural Confucianism collapsed as a self-reproducing system by the early years of the twentieth century ... Maoist Communism was strategically dead by the start of the 1980s ... the double disavowal has left an emptiness at the heart of Chinese metaphysical life—the life of meanings—that no mixture of consumerism and familism, power lust and patriotism, borrowed modernism or neo-neo-Confucian revivalism, will satisfactorily fill for long.*
>
> —Mark Elvin, *Changing Stories in the Chinese World*

Even though the Communist Party has managed to perpetuate its monopoly on political power well past its use-by date, there is a restless need in China for new ideas and beliefs to lend coherence to the emerging post-communist epoch. The most commonly cited candidate for this role is neo-Confucianism—a restoration of traditional Chinese values and beliefs. This was particularly true in the 1990s, before the Asian financial crisis took something of the wind out of the sails of the 'east Asian model', and it was implicit in Samuel Huntington's loose description of 'Confucian civilization'. To think meaningfully about all this and how to engage intelligently with it, we need to overcome some confusion over Confucianism. We need to see that, neo or retro, it can be critically analysed just as readily as the ancient systems of thought that shaped the Western world.

According to *The Analects* of Confucius, #7:8, 'The Master said: "I enlighten only the enthusiastic; I guide only the fervent. After I have lifted up one corner of a question, if the student cannot discover the other three, I do not repeat."' In the spirit of the Master, let me try to lift just one corner of the debate about Confucianism in contemporary China. The question at the bottom of the debate over Neo-Confucianism is: 'What do the Confucian classics have to teach us at the dawn of the twenty-first century?' Of course, it is not always raised precisely as a question. Nonetheless, this is the question that was implicit during the 1990s in the so-called 'Asian values' debate, giving it a very contemporary context. As discussed in chapter[1], Samuel Huntington wrote of the threat to Western civilisation arising from 'Confucian civilization'. Five years later, in 2000, Lee Kuan Yew wrote that 'There is no Asian model as such, but there are fundamental differences between East Asian Confucian and Western liberal societies.'[2]

However, I do not intend to address the Confucian question in the context of contemporary debate. I propose, instead, to put it into the context of the emergence of what I call *universal cognitive humanism*. By this I mean that what happened in China 2,500 years ago is intelligible in terms of the general development of human kind. Indeed, it is more intelligible in these terms than if we lose ourselves in the obscurities of Chinese Confucian orthodoxy. In the deeper context of universal cognitive humanism, we can set the Chinese sage, and his heirs, free of narrow interpretations based on current political agendas. We can also set both their work and contemporary debates about the 'clash of civilisations' in critical perspective. We can, therefore, see where current debates come from, before plunging into them.

Let's begin by reversing our temporal perspective on the ancient Chinese sages. We say 'ancient' because we think of them as belonging to the earliest era of world history—that is, the years 'before the Common Era'—which recedes into the mists of folk memory. This takes us back to the Yellow Emperor, if you are Chinese; or Ur of the Chaldees and the Pharoahs of Egypt, if you are from the Middle East or the West. Though the ancient sages came well after this, they still seem to come 'early' in the story of mankind. But even in terms of agrarian civilisation, these thinkers of the second half of the last millennium BCE were latecomers.

There had already been settled agrarian societies in their parts of the world for many thousands of years before they were born. Consequently, their perspective was one of looking back on an ancient past, not a forward-looking perspective suited to imagining a radically different future. Plato, for example, in the fourth century BCE, believed that Egypt had had ten thousand years of history before his own day and that Atlantis had been destroyed long, long before. Aristotle, a generation younger than Plato, believed that technology was not likely to progress much beyond what had been achieved by his time—still in the fourth century BCE.

So, how did the minds of people in that time work? To begin with, consider that human cognitive development—the development of the human mind—goes back far earlier again than the beginnings of agriculture. Archaic human beings have been in what we now call Asia for between 500,000 and one million years.[3] Modern human beings—our own species of hominid—have been in what became 'China' a couple of thousand years ago for at least 40,000 years.[4] Both genetically and culturally, in other words, the human beings of Confucius' era, who fought one another much like ancient Greeks and who also discussed ethics and politics as human ideals, were of vastly older stock than our own backward-looking historical perspective tends to allow. The same is true of Plato and Aristotle. To them, the world was already old, just as it was for the writer in *Ecclesiastes* who declared that, 'What has happened before will happen again. What has been done before will be done again. There is nothing new in the whole world. "Look!", they say, "here is something new!" But no, it has all happened before, long before we were born.'[5]

Our common ancestors would appear to have come out of Africa, about 150,000 years ago. They seem to have encountered a number of other human species abroad in the world, and to have driven them to extinction by 30,000 years ago.[6] The first great wave of 'imperialism', in other words, originated in Africa, and conquered both Europe and Asia before discovering and conquering the Americas.[7] These Palaeolithic *Homo sapiens* had the same sized brain and the same natural cognitive capacities as ourselves. They overcame all other hominids and all other creatures, during the endless millennia of the Palaeolithic, because of a *cognitive* advantage: the conceptual and communicative capacities bound up with the full-blown development of language. Whether the extinction of other kinds of hominids or of Pleistocene megafauna was experienced or discussed as an ethical issue some 150,000 to 30,000 years ago is unclear. If it was so discussed, we do not know whether cumulative conceptual progress was made. What we can state with some confidence, however, is that 'sapient' human beings uniquely negotiate their ethical and political rules linguistically.

With all our cognitive gifts it still took 140,000 years after the exodus from Africa before any of our kind invented agriculture. Why this was so is still under investigation, but it is universally regarded as the beginning of what we call civilisation.[8] It took a further 5,000 years for agrarian peoples anywhere to invent writing, by which I mean not elementary graphical devices such as body-painting, pictures on rocks, or scratches on bones, but ideographic systems.[9] Agriculture was the seedbed for the cumulative *material* development of human civilisation; writing, for its cumulative *cognitive* development. Whether we are considering Mesopotamian, Chinese, Indian, or Mediterranean civilisations, these are universal truths. It was the confluence of these developments that made possible the work of the first millennium BCE sages, in both the East and the West. They were leisured thinkers conversant with established traditions of written poetry, history, cosmology, and philosophy.

If we are to set Confucius and Mencius alongside their Western counterparts Socrates and Plato in judicious perspective, we must begin by seeing them in this long-term context. Once we do so, we can begin to see what problems they encountered as they faced the challenge of understanding a world which was changing—Ecclesiastes notwithstanding. What they had in common was access to new, more abstract ways of thinking, made possible by centuries and even millennia of cognitive accumulation. They were increasingly able to generate theories of ethics and society, because written records and the use of writing as a tool made the beginnings of comparative and logical analysis possible.[10]

It might be objected that Confucius, like Socrates, did not write, but rather engaged in conversation and verbal argument. This would be to miss the point about the nature of their conversations. We would, in any case, know nothing reliable of Confucius had his disciples not set down a written record of his sayings. Similarly, we would know nothing reliable of Socrates if Plato and Xenophon had not written down their accounts of his dialogues with others. More importantly, even in their conversations, both Confucius and Socrates drew upon—one might say moved in and out of—the world of ideas accumulated in writing over the preceding centuries. They plainly were literate men. When we get to Mencius and Plato, this tradition is even more apparent.

A third pair of thinkers readily juxtaposed is Xunzi (310-238 BCE) and Aristotle, whose comparative, analytical, and deductive work would have been impossible without close reference to, and use of, written records. This is because theories depend on the external storage and careful manipulation of ideas rather than on the intuitive, unassisted brain. Once we grasp the significance of these facts of *cognitive process*, we are able to avoid falling into the trap of mystifying the ideas of any of these thinkers. We can examine them from two dispassionate points of view. First, we can put them in comparative perspective, given our access to a vastly deeper archive of written records and a much more powerful armoury of cognitive tools than they had. Second, we can put them in analytic perspective, by relating to them as sets of propositions, rather than as mystical and authoritative wisdom.

By cross-examining the writings of the classical thinkers we are free to deepen our understanding systematically, without subscribing to an arcane set of doctrines. This has important implications for how we might then approach, for instance, Huntington's notion of Christian versus Confucian civilisation in the twenty-first century. It is also, surely, consistent with the spirit of Confucius' instruction:

> 'Be a noble scholar, not a vulgar pedant.' (*The Analects*, #6:13).

With the knowledge and methods accumulated in recent centuries, we can survey the world of the Chinese and Greek thinkers of 2,500 years ago in ways that they themselves never could.

We can see common themes emerging in the philosophies of East and West, in the second half of the last millennium BCE. If we scan an arc extending from Confucius and Mencius, via Buddha in India and Zoroaster in Iran to Isaiah and Micah in Israel, to Aeschylus, Democritus, Pythagoras, Plato, and Aristotle in the Grecian world, what do we see? We see a spectrum of wisdom, revelation, and scepticism which planted the seeds of those philosophies and religions that endured right into the twentieth century. We see cognitive breakthroughs occurring, using the accumulated records and thinking-tools of Iron Age civilisation.

We now have a much broader comparative perspective than was possible for those pioneering thinkers. Since the eighteenth century, we have uncovered their remote past, the historical world that preceded them, and the cognitive world that enmeshed them in ways previously unimagined. It was for these reasons that Arnaldo Momigliano wrote, in 1975:

> Confucius, Buddha, Zoroaster, Isaiah, Heraclitus—or Aeschylus. The list would probably have puzzled my grandfather and his generation. It makes sense now; it symbolizes the change in our historical perspective. We can face, more or less from the same angle, cultures which seemed wide apart; and we can find something in common among them. On a synchronous line, the names stand for a more 'spiritual' life, for a better order, for a reinterpretation of the relation between gods and men, for a criticism of the traditional values in each respective society ... instead of seeing *each* of them as the codifier of a new religion we now see *all* of them as reformers of the existing order (emphasis in the original).[11]

What they had in common was a sense of transcendent insight into the evils of higher civilisation: the wars, luxuries, moral abuses, and tyrannies of the historical Bronze Age and the early Iron Age. What the Greeks had, in addition, was a new kind of insight into the nature of thinking itself.

These sages all knew enough of civilisation for us to understand their most common metaphors, and they were disillusioned enough with the banalities of human evil for us to share their general moral sense. From a cognitive point of view all of them are recognisable to us as analysts of civilisation and its discontents. We can honour them. We cannot, however, turn back to them. All we can do is to gain some sense of perspective by reflecting on their example, for the human world has changed—both materially and cognitively—since they passed through it. These changes have implications for how we live and how we think. The more dramatic changes in very recent times require a profound reckoning with what manner of being we actually are and how we are transforming the face of the world.

Against this background, let's consider the specific cases, along the arc, of Confucius and Mencius. Just as Bronze Age empires rose and fell in the Indus Valley, the Mesopotamian, Levantine, and Anatolian worlds, the Cretan and Mycenaean worlds, so whole dynasties rose and fell in central China (what is now the People's Republic of China includes enormous territories that were never part of the archaic or classical Chinese states) in the same millennium. Chinese civilisation was not unique but typical in this respect. Just over two centuries before Confucius was born, the Bronze Age kingdom of the Zhou collapsed in 771 BCE with the assassination of King Lu. China subsequently broke into Iron-Age warring states that would not be brought within a single dominion again for 550 years.

The years of comparative anarchy were, however, an era of tremendous intellectual ferment in the Chinese world. Mao Zedong, in 1957, adopted the slogan:

'Let a hundred flowers bloom. Let a hundred schools of thought contend!'[12]

But when some of his citizens started to do this, his anti-Rightist campaign ensured that they were ruthlessly suppressed. In the centuries before and after Confucius, however, a hundred schools of thought did, indeed, contend in ancient China. Here is how that intellectually prolific period was described by the great historian of Chinese thought, Joseph Needham:

> The 'hundred schools' of philosophers were at their height between 500 and 250 BC, with scholars travelling with their disciples from capital to capital to act as advisers to the feudal lords, whose realms were beset by conflicts with barbarians, unrest within and vast technological changes due to the increasing use of iron. During this period, academies of scholars were set up; the most famous being the Academy of the Gate of Qi (Jixia) at the Qi capital, founded in 318 BC by Prince Hsuan. Here scholars were welcomed from other states besides Qi and all were provided with quarters and maintenance. Established not long after Plato's Academy in far off Athens, it attracted a great number of superb scholars ...[13]

The Academy of the Gate of Qi mentioned by Needham was founded 160 years after the death of Confucius. Thus, Prince Hsuan was a contemporary of Mencius, and the sage advised and admonished the prince. Whereas Plato's Academy lasted until 529 CE when it was closed by the Roman Emperor Justinian, the Academy of the Gate of Qi seems to have been a more ephemeral affair. It certainly did not survive the rise of the First Emperor in 221 BCE. According to the historian Mark Elvin, Prince Hsuan "did not found whatever it was that was going on, but rather revitalized it. The key sentence comes from Sima Qian: 'In the time of King Hsuan of Ch'i, the scholars of Jixia had a revived prosperity.'"[14] So while the Chinese Academy may have antedated that of Plato, it predeceased it by some 750 years because a Chinese Justinian shut it down.

In other words, the intellectual environment in which Confucius and Mencius lived was in some ways comparable to that in which Socrates and Plato worked in Athens, around the same time. There were in both cases numerous thinkers, natural philosophers, and logicians debating and teaching variations on the new transcendental, ethical, mystical, and proto-scientific ideas that had begun to occur to civilised human beings. If, therefore, we allow ourselves to think that Chinese philosophy was or has been in any sense always 'Confucian', we would be making the same sort of error as if we assumed that Western philosophy has always been Platonist. In both cases there was a rich variety of speculative thought that was later suppressed or marginalised by the dominant orthodoxy. In both cases, though, that suppression occurred centuries after the death of the great thinker—Confucius in China, and Plato in the West.

Like Plato and Aristotle, both Confucius and Mencius sought to influence the political and ethical cultures of their time. Plato famously tried to persuade the tyrant of Syracuse to adopt his philosophy. Aristotle tutored Alexander the Great. He also wrote a treatise on *The Constitution of Athens* and a theory of politics incomparably more empirical and practical than Plato's more famous *Republic*, or his *Laws*. Confucius spent much of his adult life wandering from state to state, seeking to persuade various tyrants to adopt his philosophy. Mencius spent most of his adult life advising the rulers of Liang and Qi, two of the states of the fourth century BCE that were to disappear under the pressure of the aggressive state of Qin, in the late third century BCE.

The influence of Confucius on China, from the Han dynasty in the second century BCE, down to the nineteenth century CE, has been so great that he has been dubbed 'the uncrowned emperor of China'. In this respect, the comparison with Plato is interesting. It was Alfred North Whitehead, himself a distinguished modern philosopher and colleague of Bertrand Russell, who remarked that 'The whole of Western philosophy consists of footnotes to Plato.' The Catholic pope is called the Vicar of Christ, but is closer than anything else in the Western tradition to Plato's philosopher king—with the many drawbacks that role entails.

Plato and Confucius have each been the genius of a whole conception of civilisation. Each placed great importance on the names and essences of things, on rites, and on music. Each believed that his true philosophy could never be put down in writing, but only imparted indirectly, by inspiration. Each believed in an educated elite being the guardians of propriety and governing the state. In each case, a set of ideas and ideals became converted into an orthodoxy—imperial in China, theological in the West—which critical and scientific thought has had to fight strenuously to shake off. And, in each case, the orthodoxy still tends to act as a beacon for conservative moral or political nostalgia.

Yet, beneath the orthodoxy, the original texts still come alive, if read freely. As Pierre Ryckmans (who writes also as Simon Leys) remarks in the introduction to his acclaimed 1997 translation of *The Analects*, Confucius, in his time, was a stirring, charismatic, and deeply thoughtful human being. Likewise, in the Western tradition, one can still read Plato and be awed by the depth of his thinking and the sweep of his intellect. One can read Mencius and be fascinated by his brilliance of style and his insights, just as one can read Aristotle and be compelled to admit that in many ways he thought further and wider than most people do today. When we look to any of these thinkers, however, we should be wary of the patina of orthodoxy and received wisdom that has become attached to them. Rather, we should be alert to three things: the pungency of their insights into human behaviour; the occurrence of anachronism in our reading of their ideas; and, above all, the role of reference in their theoretical reasoning.

Ryckmans suggests that we, in the West, can bring a freshness and innocence to a reading of Confucius that is almost impossible for those raised in 'Confucian' societies. If we do that, he advised, we will discover not the orthodox teacher of the Chinese imperial system, but 'one unique and inimitable voice ... one singular and exceptional personality'. That voice was strong and complex; the personality passionate, energetic, restless, imaginative, and humane.[15] The figure of Confucius can be rediscovered, he argues, much like the Jesus of the Gospels— that heterodox and charismatic figure so often and so long obscured behind the religious symbolism of Pauline theology and Christian orthodoxy.[16] This analogy extends to the transmission of their written texts. Just as the Gospels were written decades after the death of Jesus of Nazareth, *The Analects* were compiled some seventy-five years after Confucius' death (taking place, therefore, during the last decade of the life of Socrates in Athens).

Elias Canetti has called *The Analects* 'the oldest complete intellectual and spiritual portrait of a man'. Others are more sceptical about their value. Mark Elvin has remarked, 'Only some parts of *The Analects* have some chance of being more or less authentic and even these parts are gnomic and hard to grasp.' But the same could surely be said of the Jesus of the Gospels. And yet, in each case, through the filter of two millennia of interpretation, one can still be affected by the moral and psychological presence of the Master, as recorded by his disciples.

When we read and discuss excerpts from Confucius and Mencius, we should not do so in order to find a timeless Confucian system that might answer contemporary Chinese dilemmas. We should read them simply to encounter two remarkable human beings who, in a world already old and acquainted with human corruption, technological change, conflicting norms, and exquisite poetries, sought to think through the ethical dilemmas and political needs of their civilisations. They knew nothing of ours, and cannot provide ready-made answers to modern-day problems. (Indeed, they did not have ready-made answers to the problems of their own, though they believed they did.)

We should not make the mistake of believing that these texts alone show 'the Chinese mind'—for that mind is, first and last, a *human* brain, whose basic architecture long antedated Confucius. Rather, when we read Confucius, we should listen to his voice for precisely what it is: the expression of a singular human personality, whose reported sayings were recorded by his disciples, from memory, on the Iron Age equivalent of audiotape long since spliced and damaged. If you believe you have to master the intricacies of something called 'the Chinese mind', or two millennia of Confucian orthodox exegesis in order to understand Confucius, you are unlikely to be stimulated by the idiosyncrasies of Confucius' true voice.

What, then, might be some of our first reactions to reading Confucius and Mencius? To start with, it's clear that Confucius presents a wider range of ideas and maxims than the Gospels attribute to Jesus of Nazareth, 500 years later. From the point of view of practical ethics in a civilised community, there is more on offer in *The Analects* than in the Gospels. This may be one reason why Christianity has not swept China after half a millennium of missionary endeavours. It should be reason enough for Westerners to read *The Analects*, much as we might now read the more inspiring parts of the Bible, or the meditations of Marcus Aurelius.

Confucius does not debate ideas with his disciples, in the Socratic manner. He presents his case from an unchallenged position as the Master. In this respect, he is more like Jesus than Socrates or Aristotle. That's not to say that he has no interest in processes of enquiry to establish the truth, but he does not dwell on those processes. This didactic approach is in notable contrast with the Socratic dialectic, in which the finer points of both semantic and logical discrimination are constantly at issue. We know that Chinese philosophers debated some of these things, but you will not find them in *The Analects*.

From a cognitive point of view, this is of more than passing interest. As Joseph Needham pointed out forty years ago, there is a certain 'agnostic rationalism' in the Confucian canon that 'should have been favourable to early science', but orthodox Confucianism took little interest in natural science.[17] Confucius himself regarded scientific investigation as unimportant compared to social order—as did Plato, incidentally. Far from leading to the flourishing of Chinese intellectual life, the consolidation of the famous Confucian bureaucratic elite under the Han Dynasty entailed what the great twentieth-century Chinese liberal nationalist Hu Shih called 'the downfall of the most glorious era of Chinese thought'. Karl Popper, among others, has argued in the twentieth century that something similar occurred in the West when the profusion of pre-Socratic natural philosophers was followed by the epistemological systems of Plato and Aristotle.[18]

When Confucius talks of humanity, much of what he says is immediately intelligible to a modern Western moral ear. He tells his disciples to love men; to be courteous and magnanimous; to act in good faith; and to be diligent and kind. Esteem your humanity in these terms, he advises, above wealth, power, and even your life. And don't mistake the form of rites for the spirit of them. ('Rites, rites!' he expostulated. 'Does it mean no more than jades and silks? Music, music! Does it mean no more than bells and drums?' Here are echoes of Jesus, the Hebrew prophets, and Socrates. When Confucius tells his disciples that perfect virtue is according to the (golden) mean, he sounds like Aristotle in his *Nichomachean Ethics*. There is nothing, surely, that sounds strange to us in such teachings.

Indeed, he is far easier to 'hear' in a modern context than Jesus or Paul, because he eschews speculation about an afterlife or a spirit world. He urges that we keep a clear eye on the world of mankind, seek to live by the golden mean of reciprocity, and practice virtue and rites without mistaking form for substance. In the case of Confucius we do not have to deal with problems that are stumbling blocks of Jesus' teachings, such as miracles, godhead, sacramental meals, bodily resurrection, or a second coming. Confucius, by comparison, was simply a thinker and teacher in an epoch of upheavals and cruelties, who called for a return to ancient virtue and harmonious order.

Confucius makes reference to written records—the poems, the documents, the histories of earlier dynasties and wars, and the lives of other sages—getting some way towards theoretical reflection. In his use of classical references we can begin to recognise standard civilised discourse. He looked back to what he saw as a golden age of order under the Zhou kings, and his teachings were intended to make it possible to restore and sustain such an ideal. However, given the vastly greater archive we have to work with than that available to Confucius, as well as far more refined tools for using it, this is not something we can very realistically do any more. Confucius' uncritical monarchism is also less sophisticated or interesting than, for example, Aristotle's argument for a mixed and balanced constitution, which laid the original foundation for the modern liberal democracies.

What is most generally praised by those who admire Confucius is the emphasis he placed on education and the examination system, which was intended to bring merit and ability to the fore in the government of the realm. He is certainly still thought-provoking on this, but we should be circumspect about singing the praises of the Confucian approach to education. The education he proposed was of a particular kind, not dissimilar from that proposed by Plato for the guardians in his Republic. Although he taught that, 'In education there are no class distinctions', the form of education he advocated was highly conservative.

Confucian ideas on education did not inspire social or technological innovation throughout the long history of the Chinese empire—only conservative renovation. We should not, therefore, attribute to his influence all that is vital or impressive in the history of China: the flourishing, cosmopolitan culture of the early Tang dynasty in the eighth century CE, and the technological achievements of the Song (tenth to twelfth centuries CE) and early Ming (1368–1450) dynasties. Nor should we assume that his ideas can be of more than indirect and incidental use in the huge tasks of innovation we face globally in the twenty-first century world—whether or not we are Chinese.

Many of the same remarks could be made concerning Mencius. The emphasis he placed on human virtues is not difficult for us to identify with. Underlying his specific claims about virtue, however, is his analysis of names and definitions and inferences that is strikingly familiar to anyone who has read the dialogues of Plato. The parallel is fascinating when we consider that Mencius' life span (374 to 289 BCE) overlapped those of Plato and Aristotle[19]. The common cognitive underpinnings here are a search for the abstract, the pure, and the real beneath the surface appearance of things.

A certain depth of perspective is necessary to reach this degree of abstraction. Mencius refers to ancient kings and other states and varieties of human custom. He uses metaphors to widen the conceptual space for thinking about problems. He differentiates between what human beings tend to do and what they would do if they were virtuous. He thinks of an abstraction called 'real humanity', as distinct from merely actual or observable human nature. He claims that compassion, shame, courtesy, and a sense of right and wrong are as natural to human beings as having four limbs. While we might discuss the merits of his beliefs, what is more interesting is the mere fact that human beings had started to do this sort of thinking at all.

Our freedom, our humanism, and our capacity to widen our moral horizons are all rooted in this kind of comparative and analytical thinking. These latent capacities are built into our brains, but our depth of perspective and the systematic broadening of our horizons depend on the development of what I have called 'cognitive accumulation'. Mencius did not see this. His insights depended on it, but he took it for granted. Once we see what is going on here, however, we become free to think through the issues that concerned Mencius with greater rigour.

When we read Mencius, we not only depend on libraries and well-edited books for access to his thought, but we bring to our reading the awareness we have derived from other studies in psychology, language, anthropology, philosophy, ethics, religion, and history—all of which depend on long processes of scholarly inquiry. We do not rely on our natural abilities to think through what he wrote 2,300 years ago, although we need them as a starting point. We rely on shared access to the records that our civilisation has developed over the past five thousand years.

Our civilised conversation revolves through this vast external storage system. It is as if those of us who are educated now have access to a gigantic version of the famous Ptolemaic Library in Alexandria and can, each of us, be an Eratosthenes, learned in the accumulated knowledge of mankind and able to work at the edge of the known and unknown. We can, in other words, join in the conversation with Mencius or Plato—in the tradition of the scholars at the Gate of Qi and the sophists of Athens, but with a far wider access to the world of ideas than any of them had. In short, the key here is not what occurs to us intuitively or what has been handed down traditionally, but what we are capable of precisely as civilised human beings—what we are capable of *asking* ourselves, and how we are capable of *extending* ourselves.

Through such 'spiritual exercises' we create our philosophic and moral freedom. Reading Confucius and Mencius, Plato and Aristotle, can still be the stimulus to embarking on expeditions of discovery; but once we embark, we have a whole new contemporary world to navigate. The freedom to do just that is at stake in China as the Communist Party, with its mishmash of Leninism and neo-Confucianism, seeks to censor use of the Internet, for example, in order to dominate the thinking of its people. The freedom to break new ground and to transcend the given and the 'known' is vital in the quest for political democratisation in China. To overcome the confusion created by communism and its decay, something more than an authoritarian neo-Confucianism is required. That something more will be new in the Chinese world and will shed fresh light on the classics, rather than leaving them as merely the 'sacred texts' of a tired orthodoxy.

Chapter 10

Hu's Rhetoric: A Chinese 'Stolypin' in Australia

Democracy is the common pursuit of mankind and all countries must earnestly protect the democratic rights of the people. In the past twenty years and more, since China embarked on the road of reform and opening up, we have moved steadfastly to promote political restructuring and vigorously build democratic politics under socialism.

—Hu Jintao, in an address to the Australian parliament, Canberra,
24 October 2003

Who would have thought, a generation ago, that the heir of Mao Zedong—the architect of thirty years of inward-looking economic irrationalism in China—would one day stand before the parliament of a liberal democracy and extol markets and the international division of labour, investment and comparative advantage, diversity and mutually beneficial cooperation? Yet, in October 2003, Hu Jintao stood before the Australian parliament in a smart business suit and sang the praises of the growth of China's market, the immense economic complementarities between China and Australia, the countries' burgeoning two-way trade (up 100-fold since the early 1970s), and China's readiness 'to be your long-term and stable cooperation partner'?

President Hu's visit to Australia was remarkable for many reasons. His predecessor, Jiang Zemin, had come before him, as had the impressive Zhu Rongji when he was premier. Yet Hu's visit was truly historic. For those with long historical memories, it might usefully have prompted reflection on the visit by the great Chinese scholar and advocate of political reform Liang Qichao over 100 years ago in 1901, the year of Australian federation. For Liang is a figure whom China needs to remember; and, for that very reason, so do all of us who want to think through China's contemporary challenges.

Along with Kang Youwei, Liang Qichao was the leading proponent of constitutional reform in China under the late Qing dynasty, when the Empress Dowager first attempted to repress the reform movement and then sought to harness it. In 1901, Liang met with

Australia's first prime minister, Edmund Barton, in Sydney. He saw much to admire in Australia's constitution, and wrote for a Chinese readership of the need for a federal polity and constitutional monarchy in China.[1] A century later, Hu Jintao's meeting with Prime Minister John Howard took place in a world immeasurably changed, but constant in this respect: China is still in search of a truly workable constitution, and Australia still stands out as a model of democratic governance. But Hu Jintao did not come as an exile or wandering scholar. He came as the head of state.

Hu is at the forefront of a new generation of Chinese leaders. There is almost a determination among China's well-wishers to find in him the sort of freshness and dynamism still associated with the coming of John F. Kennedy to the American presidency in 1961. The analogy is not completely fanciful. With Hu, as with Kennedy, the torch has been passed from an older generation to a younger one. Born in 1942, Hu grew up after the communists came to power. He is the first Chinese leader of whom this can be said. He was already being groomed for the top job when in his forties, and came to the Chinese presidency with a reputation as someone, somewhat like Kennedy, who was highly articulate, able to listen to advice, and keen to gather intelligent people around him.

This persona makes it all the more crucial that we think carefully about the rhetoric used in Hu's address to the parliament of Asia's oldest and best-established democracy—and about the challenges he faces at home in what is still anything but a democracy. Three themes of his Canberra speech stood out: the promise of economic growth; the commitment to democratisation in China; and the question of Taiwan. Each of them is problematic and confronts him, far more than it does the Western democracies, with critical challenges. It was clear in October 2003 and it remains clear that how he dealt with them would define his presidency.

But before turning to these themes, it seems worth extending the unorthodox comparison between Hu and Kennedy. The differences, of course, are as striking as any similarities. Kennedy was, apart from anything else, the liberal leader of the world's greatest democracy, while Hu is the leader of a one-party dictatorship that has no electoral mandate, an appalling human rights record, and a still highly repressive attitude to critical enquiry into its own history and policy-making processes. Consider, however, not only the generational and character similarities, but the broad similarities in the policy challenges inherited by the two men. Each came to power facing significant domestic policy challenges without a clear plan to tackle them. Each faced the foreign policy challenge of a nearby island state which powerful domestic forces believed should be within their country's orbit, but which was, in reality, allied with its chief superpower rival. For Kennedy, the challenge was Cuba. For Hu, it is Taiwan.

Each also realised that his country needed to demonstrate leadership and responsibility on the world stage, because of the crucial place it held in international security and economic terms. In every case, the challenges that confronted Hu were considerably more difficult than those that confronted Kennedy: civil rights in China are in much worse shape than they were in the United States half a century ago; poverty is far more widespread; and crime more difficult to constrain—despite the highest execution rate in the world. Taiwan presents an even more delicate policy challenge for Hu than Cuba did for Kennedy, especially considering that it has governed itself in defiance of its huge neighbour for decades more than Cuba had when Kennedy took office. It is a wealthy, as well as democratic, state that cannot easily be subdued. As for global leadership and responsibility, Kennedy inherited the mantle when the United States was incontestably the world's greatest economic and military power—as it remains today.[2] Hu heads a state seeking a larger role in world affairs without triggering outright strategic competition with the US.

The claim that China has the highest execution rate in the world warrants some explanation, for the extent of violence and repression in China is not widely appreciated. According to a reputable recent study, Chinese Communist Party internal investigation reports reveal that 'more than 60,000 people were put to death in China during the four year period between 1998 and 2001, an average of 15,000 a year', including 'both death sentences and the killing of alleged criminals apprehended or in the act of flight'.[3] The same internal reports state that these figures are the highest since the beginning of the reform period in 1978–79. If these figures are accurate, an Amnesty International report which found that 2,486 executions took place in China in 2001 was a gross underestimate. Even so, the AI report put China's tally of executions at 81 per cent of the known worldwide total. AI analysts have variously estimated the true figure for China to be two to four times higher. What the internal report suggests is that the real figure was closer to six times higher, although it is not clear how many were judicial executions as opposed to police killings.

To put these figures into comparative perspective, the Chinese average of 15,000 executions in one year is the statistical equivalent, on a population-ratio basis, to 200 such executions in Australia, or 3,000 in the United States. Under the last Russian tsar, Nicholas II, the total number of executions has been estimated at 11,000 over a period of 23 years, or about 500 per year in a population of rather less than 150 million. On a population-ratio basis, this would be the equivalent of about 4,000 executions per year in China in 2001, making contemporary China a great deal more repressive in this respect than late-imperial Russia. And these figures are only of executions; they do not address the question of detention and harassment of political dissidents.

Of course, under old-fashioned communism, things were far worse. During the Red Terror under Lenin, at least 200,000 people were executed in just over six years—roughly 30,000 per year on average.[4] The equivalent in China today would be about 240,000 per year, which is vastly more than the actual figure. If the comparison were made with Stalin's Great Terror, in which some 700,000 people were executed in the two years 1937–38, the Chinese figure would blow out to a staggering 5,500,000 per year.[5]

In fact, during the worst excesses of Mao's rule in the 1950s the number of executions has been estimated at between several hundred thousand and 15 million. The latter figure is implausibly high, but there is no doubt that large-scale killing took place as the Communist Party consolidated its rule. During the Cultural Revolution (1966–76), of course, things got severely out of hand.

In the wake of the Cultural Revolution, Deng Xiaoping declared that the rule of law had to replace arbitrary rule in China, but there is still a large degree of arbitrariness in China's judicial system, and a lack of power outside the Communist Party to check, criticise, or reform it. China's judicial execution rate has declined since the Mao era, but it certainly remains at a savage level. It is made worse by the fact that executions tend to follow also immediately upon conviction, and that successful appeals against the death sentence are virtually unheard of. In short, if Hu Jintao is to bring about the rule of law in a serious way in China, he has much work to do, and there are many obstacles in his way, whether or not he is especially inclined to attempt the task.

Now that China is in a period of transition, the challenge for foreign advocates of the rule of law and human rights is even greater than it was when outright totalitarian tyranny dominated China. At the government-to-government level, there is always a trade-off between geopolitical or economic interests and basic principles. At the business level, the balance is even more delicate, since corporations in general have less leverage than governments in dealing with the Chinese authorities.[6] Nonetheless, it is important that dialogue at both levels should encourage the authorities to move steadily in the direction of replacing arbitrariness and coercion with consistency and justice in China.

The challenge of reforming an authoritarian regime prompts a second, very different, historical analogy. This time the comparison is between Hu Jintao and Peter Stolypin—one of the last great statesmen of Tsarist Russia. Stolypin, (like Kennedy) took office at the age of forty-four when, in 1906, he became prime minister and minister of the interior of Russia. He was conscious that Russia had taken giant strides economically in the late nineteenth and early twentieth century, but that it still had a long way to go. Stolypin was a cautious, conservative politician, and a tough opponent of those demanding radical political reform. It is this context that invites comparison with Hu Jintao almost 100 years later.

'Give me twenty-five years of peace,' Stolypin declared to the Russian duma in 1907, 'and you will not recognize Russia.'[7] The peace he had in mind involved a gradual move to constitutional monarchy—not the upheaval sought by any of Russia's plethora of socialists, populists, and anarchists. 'What you [the radicals] want is great upheavals; what we [the conservatives] want is a great Russia,' he declared. Stolypin was assassinated by a political radical in 1911. In the 25 years following his death, Russia was to suffer the devastation of World War I; violent revolution; a civil war even more destructive to the country than World War I had been, which included a terrible famine; the Bolshevik Red Terror; Stalin's forced collectivisation, which caused another horrific famine; and the creation of the Gulag archipelago.

And all this was merely the prelude to the catastrophes of Stalin's Great Terror during 1936–38, and World War II from 1941–45, in which 25 million Soviet citizens lost their lives. At the end of all this, one could barely recognise Russia, it is true, but not because of the kind of changes Stolypin had hoped to see. A generation of almost unimaginable brutality and suffering had turned it into an empire incomparably more violent and repressive than that of the tsars. Even now, more than a decade after the collapse of the Soviet Union, Russia is still suffering from the enormous destruction wrought by communism.

What Stolypin had hoped for was the evolution of the Russian empire into a constitutional monarchy, with an industrial economy, a modern, liberalised culture, and a great place in the comity of nations.[8] He liked to compare himself to Bismarck. His great biographer, Abraham Ascher, astutely observed that there was, indeed, a strong similarity between the two—not only in their methods and their achievements, but also in their flaws. He cited Max Weber's criticism of Bismarck for having 'left behind a nation totally without political education', and observed that Stolypin, likewise, 'did little to enable political leaders to obtain appropriate experience in the art of responsible government'. He added that Stolypin's 'insistence on excessively severe treatment of student activists did more to inflame the opposition than to restore calm to the universities, which, as he acknowledged, were indispensable in training the manpower needed in a modern state'.[9]

Why compare Hu with Stolypin? Because, beneath the surface of China's one-party political regime, there is a major, continuing debate between those who believe democratisation could disrupt the process of rapid economic reform, and those who believe it is indispensable to this same process.[10] The authoritarian conservatives—those most cautious about political enthusiasms—are China's Stolypins. Like him, they have a hopeful vision of China's future. But, like him, they need years of peace to achieve it, and believe that irresponsible dissidents could set the whole project at risk at any time.

These conservatives are inclined to authoritarian means for maintaining the stability they consider necessary to build a great China. They broadly agree with the liberal economists who recommend restricting democratisation, since it might unleash popular resistance to the costs of reform. To use a phrase made famous by Stolypin in the 1900s, it is a policy of 'banking on the strong'—that is, the new rich. This policy is controversial and its proponents might be seriously mistaken. Stolypin's hopes may have been derailed by World War I, but there can be no certainty that they would have worked, irrespective of the war. In the first decade of the twentieth century there was enormous, pent-up pressure for reform in Russia, and some form of violent upheaval may have been inevitable.

Hu Jintao and the new premier of China, Wen Jiabao, both seem to be 'Stolypins'. It is unclear if they are aware of the potential dangers of their approach. In the course of his speech in Australia in 2003, Hu talked boldly about economic development, but only obliquely about democratisation. Wen has said that he admires Singapore, and believes that China needs 'a detailed system of management through laws' in order to avoid 'chaos'.[11]

Because they are Chinese 'Stolypins', Hu and Wen believe that there should be a 'strengthening of internal party mechanisms to rectify the behaviour and quality of cadres'.[12] This is a dubious tradition that owes more to Lenin's last pamphlets of 1922–23 than to Stolypin.[13] Yet these men and their staffs are not mere Leninists—they are increasingly well educated in political and economic theory, and are searching for solutions to China's problems, as Stolypin sought solutions for Russia's a century ago.[14] Or so, at least, we might allow them.

These two historical analogies—with Kennedy and Stolypin—offer useful alternative lenses through which to read Hu Jintao's rhetoric in 2003 and his politics more generally.

When he evokes the promise of economic growth, the commitment to democratisation and, more negatively, the question of Taiwan, there are a number of ways open to us for making sense of his positions. Much depends on the antecedents and assumptions that make up our own mind-sets. Whether we are China specialists too immersed in the specifics of Chinese politics to take a wider view, or Western citizens too ignorant of China's history and politics to see them with any clarity, we can benefit from analogies that enable us to see what is happening in China in more imaginative and instructive ways.

At the centre of any critical understanding of Hu's world view lies the vexed question of political reform in China. We can broaden our thinking about how this could play out by looking at it through the alternative lenses just polished: Kennedy for the possibilities; Stolypin for the uncertainties. The question of political reform, or democratisation, is central, because of its relationship to the promise of economic growth. 'China enjoys a vast market, abundant labour, social and political stability and a vibrant momentum for development', Hu stated. The first two parts of this claim are relatively uncontroversial, but the latter two are more problematic.[15]

In *The Coming Collapse of China*, a hard-hitting polemic written two years before Hu visited Australia, Gordon Chang argued that China's rapid recent economic growth is like a house of cards. He predicted the regime's probable collapse because of a massive financial crisis, and because the party's insistence on maintaining 'stability' prevents it from dealing with the fundamental sources of instability.[16] Similarly, in a provocative essay entitled 'The Chinese Sickness' (published in the July 2003 issue of *Commentary*), historian Arthur Waldron argued that China's regime is corrupt and incompetent, and that its financial institutions are teetering on the brink of collapse while discontent boils to the surface in the vast Chinese hinterland.[17]

Many China specialists strongly contested Waldron's argument. Henry Rowen said it was 'a collection of truths, half-truths, and misconceptions'. In a collective letter to *Commentary*, Michael Swaine and eleven others complained, 'We have heard all this before, many times. Unfortunately, it does not become more convincing with the retelling.'[18] Yet William Odom, former director of the US National Security Agency, greeted Waldron's essay as 'an excellent antidote to the conventional wisdom on China'; and James Lilley, a former US ambassador to China, and two China specialists at the Heritage Foundation, John Tkacik Jr and Larry Wortzel, were also supportive. Harvard University's Ross Terrill wrote that 'simple prudence requires the United States and the rest of the world to prepare for drastic political discontinuity within China.'[19]

Waldron's response to his critics was, in essence, that they had conceded all his major claims, but baulked at drawing the appropriate conclusions. He argued that they were in denial. He recalled a 'comparable intellectual scandal that afflicted the field of Sovietology during the period of the USSR's existence', and quoted leading Sovietologist and historian Richard Pipes on 'the groupthink then dominating Soviet studies' that made it 'permissible to maintain that the Soviet regime was more stable or less stable, but not that it was unstable'. Waldron conjectured that 'something about my analysis—something, perhaps, too candid—[seems to have] crossed the line of the permissible'.

Through the Stolypin set of lenses, we can see that, for the reasons Chang, Waldron and others adduce, a possible political and social abyss yawns beneath the presidency of Hu Jintao; that he and his colleagues understand all too well the possibility of a crisis. Hu's remarks about China intending to 'move forward our political restructuring in a vigorous and cautious manner as our national conditions merit' are thrown into somewhat higher relief, when seen in this context. The Kennedy set of lenses, conversely, puts the question of democratisation in a very different light, and would have us focus on bright prospects, stirring rhetoric, and the liberal hope for a political reform process that matures in step with the growth of China's new middle classes.

'In the past 20 years and more, since China embarked on the road of reform and opening up', Hu declared, 'we have moved steadfastly to promote political restructuring and vigorously build democratic politics under socialism'. Without question, there has been some political restructuring in China since 1978–79, which is why it was possible for Hu Jintao, Wen Jiabao, and the other fourth-generation leaders to succeed Jiang Zemin and the rest without a violent struggle. The most impressive aspect of the handover was the resignation of Jiang Zemin even from the chairmanship of the Central Military Commission in 2004.

But Hu's claim is plainly false. China has clearly not been building 'democratic politics under socialism'. On the contrary, since Deng Xiaoping suppressed the democratic movements of the 1980s, the Communist Party has steadfastly obstructed the emergence of democratic politics in China. It is far from clear what Hu meant by 'socialism', but certainly what has passed for socialism in China since 1949 has been anything but democratic. Political reform has been demanded for precisely that reason, and there is still a very long way to go. Disturbingly, Hu Jintao declared, in 2005, that he thinks North Korea has got its politics pretty much right.[20]

The vigorous *unbuilding* of democratic politics in China in the era of reform began with the suppression of the Democracy Wall movement in 1979, and the imprisonment of

Wei Jingsheng, and climaxed with the brutal crackdown in Beijing that centred on Tiananmen Square in 1989. It also includes the bloody suppression of Tibetan dissent, the Falun Gong religious movement, and the China Democratic Party, as well as the arbitrary arrest and detention of scholars and journalists for 'revealing state secrets'. Since Hu became president, harsh crackdowns on political dissent, on investigative journalists, on the internet and on religious freedom have not abated, and there has been no sign of any fundamental opening-up of the political system.

'Our world is a diverse place like a rainbow of many colours', Hu declared in the most flamboyant phrase of his Canberra speech. Unfortunately, the Chinese polity itself is no such thing. A future in which diversity truly flourishes under the rule of law in China is something the democratic world would join the Chinese people in celebrating. Achieving it, however, will require fundamental restructuring of the state, as well as the end of the party's monopoly on political and judicial power, and its relentless censorship of the press. What is crucial for outsiders to appreciate is that such demands are not Western impositions or pipe dreams, but things that have been repeated by every free voice in China for decades—just as they were in Taiwan under the Guomindang, until martial law was finally lifted there and dictatorship ended.

This brings us to the third theme of Hu's address—the matter of Taiwan. 'Taiwan is an inalienable part of China's territory', he asserted toward the end of his speech. 'The complete reunification of China at an early date is the common aspiration and firm resolve of the entire Chinese people ... The greatest threat to peace in the Taiwan Straits is from the splittist activities of the Taiwanese independence forces.' This is wearisome and sterile rhetoric. Hu and his colleagues must, by now, understand that their endless repetition of this mantra has only contributed to the alienation of the majority of Taiwanese from unification with China. The threat to peace in the Taiwan Strait is not Taiwanese aspirations, but the obduracy of the regime in Beijing.

Yet, on this point at least, one may allow a closer comparison with Kennedy than with Stolypin. Kennedy did not feel politically free to accept Castro's government in Cuba, because of powerful conservative sentiment in the United States that demanded Castro's overthrow. Indeed, from the very beginning of his presidency, Kennedy made extraordinary efforts to undermine Castro—beginning with covert invasion of Cuba and including a series of attempts to assassinate Castro himself.[21] Hu cannot be accused of having attempted any such thing in regard to Taiwan, and it is to be hoped that he does not. Likewise, Hu is in no position to simply renounce China's claims to sovereignty over Taiwan; his political rivals would certainly denounce him should he attempt to move in that direction.

Hu Jintao, Wen Jiabao, and their colleagues have their work cut out for them. We should not demand more of them, given China's challenges, than Kennedy was able to achieve in America. We should understand that they are, in some respects, more in Stolypin's circumstances than Kennedy's, and should do what we can to help them enjoy 'twenty-five years of peace'. We should also recall, with a sobering sense of how the best-laid plans can go awry, that both Stolypin and Kennedy were assassinated. In China's twentieth century, many of those who sought democratisation were assassinated or defeated—not least among them the promising young Guomindang leaders Song Jiaoren, in 1913, and Liao Zhongkai, in 1925. Yet somehow China has overcome enormous setbacks to get to where it is today.

The twenty-first century beckons with the linked prospects of successful economic development and political democratisation. The question is only how to achieve these goals. Many dared to hope that the answer would at last be found with the accession to power of Hu and Wen. At mid-decade, it is by no means clear that such hopes are set to be fulfilled; but if they are not, the future of China could be grim. None of us should want that.

Part Four

Democracy and Human Rights in the Chinese World

Chapter 11

Wei Jingsheng and the Communist Party

Although an enormous diversity of opinion was behind bars in the Gulag, dissidents shared one belief in common: We all wanted to live in a free society. And despite our somewhat contradictory visions of the future, the dissident experience enabled us all to agree on what freedom meant: A society is free if people have a right to express their views without fear of arrest, imprisonment or physical harm.

—Natan Sharansky *The Case for Democracy: The Power of Freedom to Overcome Tyranny and Terror.*

The lack of authentic democracy or the effective rule of law in Hu Jintao's China has been demonstrated again and again by the arrest of those who attempt to practise freedom of speech, assembly or religion, where these practices are seen by the Communist Party as even remotely threatening. The arrest of leading Hong Kong–based journalist Ching Cheong and two staff of the Chinese Academy of Social Sciences in late April 2005 on charges of 'spying' was merely the latest episode in a long and grim history. The real reason for their arrests was that they were trying to collaborate in the publication of an underground manuscript of secret interviews conducted with former premier Zhao Ziyang before his death in early 2005.[1]

In order to bring more pressure to bear on the party for its abuses of power, the names and personalities of those it represses need to be better known. Ching Cheong was once a journalist for the Communist Party–controlled Hong Kong paper *Wen Wei Po*, but quit in disgust after the Tiananmen Square bloodshed of 1989. He has at least some profile outside China, if only because he was working for the Singapore-based *Straits Times* when arrested. Too often, however, when dissidents or journalists are arrested in China, their names and fates rate only with small circles of scholars or human-rights specialists in the outside world.

During the last decades of the Soviet Union, a small number of dissidents earned international notoriety and had a disproportionate influence on calling the Soviet Communist

Party to account over its abuses of power. The most famous are Alexander Solzhenitsyn and Andrei Sakharov.[2] But there were also many others—not least among them Andrei Amalrik and Natan Sharansky. As early as 1970 Amalrik was questioning the viability of the Soviet Union. His prediction of its demise by 1984 was out by less than a decade—though it was not the disintegration of the Soviet Union Amalrik sought, so much as its democratic transformation.[3] After serving nine years in Soviet prisons, Sharansky left the Soviet Union and has since become a citizen of Israel. His recent book, *The Case for Democracy: The Power of Freedom to Overcome Tyranny and Terror*, was dedicated to Andrei Sakharov, 'A man who proved that, with moral clarity and courage, we can change the world.'[4]

Wei Jingsheng, a genuine *bête noir* to the Chinese Communist Party, has exemplified moral clarity and courage since 1978, and has paid very heavily for doing so. Although China has had many dissidents who have suffered as Soviet dissidents did, none of them has so far achieved the iconic status of Solzhenitsyn or Sakharov in the Brezhnev era (1964–1982). But of those who have stood out, and at least briefly captured the imagination of the outside world, Wei Jingsheng is among the more notable. His stand against the dictatorship of the party in China was based on precisely the principles that animated Soviet dissidents—and his fate was every bit as harsh as theirs. Like Solzhenitsyn, Sakharov, Amalrik, and Sharansky, he was imprisoned simply for daring to write and say things the party did not want people to read or hear.

What Wei Jingsheng stood for, and was imprisoned for, was, quite simply, freedom of speech. He made this point clear in 1978–79 when he was a leading democratic activist in the so-called Democracy Wall movement in Beijing. At the time, he wrote a major manifesto called 'The Fifth Modernization: Democracy' in which he denounced the delusions of communism. 'For three decades', he declared, 'we've been acting like monkeys grabbing for the moon's reflection in a lake—no wonder we've come up empty-handed!'[5] He expressed contempt for the party's propagandist line about China needing dictatorship, and described the party's apologists as political swindlers and fascists. 'The Chinese people don't need democracy, they say, for unless it is a "democracy under centralized leadership", it isn't worth a cent. Whether you believe it or not is up to you, but there are plenty of empty prison cells waiting for you if you don't.'[6]

One of those cells was waiting for him. Arrested for his activism and put on trial in October 1979, Wei defended his right to advocate democracy and criticise the party. Such rights had already been defended in the Democracy Wall journals such as *Exploration* and

April Fifth Forum in 1978 and early 1979 as the legitimate exercise of freedom of speech recognised under the Chinese constitution. Defying Deng Xiaoping's call in early 1979 for an end to the Democracy Wall movement, he wrote a stinging essay called 'Do We Want Democracy or a New Autocracy?' which was published in a special edition of *Exploration* on 25 March 1979. It read, in part, 'Does Deng Xiaoping want democracy? No, he does not. He says that the spontaneous struggle for democratic rights is just an excuse to make trouble, that it destroys the normal order and must be suppressed. Especially in politics, only if different kinds of ideas exist can the situation be called normal.'[7]

Wei was arrested four days later. Deng Xiaoping did not want democracy; what's more, he didn't want ordinary citizens to shout this from the rooftops, as Wei Jingsheng was doing. He is said to have personally ordered Wei's arrest, and determined his sentence and conditions of imprisonment.[8] Their confrontation set the stage for the party's failure over the next decade to allow its most imaginative and freest spirits to shape a political-reform agenda. Such reform might have made possible a dignified retreat from dictatorship. Instead, their failure culminated in the debacle of 4 June 1989 when soldiers of the People's Liberation Army—on the direct orders of Deng Xiaoping—marched into Beijing and other Chinese cities, and bloodily crushed the peaceful and principled demands of educated and ordinary Chinese for democratic reform and the accountability of their leaders.

Wei Jingsheng watched the entire decade that included the Beijing massacre from a prison cell. Such is the gulf between a 'people's democracy' and an actual democracy. His prison conditions, especially in the first three or four years, were so harsh that he deduced they were intended to bring about his death from 'natural causes'. He was not permitted to write at first, and his reading was strictly controlled. He was condemned to solitary confinement for long periods, and almost lost the capacity to speak.[9] He was fed so badly that his health declined dangerously. Yet, from the time of his arrest and throughout the years during which he passed from youth into middle age, into the early 1990s, he did not permit the dictatorship to break his will. Once permitted to write, he penned a long series of letters from prison addressed to the party's most senior leaders, challenging them relentlessly. As a prisoner in the 1980s, he became, in the words of Sophia Woodman, 'living proof of the party's bad faith' as regards the rule of law and political reform.[10]

'I see as unfounded and unsubstantiated the charges in the indictment brought by the Beijing Municipal People's Procuratorate', the 29-year-old Wei declared at his 16 October 1979 trial in Beijing. 'My editing of publications and my writing of posters were both in accordance with Article 45 of the Constitution: 'Citizens enjoy freedom of speech, correspondence, the press, assembly, association, procession, demonstration and ... have the right to speak out freely, air their views fully, hold great debates and write big-character posters.'[11] One after another, he confuted all the charges against him. Indeed, he made nonsense of the charges so comprehensively that, had the trial been anything other than a political kangaroo court, he would have certainly been acquitted and carried from the courtroom on the shoulders of a cheering throng. Instead, he was sentenced to fifteen years in prison, and deprivation of all political rights for three years after completion of his sentence.

Given that the Chinese dictatorship continues to arrest and imprison journalists, scholars, democratic dissidents, and human-rights activists on spurious charges of counter-revolution, revealing 'state secrets', and 'disturbing the social order', Wei Jingsheng's cool and devastating refutation of the logic of such charges in 1979 deserves to become part of the collective memory of all those thinking about or dealing with China. His bold defence should be recited at will and at need—and the need is certainly continuing. After Wei's expulsion from China in 1997, Xiao Qiang, executive director of the US-based group Human Rights in China, declared that China should unconditionally release 'thousands of other political prisoners' and not be granted any favours merely because it released one man who should never have been in prison in the first place. 'Sending one more dissident into exile does not represent an improvement in China's human rights situation,' he said.

There has been no significant improvement since then in China's human-rights situation, despite some hope in 2004 that Hu Jintao might prove more liberal than Jiang Zemin. Among other things, the arrests and imprisonment of the *New York Times'* Beijing correspondent Zhao Yan in September 2004, and the arrest of Singapore's *Straits Times* Hong Kong–based correspondent Ching Cheong in April 2005, demonstrate that little has changed. They, too, faced charges of revealing, or seeking to reveal, 'state secrets'. In this context, Wei Jingsheng's self-defence reads especially powerfully, and should be used by both the New York and Singapore papers to challenge—indeed, to taunt—the Chinese government.

When charged with providing foreigners with national military information, Wei responded,

> If my memory serves me correctly, the new penal code and the old 'Act of the People's Republic of China for the Punishment of Counterrevolution' read alike: 'Providing military information to the enemy constitutes the crime of treason.' Yet in the eyes of the public prosecutor, my discussions with English and French foreign correspondents are seen as treasonable acts. Is this not as good as describing the English and French journalists as the enemy? I would like to draw the attention of the prosecution to the

fact that when party chairman Hua Guofeng met with journalists from four Western European nations, he quite clearly addressed the correspondents from each nation as 'my friend'.[12]

As for revealing 'state secrets', he went on, any requirement that citizens keep them must presuppose that they know what is and is not secret. Wei testified that, as he had never once had access to anything classified, '... there is no question of my furnishing anyone with anything that can be described as secret by the terms of the legal definition.' He then used a beautiful rhetorical challenge to the supposedly post-Mao leaders of China:

> When the Gang of Four was still in power and a policy of isolation held sway, anything that appealed to the authorities became a national secret, and just to say a few words to a foreigner could, if the powers wished, be construed as having illicit relations with a foreign country. Does the public prosecutor want all citizens to abide by the established practices of the Gang of Four era? Or does he want them just to adhere to the law?

Then, as now, the reality is that the communist regime arrests and imprisons people on the Gang-of-Four rule, just as Wei charged, even while it talks of 'law'.

When he was charged with counter-revolution and with writing 'reactionary' things in the democratic journal *Exploration*, Wei pointed out that, even to make sense of such charges, 'we must first make it clear what is meant by such terms as "revolutionary" and "counter-revolutionary".' The consequence of many years of propaganda and dictatorship, he argued, was that 'there are still people who feel that "revolutionary" means doing things in exact accordance with the will of the leadership currently in power, and to run counter to this will is "counter-revolutionary". I cannot agree with such a vulgar debasement of the concept of revolution.' Instead, Wei maintained that democracy is the 'revolutionary current of the present day and those autocratic conservatives who stand in opposition to it are the real counter-revolutionaries of the day.'[13]

The trial continued as Wei responded to the indictment that he had 'slandered Marxist-Leninist-Mao Zedong Thought' by calling it 'an even more brilliant piece of quackery than any of the old itinerant pox doctors' panaceas and poultices.'[14] But there is no slander in stating the simple truth, as he did, that Marxist–Leninist regimes have 'without exception deteriorated into fascist regimes, where a small leading faction imposes its autocracy over the large mass of ordinary labouring people'. To the charge of 'flaunting the banner of "so-called free speech"', he responded, 'Allow me to point out that there is nothing whatsoever "so-called" about free speech. On the contrary, it is stipulated by the Constitution as a right to be enjoyed by all citizens.'[15]

When charged with 'conspiracy to overthrow the government', he countered that the charge was 'demonstrably false, since I have done nothing conspiratorial and nothing violent, but have simply argued publicly and peaceably for the democratic reform of the political system. I have criticised political leaders, but this is the "sovereign right" of citizens "with which no individual or government organisation has a right to interfere."' He insisted that such criticism is necessary to hold political leaders accountable, and that only if their leaders are held accountable 'will the people be able to breathe freely'. Wei put forward a stark choice between the 'blind faith in the leadership as advocated by the Gang of Four' or 'democratic reform of the socialist system based on criticism and discussion uninhibited by the preference of political office holders and party apparatchiks'.[16]

None of this made any impression on the judge, who was not required to answer Wei's questions. He simply reiterated the charges: 'Wei Jingsheng betrayed his motherland by supplying a foreigner with state military information. He violated the Constitution by his writing of reactionary articles and, by his propagating counter-revolutionary propaganda and agitation, he endangered the basic national and popular interests. All of this constitutes a serious counter-revolutionary crime of a most heinous nature.' In sentencing Wei to fifteen years in prison, the judge asserted that such imprisonment was necessary to 'safeguard the socialist system and consolidate the dictatorship of the proletariat ...'[17]

After a decade in prison, at the height of the Beijing spring that was to climax only a month later in mass bloodshed and political regression, Wei Jingsheng wrote a letter on 4 May 1989 addressed to hardline Premier Li Peng. The date marked the seventieth anniversary of the famous student protests of 1919 that had done much to inspire the founding of the Chinese Communist Party in 1921.[18] 'In China', Wei wrote, 'our traditional mentality and thinking about "benevolent dictators" has frequently led to great tragedy. Not only have those in power ended up being swept into the garbage heap of history, but the blood of the ordinary people has flowed like rivers.'[19] These lines read grimly in retrospect, given the events of June 1989, but may be vindicated again by what lies ahead.

Wei wrote that the time had come for democratisation and there should be no pretence that China was not ready for it. On the contrary, he argued, 'there is no democratic country in the world that had better conditions in the areas of education, ideology, politics, social fabric, economics and the news media for taking the first steps toward democracy than can be found in present-day China.'[20] He argued that democracy would more effectively contribute to the reduction of corruption than any 'iron fist', and would gain the people's trust better than any state propaganda. Therefore, he urged the premier to 'expand the scope of dialogue with the students and all facets of society and directly involve the public in order to ensure that political and economic policies are appropriate'. Wei concluded that Deng Xiaoping's problems were not due to some minor thing going wrong in the spring of 1989, but were 'ten years' worth of mistakes that have accumulated into one great big one'. He counselled Premier Li not to follow 'this disastrous path' any further.[21]

The next letter in Wei's published collection is dated 15 June 1989, and was addressed to Deng Xiaoping himself: 'So, now that you've successfully carried out a military coup to deal with a group of unarmed and politically inexperienced students and citizens, how do you feel? ... Going down in infamy for carrying out a military coup doesn't sound too good to you, does it? Even the likes of Yuan Shikai ... had trouble accepting such a terrible reputation.' With exquisite moral irony, he thanked Deng for having 'bestowed so much honour upon me. I wouldn't be what I am today without you. You can take these words however you like; it's up to you.'[22]

He then proceeded to berate the old party strongman for his betrayal of the cause of twentieth-century China, comparing him not only to Yuan Shikai but to the Empress Dowager Cixi herself:

> You old men love to talk about carrying on the 'cause of the pioneering party martyrs', and so on, yet you need to clarify yourselves exactly what sort of cause these martyrs died for. Did they die so that a few people could act as they please and commit all kinds of outrages, foster corruption and use tanks and planes to suppress the people? ... If you tell me that the early martyrs spilled their blood for the recent triumph of greed and tyranny, then was not their blood spilled in vain? ... Who betrayed these martyrs?[23]

It's a pity that there is no record of Deng Xiaoping having read this letter, let alone of his response to the moral challenge with which he was confronted.

The final year of Wei's sentence began in March 1993 as the party was bidding to host the 2000 Olympic Games in Beijing. On 14 September, nine days before the International Olympic Committee was to vote on the bids, the dictatorship decided to release its most famous political prisoner on 'probation' in a transparent effort to improve its image on human rights. Wei himself denounced the move to the *New York Times* as a 'dirty and abnormal' piece of opportunism on the party's behalf. He went so far as to refuse to accept release on probation unless he was allowed to take with him from prison the hundreds of pages of letters he'd written over the years, which had been kept on file by his jailers.[24]

Wei had been informed that he was 'prohibited from speaking to the media or expressing his opinions', but shortly after his release he broke the prohibition to inform journalists that he would 'continue to press for democratisation and respect for human rights and would bring a lawsuit challenging his conviction'. He fully expected to be jailed again, he said, because he rejected the validity of restrictions on his right to free expression.[25] He told the journalists that his greatest concern was that there would be civil conflict in the future because the party had lost all vital connection with the people. In a display of extraordinary moral courage, he spent the months of his 'probation' talking endlessly to journalists and fellow dissidents, and even writing opinion pieces for Hong Kong papers and the *New York Times*.[26]

One of these pieces, dated 18 November 1993 and appearing on the eve of a summit in Seattle between Jiang Zemin and Bill Clinton, called on the United States to put more pressure on China over its appalling human-rights record. The message got through in the United States, though there was—and still is—intractable uncertainty over what to do in this regard. In China, on the other hand, Wei's bold call was seen by the dictatorship as treasonous. Wei was uncompromising. He told a journalist in late 1993, 'If there wasn't international pressure, a lot of political prisoners wouldn't have been set free, including me. According to the standards of the CCP, many of us, including me, would have been executed.' He said that it was because of international protest and pressure that 'many Communist Party cadres at least now have the concept of human rights and the violation of human rights.'[27]

As Natan Sharansky has argued, and Australian scholar Robert Horvath has shown in a recent major study, the same process of international pressure was what helped to undermine dictatorships in the Soviet Union and Eastern Europe during the 1970s and 1980s.[28] The Chinese dictatorship had already responded to that reality with the repression of 1989, however, and throughout the 1990s and into the 2000s made plain both through its actions and its propaganda that its strategists were all too aware of the dangers that freedom of expression and the rule of law posed to their rule. Wei himself soon felt the full force of their fear and anger. On 1 April 1994, he was kidnapped by the security forces and 'disappeared'. His secretary, Tong Yi, was also arrested four days later, detained without right of redress, and sentenced on 22 December 1994 to two-and-a-half years in prison ('reform through labour') without even a trial. The charge had been 'disturbing social order'.[29]

Wei's disappearance, like his original trial and sentencing, was in clear violation of Chinese law, but was perpetrated on orders from senior officials without regard to the law, in the customary manner of the Communist Party. For some twenty months while he was being held incommunicado in Beijing, the Chinese authorities officially denied knowledge of Wei's whereabouts. During this period, there was a systematic campaign by the government of Jiang Zemin against the democracy and human rights movement in China, with almost all of its leading figures being arrested. Finally, on 21 November 1995, it was announced that Wei Jingsheng, too, had been arrested. It was indicative of the absolutist nature of the government that when a group of dissidents in Zhejiang had the courage to protest at Wei's arrest, they themselves were arrested. Wei's lawyers were only allowed to meet him a few days before he went to trial, on 13 December 1995, and were given only one day to review the dossier compiled on him, which ran to almost 2,000 pages.

There was, of course, never going to be any kind of fair or open-ended trial. The much-ballyhooed 'rule of law' that Deng Xiaoping had spoken of in the late 1970s was a farce. Police prevented the press, foreign diplomats, and even Wei's friends and supporters from attending the trial. The 'charges' against him were based almost entirely on his letters from prison calling for democratisation and human rights, less repressive policies in Tibet, and a rational approach to Taiwan. He was 'accused' of urging the United States to put pressure on China to improve human rights, and also of collecting the names of the victims of political repression in order to enable overseas human-rights groups to aid them. Such were the 'crimes' of this ailing, but unflinching, man.

His defence was as eloquent and uncompromising in 1995 as it had been in 1979, and its key phrases should be repeated like a mantra in the face of the communist dictatorship's continuing evasions, denials, and abuses. 'Actions to promote human rights and democracy and to expose and fight against the enemies of democracy and human rights do not constitute a crime,' he told the prosecutors, who made no effort to answer his argument. He was sentenced, again, to fourteen years in prison to be followed by three years' deprivation of political rights. His appeal was dismissed without a serious hearing on 28 December, and he was sent back to prison. There he would have remained and perhaps died—such was his state of health—but for the international protests that led to his release and expulsion from China in November 1997.[30]

The protests included four nominations for the Nobel Peace Prize and, in 1996, the award by the European Parliament of the Sakharov Prize for Freedom of Thought. The Chinese dictatorship angrily denounced this prize on the grounds that Wei Jingsheng was a 'criminal' and could not, therefore, qualify for such an award. In truth, the criminals were those running the Chinese government, who were relentlessly and lawlessly suppressing freedom of expression, along with other basic civil rights, despite the fact that the Chinese constitution expressly enshrines these freedoms. Any government—democratic or authoritarian—will suppress violent and lawless efforts to overthrow the social and political order. No government, however, can sustain its legitimacy by itself violently suppressing lawful efforts to uphold and rationally reform the social and political order.

Those who imprisoned and then exiled Wei were behaving in the worst traditions of the old China. They simply wanted to shut him up because his lucid insistence that 'without democracy there is no modernization' struck at the very foundation of their rule. When they exiled him they appear to have calculated that, cut off from his roots, he would wither and die. But he has not done so, although he has struggled to find his feet and find a coherent purpose in exile. It is, after all, notoriously hard to keep one's morale up in the linguistic and cultural isolation of exile. Having become socially and politically marginal, exiles squabble like theologians over obscure niceties, for want of more substantial things on which to expend their energies.

When Wei arrived in exile in the United States, he found the Chinese dissidents-in-exile very factionalised and not at all disposed to looking to him for leadership. He struggled to build connections because of his lack of English, and because he had spent so much time alone in prison that it had become difficult for him to work closely with others. Over a period of years, however, Wei put together the Overseas Chinese Democracy Coalition and established an eponymous foundation as a base of operations. Safe from the continuing threat of incarceration, he renewed the rallying cry that he had put up on the famous Democracy Wall in Beijing back in 1978: 'Comrades, I appeal to you: Let us rally together under the banner of democracy. Do not be fooled again by dictators who talk of "stability and unity". Fascist totalitarianism can bring us nothing but disaster. Harbor no more illusions; democracy is our only hope.'[31]

When Jiang Zemin visited Australia in 1999, Wei Jingsheng also travelled to Australia to raise public awareness of the human-rights abuses and suppression of democratic norms in Jiang's China. His approach was as it had always been—addressing his vision of what was necessary in his country not only to the general public, but to the leader himself. He wrote the following brief note to the Chinese president, and asked leading Australian China scholar John Fitzgerald to hand-deliver it to Jiang at an official function:

> Honourable Mr Jiang Zemin,
> This is not our first encounter, and as you can already hear what I have to say through public channels there is no need for me to go into any detail here. I simply want to alert you to something.

> China is bound to change. In thinking about the changes that lie ahead, do you want to deal with reasonable people, or do you prefer dealing with unreasonable people? This is the biggest question that you face, and the biggest question confronting your party.

Once again, Wei's words are haunting when read in retrospect. That very year, Jiang Zemin was suddenly confronted by Li Hongzhi's religious sect Falun Gong, the rapid rise of which had caught even the party's vigilant security services by surprise. The party's ruthless and controversial suppression of Falun Gong as a dangerous cult reeks of political panic, but the strange beliefs and millenarian appeal of the sect evoke memories of the Taiping sect of the mid-nineteenth century, whose rebellion against the corrupt Qing Dynasty led to a colossally bloody internal war in China estimated to have cost tens of millions of lives.[32] Wei was, again, implying that reform would be far better for China than a mass upheaval.

At the time of writing, Wei Jingsheng remains in exile, and the Communist Party remains in power. Nonetheless, Wei has made an inestimable contribution to the cause of Chinese democratisation by having the moral backbone to articulate a sustained critique of the Communist Party against all odds. As John Fitzgerald remarked in a perceptive essay on the moral underpinnings of democratic sentiment in China, Wei had wanted to show, in 1979, that the Chinese democrats were 'not "a bunch of spineless weaklings", and that when individual citizens learned to straighten their spines, China would stand tall in the world'.

In Ha Jin's *Waiting*, doctor Lin Kong wants to divorce his wife, Shuyu, in order to marry his true love, Manna Wu. But he can't quite get a divorce and so he has to wait, year after year, hoping that an easy and legal divorce will finally become possible so that he can make a new life with Manna.[33] Manna's wry judgement after years of waiting for Lin is that 'he would always choose the easy way out.'[34] The same comment is true of many who would like to see democratisation in China, but shy away from a messy divorce from the Communist Party. It is particularly true of those who engage in serial wishful thinking about China, and excuse or extenuate its relentless political repression on the grounds that 'stability' is vital. Wei Jingsheng has divorced the Communist Party and proclaimed his love for freedom. He's just waiting for that 'vigorous democracy' that Hu Jintao claimed the party is building, so that he can openly declare his love in his native land.

Chapter 12

The Truth about Tiananmen

If you were to go privately to the top one hundred officials in China and ask them whether the verdict on the June 4th incident should be reversed, I can guarantee you that more than eighty of them would say sooner or later it has to be done.

—Zhang Liang[1]

Ten years after Wei Jingsheng was incarcerated for exercising his rights under the Chinese constitution, the democracy movement in China was brutally crushed on the orders of Deng Xiaoping. This remains the defining moment of the post-Mao regime in China. It demonstrated that the Communist Party was bereft of the means for dealing with serious dissent in a civilised manner. Since it had never demonstrated any such capacity, this should not have come as any great surprise. Yet the decade of the 1980s had given rise to the hope that Deng Xiaoping would move cautiously down the path of political reform, despite the nervousness he had exhibited in suppressing the Democracy Wall movement in 1979. Those hopes were to prove unfounded.

The Tiananmen Papers are a remarkable set of documents that were smuggled out of China to the United States, edited by Andrew Nathan and Perry Link, and published there, and in Britain, in early 2001. These documents come as close as anything on the public record to exposing the high-level party decision-making that led to what Wei Jingsheng caustically described as a coup against unarmed and inexperienced students. They reveal how the extraordinary nationwide protest movement that challenged the Communist Party government in 1989 was viewed from the top of the party. This makes them rare, indeed—for the Chinese government guards its secrets with a paranoia that makes Richard Nixon look candid, and is extremely averse to honest and critical political or historical reporting about itself. Nathan, a specialist on Chinese democracy movements, described them as 'the richest record I have ever seen of political life in China at the top.'[2]

Not only do *The Tiananmen Papers* form a rare record; they also offer an intriguing study in the legitimation crisis of a dictatorship. They put on stage, as it were, a gripping drama of state authority versus citizen protest, with all the elements of a Greek tragedy. They also provide a fascinating insight into the cognitive failures of human beings under pressure. The real thinking and motives of Deng Xiaoping and his senior party colleagues are recorded here, more or less directly. They make compelling reading. Given the critical importance of reform and political evolution in China in the years immediately ahead, they are a valuable source of insight into how the process can break down or be thwarted.

The chief preoccupation of many critics—including the party itself, which strove to discredit the book, even as it sought to identify and punish those who had made it possible— was with the authenticity of the documents. There are, of course, precedents for allegedly long-secret documents that turned out to be hoaxes. Perhaps the most famous case was the publication of the *Hitler Diaries*, in 1983, to which distinguished historian Hugh Trevor-Roper gave his imprimatur, only to later find that he was in error. *The Tiananmen Papers* raised questions because their sources were obscure; the motives of the individual who supplied them to the American translators and editors were unclear; and because many of the documents themselves were clearly summaries rather than original records, so their wording could not be taken literally. But Nathan, Link, and another leading Sinologist, Orville Schell, all concluded that the documents were authentic and that they were of pathbreaking significance in opening up to scrutiny the innermost sanctum of the intensively secretive Chinese government.

They argued that the papers were genuine on the basis of internal evidence and familiarity with the Chinese originals, as well as from acquaintance with their pseudonymous source, Zhang Liang. There is further reason to judge them as authentic. Had they been the product of a hoax, one would have to ask: *cui bono*? Who would have tried to perpetrate the hoax, and why? Certainly not the editors, whose reputations as serious scholars remain beyond reproach. That leaves only Zhang Liang, or those who supplied him with the documents. If Zhang's motive was to make a killing with a sensational but fraudulent exposé, he was not only very clever, but also extraordinarily subtle—for while *The Tiananmen Papers* make gripping reading they are not at all sensationalist. They are fascinating for those with a serious interest in contemporary Chinese politics, but probably of little interest to those whose imaginations are not already engaged with the subject. There is no meretricious dramatisation in them, only a sense of complex events unfolding with often unintended consequences.

An alternative explanation might have been that the documents were a hoax perpetrated for political reasons. The problem with this claim is that the book does not, on the face of it, serve any clear agenda other than documenting the events of 1989. Three mutually incompatible political agendas might be imagined: to discredit the Communist Party by revealing the guilt of senior leaders in the Tiananmen crackdown; to justify the very same leaders and buttress the legitimacy of the Communist Party, by showing that what happened in June 1989 was understandable and even necessary; or else to advance the interests of a particular faction within the Communist Party. While any one of these might seem plausible as a motive for someone to put together a false record of the matter, neither the documents themselves nor the preface by Zhang Liang lend support to any such hypothesis.

The Tiananmen Papers did not discredit the party any more than it was already discredited. They show in detail how difficult it was for the party leaders to agree on what to do and how anxious they were to avoid bloodshed. They actually put key figures—notably Deng Xiaoping, Yang Shangkun, and Li Peng—in a somewhat better light than most speculation and reporting in the years after the crackdown had done. Yet they do not, conversely, justify or legitimise the decisions made by the party leaders, because they show glaringly where their blind spots and failures of judgement occurred. Moreover, Zhang Liang declares that 'June Fourth weighs on the spirits of every Chinese patriot', and predicts that a reinterpretation of the crackdown, based on the documentary record, will be made by liberal elements as they 'move toward discarding the Communist system'.

As for the papers possibly serving the cause of a faction within the Communist Party, one would have to ask what faction this might be. In the preface, Zhang Liang refers to 'the pro-democracy faction in the party', but also to the party as a whole now being 'a melange of factions with diverse goals and differing ideologies'. He does not offer any clues as to who made up the 'pro-democracy faction'. In an interview in 2001, he claimed that such pro-democracy sentiment was widespread within the party, but declined to name names, because doing so could put those named in an invidious position. The evidence available would suggest that there are, in fact, many different views within the party as to what 'democracy' means, and how much of it is desirable in China, but not a cohesive 'pro-democracy faction'. It is far from clear, therefore, by which factional interest the documents might have been fabricated.

Zhang Liang calls upon 'people committed to democracy and freedom' to imitate Zhao Ziyang (the reformist premier forced out of office by Deng Xiaoping in May 1989) and to risk 'self-sacrifice' for the cause, without elaborating on what form this risk should take. One might argue that if Zhao Ziyang did indeed sacrifice himself in 1989, perhaps he should not have done so. A more effective political leader might have openly challenged Deng Xiaoping and publicly demanded that the Communist Party at long last accept democratic reform. Instead, he meekly accepted political defeat, resigned, and acquiesced in house arrest and official obloquy. He then lived in the time-honoured tradition of Chinese sages, until his death in January 2005, when he was interred by the party with minimal ceremony. While Zhang Liang was an admirer of Zhao, he did not make a case, from *The Tiananmen Papers*, that Chinese democrats could look to him as a leader.

For all the reasons above, I believe we can regard *The Tiananmen Papers* as substantially, if not wholly, authentic. I agree with American China scholar Jeffrey Wasserstrom, who pointed out that their chief defect is that they are *incomplete*. We would like to know a good deal more, both in the detail and as regards the original sources and nature of the documents, given that they are heavily redacted in their published version. Such incompleteness is not, however, entirely the fault of Zhang Liang or his American translators and editors; it is the simple consequence of the obsessive secrecy of the Chinese government. When the state and party archives in China are opened to scholarly scrutiny, we may very well find the record to be even more complex and interesting than these documents attest. In the interim, there is no sound reason to accept the claims of fraudulence that emanated from Beijing in 2001. What such denunciations suggested was that the documents may have been painfully close to the truth, and made the party uncomfortable—as well they should have.

It is worth drawing a comparison between this question of *The Tiananmen Papers* and other unpleasant secrets over which the Chinese government remains a jealous guardian. In his path-breaking study of the horrendous famine caused by the Great Leap Forward, Dali Yang observed that, despite the deaths of 30 million people, the catastrophe has received meagre attention 'because, with rare exceptions, archives on the Great Leap Famine remain tightly guarded'[3] The opening of such archives is an indispensable precondition for China's general process of 'reform and opening'. Until it occurs, self-righteous official statements by the Chinese government about foreign or dissident scholars distorting the historical record do not deserve to be treated seriously.

Yang's excellent study is relevant to the case of *The Tiananmen Papers* in another respect. He was interested in the cognitive processes that shaped both catastrophic decision-making and subsequent learning in China, between the late 1950s and the beginning of the reform era under Deng Xiaoping. To explore these processes, he turned to 'recent developments in cognitive psychology'.[4] He looked especially at studies in the way human beings cope with complexity and uncertainty, use judgemental heuristics to reduce complex inferential tasks to simple operations, and often fail to learn because of persistence of belief. His application of these concepts to the case of the Great Leap famine and its aftermath is both intellectually rigorous and extremely interesting.

What emerges from reading *The Tiananmen Papers* is that similar cognitive failings can be seen, also, in this more recent case. Nowhere is this more evident than in the ineradicable belief of the party elders that they knew China required party leadership rather than 'bourgeois liberalism'. The quote cited by Yang from Francis Bacon's *The New Organon* (1620) might well be placed at the head of *The Tiananmen Papers*:

> The human understanding, when it has once adopted an opinion ... draws all things else to support and agree with it. And though there be a greater number or weight of instances to be found on the other side, yet these it either neglects and despises, or else by some distinction sets aside and rejects, in order that by this great and pernicious predetermination the authority of its former conclusions may remain inviolate.

In May 1919, and again in May 1989, Chinese students demonstrated in Tiananmen Square to call for science and democracy in China. What are science and democracy but methods for overcoming the 'pernicious predetermination' of knowledge and public policy by arbitrary authority? But in 1989 the arbitrary authority exercised by Deng Xiaoping and his senior colleagues (with Zhao Ziyang dissenting) enforced the fiat that the dictatorship of the Communist Party must be preserved at all costs.

The editors of *The Tiananmen Papers* made no reference to cognitive psychology. Yet the documents show just how relevant it is to understanding the errors and biases which shaped the thinking of decision-makers in Beijing in 1989. Above all, they show that the bloody denouement to the confrontation between citizens and government came about because there was no legitimate process by which the government could be held to account for its arbitrary exercise of authority. That, of course, was precisely why there was a democracy movement in the first place. It is also why there remains an enduring need for such a movement in China, and why the decisions made in 1989 must ultimately be renounced by any Chinese government that wants to lay claim to genuine political legitimacy.

From a cognitive point of view, nothing is more disconcerting than the evidence provided in the documents that the party leaders consistently misinterpreted the nature of the movement they were facing, and locked themselves into a course of action that was to bring about tragedy. They operated under the sway of fixed ideas, believing that they were responsible for the future of the country, and that stability was vital to that future. They told themselves that the students were being manipulated by 'black hands' from Taiwan and the United States, and by a 'tiny minority' of 'bourgeois liberals'. The country was grinding to a halt. Anarchy threatened. These young people didn't know how good they had it. Why didn't they get off the streets and back to their studies?

To a remarkable extent, the whole episode reads like a weird inversion of student demonstrations in the West in the 1960s. Instead of Richard Nixon or Charles de Gaulle confronting mass demonstrations and seeing them as the irresponsible antics of 'bed-wetting' youths (as de Gaulle phrased it, in 1968) manipulated by a tiny minority of Marxists, one finds Deng Xiaoping and his old party colleagues confronting similar demonstrations and simply substituting the term 'bourgeois liberals' for 'Marxists'. The outcome in Beijing was far bloodier than in Paris in 1968, or Kent State in 1972, but the underlying issue was the same: authority versus the conscientious revolt of the citizenry.

The tragic scenario revealed by the documents is precisely that which Hegel described as the collision between *Kriegstaat*, 'war-state', and *Privatrecht*, 'private conscience', in *The Phenomenology of Mind*. One is reminded of the collision, in Sophocles' classic Greek drama, *Antigone*, when Creon insists on the authority of the state against an unyielding young woman, who insists on the higher authority of natural law. When Antigone will not yield, Creon has her put to death. The sculpted 'goddess of democracy' brought by the students from the Central Academy of Fine Arts into Tiananmen Square, on the night of 29 May 1989, was clearly modelled on the Statue of Liberty, but it could equally have been conceived as an image of Antigone.

Alas, in contemporary China (as in ancient Greece), 'Antigone' was put to death by 'Creon'. *The Papers* recount in detail how the drama unfolded, in 1989, from the unrest in March, through the April demonstrations and the astonishing globally televised spectacle of mass protest in May, to its shattering climax on the night of 3 June and in the early hours of 4 June. The editors' prologue sets the stage for the 'Greek tragedy' by briefly recounting how, in the aftermath of the suppression of the Democracy Wall movement in 1979 and the imprisonment of Wei Jingsheng, divisions arose within the Communist Party itself in the mid-1980s. Those around party General Secretary Hu Yaobang and Premier Zhao Ziyang believed that political liberalisation was essential, if economic reform itself was to be successfully pushed forward. Others were fearful of where liberalisation might lead.

The struggle within the party reflected ferment and unrest across the country. Deng Xiaoping saw it as his job to hold the reins of power steady, ensuring that a broad program of economic reform went forward without criticism of the Communist Party running out of control. In September 1986, the Politburo appointed a top-level body called the 'Small Group for Research on Reform of the Central Political System'. Zhao Ziyang headed the group. His chief aide was Bao Tong, who was himself to become a significant actor in the drama of 1989, and has remained a critic of the party ever since. It was clear from the start that the small group had its work cut out for it. The volatility of the political situation was underscored when social unrest among students, and others, in late 1986 enabled the conservatives to press for Hu Yaobang's resignation as general secretary in January 1987.

Then, in the spring of 1988, the position of Zhao Ziyang was weakened when his plans for radical reform of state-set prices for major industrial inputs and products led to widespread panic about possible shortages. The unsettling social and economic consequences shook Deng Xiaoping's confidence in his premier. By early 1989, Deng's perennial uncertainties about how, or, indeed, whether to proceed with political reform, and even economic reform, had led to Zhao's plans for both being stalled.[5] At the same time, there were numerous signs, according to the party's security organs, of crime rates spiralling out of control, ideological problems in the military, and a common view among educated and younger people that communism had been bad for China. The growing sense was that moderate political reform would have been better for China than 'revolution', and that the classic May Fourth Movement of 1919 had stood for the introduction of Western values—above all, individual freedom.[6]

Leading intellectuals openly called for serious political reform. Three who were particularly prominent—astrophysicist Fang Lizhi, journalist Liu Binyan, and writer Wang Ruowang—had already been expelled from the party as supporters of Hu Yaobang, in early 1987. Far from intimidated, they pressed the case for change. On 6 January 1989, Fang wrote an open letter to Deng Xiaoping in which he called for amnesty for Wei Jingsheng and other political prisoners, as a way to commemorate the bicentennial of the 1789 French Revolution, the seventieth anniversary of the May Fourth Movement, and the fortieth anniversary of the founding of the People's Republic of China.[7] On 13 February, a letter along similar lines that was signed by 33 leading poets, novelists, historians, film-makers and philosophers was sent to the party's central office.[8] On 26 February, 42 top intellectuals, many of them famous scientists 'who had hitherto not spoken out politically', issued a letter 'urging faster and more radical political reform' and, on 14 March, a further 43 'younger social scientists, humanists and journalists' signed a letter to the National People's Congress calling for the release of political prisoners.[9]

The Chinese political system was in such a state of gridlock that these various appeals by the country's intellectual elite for political reform only angered party conservatives. The appeals also seemed to so confront even the leading reformers that they collaborated in suppressing publication of the letters. In what can only be seen as a remarkable emasculation of their own political position, Zhao Ziyang and fellow Politburo reformer Hu Qili themselves ordered that the official print and electronic media not publish or give any air-time to letters, petitions, or any other writings by the petitioners.

The official media repeated the mantra that it still uses now: that China did not have any political prisoners, so it could hardly grant them amnesty. Wei Jingsheng, it was insisted, was guilty as charged of leaking state secrets to foreigners. And the famous petitioners themselves, it was brazenly asserted, had been duped by the New York–based Alliance for Democracy in China into signing things they did not truly believe. It was darkly insinuated that this organisation had secret ties to Taiwan.

Thus did the Communist Party's propaganda machine react to reasoned calls for basic civil rights and democratic norms from scores of its most distinguished citizens. Deng Xiaoping had imprisoned Wei Jingsheng for insisting on speaking plainly, but had himself declared, in August 1980, that 'unsound systems and institutions' had led to 'grave misfortunes' for both the party and the country. He was absolutely right—and those same unsound systems and institutions, unreformed at his insistence, were now set to lead to yet another grave misfortune.

According to Nathan and Link, the death of Hu Yaobang from a heart attack on 15 April 1989 'fell like a spark into the highly flammable atmosphere of elite division and popular disaffection.'[10] Students across the country regarded him as 'a symbol of liberal reform and clean government.' Certainly his long career had clearly demonstrated that clarity of mind and moral integrity could survive decades of work at the highest levels of the Communist Party. He had joined the party at the nadir of its fortunes in 1933; was almost executed as an 'anti-Bolshevik' during an internal party purge in the 1940s; had endeavoured, during the 1957 anti-Rightist campaign, to moderate its impact; had been purged and punished during the Cultural Revolution; was brought back into serious work by Deng Xiaoping in 1973; was purged again by the Gang of Four in 1976; was brought back yet again by Deng in 1977; and had been the leading proponent of thoroughgoing political reform within the top leadership for a decade after that.[11]

In 1977, at the very beginning of the Deng Xiaoping era, Hu Yaobang established the 'Theory Research Office' within the Central Party School, with the agenda of exploring 'the obstacles socialist countries faced in establishing truly democratic governments and the ways they might overcome these difficulties.'[12] Between 1977 and 1986 Hu brought into his circle theorists who had struggled against the tyranny of totalitarianism throughout the Maoist era. Through the Theory Research Office and then the Chinese Academy of Social Sciences (CASS), created in 1978, Hu sponsored calls for political democratisation. Within his domain, the party's own intellectual elite articulated the same ideas that were being espoused by Wei Jingsheng and his Democracy Wall colleagues.

It was researchers at CASS who pointed out that the civil rights stipulated in China's constitution—freedoms of speech, correspondence, the press, assembly, association, procession, demonstration, and the right to strike—were violated by the party because of the lack of a 'civil code' to uphold them. An article by Su Ching and Wang Chiafu stating precisely this appeared in the *People's Daily* on 24 November 1978. At a conference held under the auspices of CASS's Institute of Law in November 1978, Yu Guangyuan (one of Hu Yaobang's advisers) told 160 participants that 'without democracy there can be no modernizations'. On 3 January 1979, this message was repeated in an editorial in the *People's Daily*. (The paper's editor, Hu Jiwei, was another confidante of Hu Yaobang.) 'The four modernizations,' read the editorial, 'must be accompanied by political democratization.'[13]

With Hu Yaobang's death, in April 1989, it became clear that his hopes had been thwarted by conservatives within the party. Students in Beijing marched to Tiananmen Square to mourn the death of a genuine hero and, in doing so, raised the call once more for the political reform that he had championed. As the students conducted a vast sit-in over the following week, party conservatives became worried that a political challenge to the regime could develop. Zhao Ziyang urged his colleagues to relax, saying that the students would make their point and then return to their classrooms. 'On the whole,' he told Yang Shangkun by telephone on 18 April, 'I think we should affirm the students' patriotism.'[14] On 22 April, Zhao left for a week-long state visit to North Korea.[15] It was during this time that things started to get out of hand.

In Zhao's absence, Deng Xiaoping swung towards a hard line. In a top-level meeting at Deng's private residence, Li Peng told him,

> There are open calls for the government to step down, appeals for nonsense like 'open investigations into and discussions of the question of China's governance and power' and calls to institute broader elections and revise the Constitution, to lift restrictions on political parties and newspapers, and to get rid of the category of 'counter revolutionary' crimes. Illegal student organizations have already sprung up in Beijing and Tianjin.[16]

Deng's assessment, based on such briefings, was that 'a tiny minority is exploiting the students. This is a well-planned plot, whose real aim is to reject the Chinese Communist Party and the socialist system at the most fundamental level.'[17] On 26 April, a harsh editorial appeared in the *People's Daily* (no longer under the editorship of Hu Jiwei) reflecting Deng's grim judgement of the student movement as 'a well-planned plot ... to confuse the people and throw the country into turmoil'.[18]

What Li Peng had reported was, of course, fundamentally true; the democratic reformers were indeed calling for radical change. Moreover, there were exceptionally good reasons for such calls, which had emanated not from any dubious 'tiny minority', as Deng arbitrarily suggested and as the official editorial claimed, but from the highest and most enlightened elements of the party and the Chinese intelligentsia. There was no plot—unless it was a plot by the old guard of the party to cling to power regardless of the constitution or the will of the people. At this juncture in the history of the People's Republic, there was scope for extraordinary statesmanship in appealing to the idealism of the mass of demonstrators, and articulating a program of reform of which the deceased and popularly mourned Hu Yaobang would have been proud. But neither Deng Xiaoping nor any of his party colleagues exhibited such statesmanship.

Was it delusion or mendacity that led old Deng to describe the mass demonstrations as the insidious work of a tiny group of malign plotters seeking to bring chaos to China? *The Tiananmen Papers* do not answer this question decisively. What they do clearly show, on the other hand, is that his strategy of denouncing the demonstrations outright backfired disastrously. The editorial had the opposite effect to that which Deng and the hard-liners seem to have anticipated: it galvanised truly massive protests all over the country. To quote Nathan and Link:

> On April 27, huge student demonstrations in opposition to the editorial swept major cities. They occurred not only in cities where demonstrations had already taken place, such as Shanghai, Tianjin, Changchun, Xi'an, Wuhan, Nanjing, Hangzhou, Hefei, Changsha, Chengdu and Chongqing, but also in cities where demonstrations now broke out for the first time: Shenyang, Dalian, Shijiazhuang, Jinan, Nanning, Kunming, Shenzhen, Yinchuan and Guilin.[19]

Among the many uses of *The Tiananmen Papers* is that they show the party's own internal security organs, propaganda specialists, and political leaders registering both the scale and political significance of the student protests. Again and again, *The Papers* reveal fascinating remarks by key figures that would have been expunged from the historical record if the hardliners had had their way. Few such remarks are more telling, both in their context and in the present, than an observation of senior propaganda official Rui Xingwen at a meeting of the heads of the Xinhua News Agency on 27 April 1989. (Xinhua publishes the *People's Daily*, *Guangming Daily* and other state-run newspapers. Many of its senior journalists were frustrated at the time by the official censorship of reporting on the student movement.)

Rui remarked, 'There are, actually, a lot of reforms we should make on the news front. We can't just stay the same decade after decade. The big forces of change in society are forcing reforms in the news and those reforms are just what the people want ... News reports have to tell the truth; we absolutely mustn't put out fake news.'[20] At the meeting, Hu Qili (the Politburo member in charge of ideology and news editorials) and Rui told the senior editors that they should feel free to be bolder in reporting what the students were saying. On the same day, Jiang Zemin (then mayor of Shanghai) and his political strategist Zeng Qinghong shut down the liberal *World Economic Herald*, because it had championed Hu Yaobang's ideas as the nationwide demonstrations spread. Both Hu and Rui were removed from all party posts after 4 June.

Zhao Ziyang returned to Beijing from North Korea on 30 April and, on 1 May, clashed with Li Peng at a Politburo meeting during which Zhao declared that the government should respond to the student protests by accelerating political reform, while Li insisted that 'order' had to be restored. The minutes of this meeting, as summarised in *The Tiananmen Papers*, make especially poignant reading, and show two things with crystal clarity: first, that even hard-liners like Li Peng and Bo Yibo understood the need for political reform (though they understood little of how to bring it about in any meaningful way), and also that Zhao Ziyang defended systematic democratisation as 'a worldwide trend' that the party had to embrace. 'If the party doesn't uphold the banner of democracy in our country, someone else will, and we will lose out,' Zhao claimed. 'In sum, we must make the people feel that under the leadership of the Communist Party and the socialist system they can truly and fully enjoy democracy and freedom.'[21]

This is the critical issue to ponder, as we look back to the events of 1989, and forward to the prospect of democratisation in China. The 'someone else' to whom Zhao referred at the time was none other than the mass of educated people in China, and many of the brightest members of the party itself. And the party failed abysmally to rise to the Zhao's challenge. *The Tiananmen Papers* document, step-by-step, how the men around Deng Xiaoping retreated into fear and defensiveness, persuading themselves that a few foreign 'black hands' were behind the 'turmoil' in China and that 'stability' required first martial law (which was declared on 20 May) and then the use of massive force to crush the last of the demonstrations. The violence was followed by lies about what had happened, sackings of all those who had 'wavered', and a nationwide campaign to root out and repress all vestiges of the democracy movement. Lamentably, such repression has continued unabated since the accession to power of Hu Jintao and Wen Jiabao.

'We should meet the students' reasonable demands through democracy and law, should be willing to reform, and should use rational and orderly methods,' Zhao Ziyang declared on 4 May in a speech to the board of governors of the Asian Development Bank. 'What we need most right now is calm, reason, self-restraint, and order as we move to solve problems through democracy and law.'[22] Such an agenda had, and still has, an enormous reservoir of goodwill to draw on, both in China itself and around the world. What made the events of the following month so tragic and so defining a characteristic of the communist regime is that the exact opposite took place, wholly because the party leadership failed to imagine, or refused to contemplate, the kinds of reform that would have turned the mass demonstrations from a 'threat' of chaos into a triumph of 'people power'.

This was Zhao Ziyang's failure as much as that of Li Peng, for there was recognition by almost all the leadership (including both members of the old guard such as Yang Shangkun and Bo Yibo, and younger leaders, such as Qiao Shi and Hu Qili) that, in Bo's words, 'the Beijing populace sympathises with the students', and that the use of force would have profoundly negative consequences for the legitimacy of the regime. As Qiao Shi remarked during a Politburo standing committee meeting on 8 May, 'Now is the time to take concrete steps to clean up the government and to build democratic politics. If we move boldly and can guide the masses skilfully, then the students' demands for reform ... and their underlying patriotism can all be channelled toward political reform ...'[23]

The problem was that they could not, between themselves, manage to move beyond old and tired Marxist–Leninist methods of trying to 'guide the masses skilfully'. As Hu Qili pointed out at the same meeting of 8 May 1989, 'I'm afraid some of the methods of leadership and political agitation that worked so well for our party in the '50s, '60s and '70s are no longer so effective ... we should reform the political system, advancing concrete proposals that will show the people the party is serious about proposing democracy.'[24] The party failed this test. Deng Xiaoping himself, trapped in his assumptions about Marxist dictatorship and the 'chaos' that 'bourgeois liberalism' would entail, summed up the party's paralysis when he remarked on 11 May, 'We've never run into this before ... We're left fumbling over what to do.'[25]

In fact, he was not 'fumbling' in 1989 any more than he had been a decade earlier when he had Wei Jingsheng arrested, tried, and sentenced for espousing political principles championed by Hu Yaobang and his circle. And, in 1979, he was not 'fumbling' any more than he had been in 1957 when he played a leading role in the anti-Rightist campaign that suppressed liberal criticism of the party's totalitarian rule. He was simply reverting to the only methods he truly understood—enforcing Marxism–Leninism by extra-legal means. He must be assigned the major responsibility for what finally happened on 4 June 1989 because he was the architect of the post-Mao era, and he had refused to countenance reform and opening in the political system. Confronted by mass demands for change, he said to Zhao Ziyang on 13 May 1989, 'We must not give an inch on the basic principle of upholding Communist Party rule and rejecting a Western multiparty system.'[26]

The party leaders met again on 17 May and the consensus, as expressed by Yang Shangkun, was that they had their 'backs to the wall'. 'If we retreat any further, we're done for,' he said. Bo Yibo agreed, asserting that the student movement was 'a consequence of the long-term spread of bourgeois liberalism in China. It aims at the West's so-called democracy, freedom, and human rights.' But, as Wei Jingsheng would have said, there is nothing 'so-called' about democracy, freedom, and human rights. The demand for them had arisen out of revulsion from the abuses of tyranny and misgovernment in China, not out of any foreign plot. The party had its back to the wall because it was unable, under Deng Xiaoping and the other old revolutionaries, to acknowledge this reality. Lacking any other perspective, Deng concluded that 'we should bring in the People's Liberation Army and declare martial law in Beijing ... to suppress the turmoil once and for all.'[27] With this decision, the die was cast.

The denouement is graphically described in *The Tiananmen Papers*. As elements of the 38th Group Army attempted to march to Tiananmen Square to clear it, they encountered huge crowds blocking their way on Fuxing Road, seven kilometres west of the Square. According to Martial Law Command and State Security Ministry reports of late 3 June and the early hours of 4 June, tens of thousands of Beijing citizens defied bullhorn appeals, tear gas, and rubber bullets for an hour before the troops (under a barrage of rocks and bottles) finally fired into the crowd at Muxidi Bridge.[28] From that point, at 10.30 p.m. on 3 June, the violence spiralled out of control.

An after-action report to the Central Military Commission by the 38th Group Army reported that: '[troops] broke through twelve intersections ... cleared away seven blockades of burning cars ... and overwhelmed a forest of roadblocks ... ' before reaching Tiananmen Square at 1.30 a.m. By then, about 3000 students remained in the Square, and they gathered around the Monument to the People's Heroes and began to sing, of all things, 'The Internationale'. 'The clearing itself began at 4.30 a.m.,' the report relates. 'Two thousand soldiers ... plus forty-two armoured vehicles ... cleared the Square, moving from north to south ... and we smashed the Goddess of Democracy, which was the rioters' spiritual pillar.'[29]

The Communist Party's suppression of what had been a huge nationwide protest movement left it with a deep legitimacy problem. This problem has never been entirely overcome, though there has been a marked rise in nationalist sentiment in the past few years that tends to put the 1989 events into a somewhat different context. Those who are well-disposed to China are likely to agree with Andrew Nathan when he remarks that democracy will be more firmly established in China 'if it evolves from the current system rather than being set up on the shards of a broken system'. This seems, also, to have been Zhang Liang's view. But if it is to evolve, the Communist Party will have to break out of the mind-set that over-determined its decision-making in 1989.

It remains to be seen who will find the courage and the political means to go beyond where Hu Yaobang was stopped in January 1987, and where Zhao Ziyang threw in his hand by resigning in May 1989. There is no present sign of Hu Jintao or Wen Jiabao doing so. They might have signalled some inclination to move in this direction if they had used the death of Zhao Ziyang in January 2005 to express regret for the political debacle of May–June 1989, and to praise Zhao as a good servant of the people. At the time of Zhao's death, Hu Jiwei urged that his reputation be restored.[30] Bao Tong and Yan Jiaqi, another of the pro-democratic intellectuals of the 1980s long since in exile, also called for Zhao to receive due recognition. Instead, the party did everything it could to bury the old reformer as quietly as possible. And, in April 2005, it arrested those who sought to obtain and publish a record of his thoughts during his last years.

In short, the party has not moved on from the hopeless conceptual impasse that crippled Deng Xiaoping and his colleagues in the 1980s. It has solved none of the problems that led to the mass protests of 1989, and has made progress only in the sophistication of its monitoring and repression of dissent. If serious thinking is being done inside the party as to how the regime is ever going to transcend Marxism–Leninism and subject itself to the rule of law, it is both muted and terribly compromised by propaganda. However, the necessary thinking is happening, not only among exiles but also among critical intellectuals in China. One notable figure in the Jiang Zemin years was Wang Hui, chief editor of *Dushu* (*Reading*), China's leading intellectual monthly, until 2000, with a circulation of about 110,000.

Wang is the heir of those major free thinkers of 80 to 100 years ago in China—Yan Fu, Liang Qichao, and Lu Xun—who hoped to see China became a modern civilisation with liberal characteristics. He is also the heir of the dissidents of the 1980s who petitioned Deng Xiaoping for political reform and an amnesty for political prisoners, only to be let down even by Zhao Ziyang. His first book, published in 1990, was hauntingly called *Revolt Against Despair: Lu Xun and His World*. In the shadow of the tragic events of 4 June 1989, political reform in China is, indeed, a matter of 'revolt against despair'. What Wang called for, however, was not 'revolt' as mobilisation but 'an unprejudiced intellectual curiosity' about the way to political reform.

Wang's later book, *Rekindling Frozen Fire*, which contains essays on the theme of modernisation, unsettled not only communists but Friedmanites with its criticisms of corruption and inequity in 'marketising' China. This stance led to Wang being called a representative of a 'New Left', although his arguments are more intellectually interesting than this label suggests. He seeks to articulate what his hero, Lu Xun, called 'thunder from the silent zone'—the explosive anger that lies just beneath the surface of a deeply repressed society. The anger does not necessarily dissipate with time. The leaking and publication of *The Tiananmen Papers* were an expression of such undissipated anger, such 'thunder from the silent zone', for it puts the truth about Tiananmen on the record, despite all the party's lies and all its efforts to suppress those who, in 1989, stood for democratic liberalism in China.

Chapter 13

Green Island: from prison camp to memorial

The Chinese 'Gulag' is a gigantic topic that has been well described by firsthand witnesses ... The reading of these accounts is a basic duty for everyone who professes the slightest concern for China ... [They demonstrate] the central relevance of the labor camps for any meaningful analysis of the nature of the Maoist regime ... [W]hoever wishes to dispose of the human-rights issue in China without first tackling this particular subject is either irresponsible or a fraud.

—Simon Leys[1]

Those calling for an end to arbitrary repression and dictatorship in China have a clear example to draw upon: Taiwan. During the first three decades of the Cold War, the question of whether the right-wing dictatorship in Taiwan (the Republic of China) was as bad as the left-wing dictatorship in China (the People's Republic of China) was the subject of some debate. The overwhelming evidence showed that the left-wing dictatorship was worse by orders of magnitude. Certainly, the regime on Taiwan was repressive in years past, but it is not now. The story of Taiwan's reform from within is a remarkable one, which should be much more widely understood by those committed to bringing about reform in China.

What has been achieved in Taiwan stands in striking contrast to the sheer scale of repression that has occurred and continues to occur in China. As with repression in the Soviet Union, so with China: it is difficult to get accurate data on the number of people executed during the mass terror of the Maoist years, or confined to forced-labour camps and so-called 're-education through labor' camps during that era. It is not even easy to get wholly reliable data on the numbers of those executed, imprisoned, or sentenced to forced labour during the generally less savage post-Mao era. The overriding reason for this, however, is the secrecy of the regime. What is clear beyond serious dispute is that repression on an enormous scale took place under Mao Zedong, and that large-scale repression has continued over the three decades or so since his death.

Estimates of the number of those who have died as a direct result of communist rule in China have always been the subject of polemic, and it seems highly probable that the total is considerably lower than the most extravagant figures suggest. As early as 1956, for example, Richard Walker, a professor of history at Yale University, credited estimates by the Free Trade Union Committee of the American Federation of Labor that Mao Zedong and the Communist Party 'had been responsible for the deaths of more than 14,000,000 people over the previous five years.'[2] But, as Stuart Schram remarked a decade later, such figures are surely far too high, if only because it is extremely difficult physically to kill so many people so quickly. Yet Schram estimated that, in the same period to which Walker had referred, a reasonable estimate of the number of people executed by the communists would be one to three million. And he did not consider this figure all that large a toll 'for a social revolution of this magnitude, carried out in the wake of a long and cruel civil war which had taken even more victims on both sides.'[3]

In her devastating biography of Mao Zedong, Jung Chang has claimed that well over 70 million Chinese people died as a result of his rule. This gigantic figure must arouse scepticism, but it is buttressed to some extent by three considerations. First, by general agreement the appalling famine of 1959–61, triggered by the Great Leap Forward, took 45 to 55 million lives and led to about 30 million postponed births. The unmistakeable drop in the graph of China's population surge suggests that there is no ground for dismissing these staggering figures as the product of fevered or polemical imaginations.

Second, there was mass repression in the early 1950s—even the party claimed quite openly at the time that it had executed hundreds of thousands of 'bandits' and 'counter-revolutionaries'. It also confined millions to forced labour, and by all accounts the conditions in the labour camp system were as destructive of life as those in the Soviet Gulag under Stalin, on which the Chinese system was modelled.

Third, the Cultural Revolution generated enormous chaos and violence in China, during which Deng Xiaoping himself estimated that 100 million people were 'repressed'. He does not seem to have meant by this that they were all killed, although very large numbers were—anywhere in the order of two to ten million. Only a massive research project in Chinese central and provincial archives could begin to get the figures right; and even then, as the Soviet case reveals, there would almost certainly be considerable room for debate. As the leading Russian specialist on the Gulag, Oleg Khlevniuk, concluded in 2004, 'Exact quantifications are impossible.'[4]

In a judicious reflection on what had been learned from the archives of the former Soviet Union, Anne Applebaum made an observation in 2003 that will likely hold true in the Chinese case when the state archives are finally opened. She wrote:

> Though the Soviet Union contained thousands of concentration camps, and although millions of people passed through them, for many decades the precise tally of victims was concealed from all but a handful of bureaucrats. As a result, estimating their numbers was a matter of sheer guesswork while the USSR existed and remains a matter of educated guesswork today ... Those inclined to dislike the Soviet Union tended to choose the higher figures of victims. Those more inclined to dislike the American or Western role in the Cold War chose the lower figures. The numbers themselves ranged wildly ... As it turned out, the opening of the Soviet archives gave neither school complete satisfaction ... [since they showed] numbers lying squarely in the middle of the high and low estimates.[5]

While there has always been ample circumstantial evidence that the Chinese communist regime was ruthless and murderous, there has long been a tendency in many circles in the West to turn a blind eye to its atrocities. In order to justify our willful ignorance, it has been variously claimed that there has been insufficient information to verify the rumours; that being frank about the appalling abuses of human rights in the name of 'liberation' would harm relations with China; or even that China was so different that democracy and human rights were concepts foreign to Chinese culture. Simon Leys' classic essay 'The Burning Forest' (written in 1978, at the height of the Democracy Wall movement and not long before Wei Jingsheng's arrest) comments scathingly on this tendency, pointing out that the same had happened in regard to the Soviet Union until very late in its history.

In the case of China, the debate over numbers has ranged at least as widely as in the Soviet case. In 1971, in formal estimates presented to the U.S. Senate, Richard Walker estimated the number of those killed in China at between 34 and 64 million.[6] Moreover, these enormous figures included extremely low estimates for fatalities during the Cultural Revolution (250,000 to 500,000) and the Great Leap Forward (one to two million). What they were based on was very high estimates for victims of political liquidation campaigns (15 to 30 million) and forced labour (15 to 25 million). Writing in 1984, Stephen Shalom argued that Walker's figures were worthless, and estimated the total fatalities at 4.5 to 5.5 million, but allowed only one million deaths during the Great Leap Forward, thus understating the total by as many as 55 million.[7]

In 1991, in another study of mass deaths in China under communism, it was concluded that a 'prudent' estimate for the total number of those who had died by execution, starvation, or forced labour would be around 38 million, while the actual number could not be lower than 6 million and could range as high as 100 million.[8] Then, in 1992, Harry Hongda Wu, who had fled China in 1985, produced a book titled *Laogai: The Chinese Gulag*. He claimed that between 40 and 50 million people had passed through the Laogai since 1949—many never to be heard from again—and that, even in the early 1990s, there were millions of prisoners still in the Chinese camps.[9]

Unfortunately, Wu was at best careless in his use of figures. As another exiled dissident and former inmate of the Laogai commented:

> Why is it that the world's foremost Laogai 'expert' can't get his numbers straight? ... In fact, Wu's claims seem to vary erratically. For instance, Wu ... claimed, in 1997, that China has 1,100 Laogai prison camps, overseeing six to eight million Laogai prisoners. He also said that out of every 100,000 people in China, 500–667 are prisoners. Yet in his book ... Wu asserted that there are at least 3,000 labour camps, controlling 12 to 16 million prisoners. On the other hand, Wu claimed in the *London Daily Telegraph* that there are 30 to 40 million political prisoners.[10]

This sceptical treatment of Wu's figures drew, in part, on the work of Richard Anderson and James Seymour, which had argued that the Laogai was much smaller and less significant than Wu had alleged.[11] Although they, too, indicated that millions had been confined in the Laogai during the Mao years, and that very large numbers remained there at the end of the twentieth century, their estimates fell well-short of the huge numbers alleged by Wu.

Exaggerations and inconsistencies do not help the cause of human rights in China; but the reality is that millions died violently, or through forced labour, or starvation caused by state policies in China under Mao. All the while, the party that perpetrated these enormities remains in power, admits only to some mistakes, denies that it now has any political prisoners, and imprisons anyone who attempts to find out the truth about its past or present practices.

Across the Taiwan Strait, the history of the recent past is quite different. Only by registering this difference can the still grim realities of the dictatorial repression and lies in China be appropriately kept in a contemporary moral and political perspective. One of the most poignant monuments to the past, and to the recent achievements of human-rights reform in Taiwan, is Green Island. This little island, which lies just off the south-east coast of Taiwan, was one of the key sites of the Guomindang's system of repression for 35 years. For decades it was the most notorious place of incarceration for the Republic of China's political prisoners. The prison on Green Island was built during the so-called White Terror of the early 1950s and was large enough to hold thousands of political prisoners. Official figures indicate that there were 14,000 prisoners on the island in the mid-1950s.[12] Thereafter, numbers declined, although the prison was not closed until after the end of martial law in 1987.

Between 1947 and 1987, in Taiwan, 29,407 people were officially imprisoned for political reasons, almost all of them before 1975. Unofficially, Guomindang insiders have put the total at up to 70,000. According to none other than Wang Sheng, a leading figure in the Guomindang repressive apparatus for many years, the number executed was around 15 per cent of the total, which could mean between 4,500 and 10,000 people. The Ministry of Justice claims that the execution files have long since been burned, which is a great pity because it prevents fuller accounting that could have been held up as an example to the Communist Party.[13] Yet the basic truth is now officially acknowledged and the reality has radically changed.

In the 1990s, a memorial was built on Green Island to commemorate those imprisoned and executed in the harsh years before Taiwan was democratised. The structure is simple and austere. Standing at its entrance, one can look out over the vast Pacific Ocean and contrast its immense expanse with the grim confinement to which the memorial bears witness. Descending into the court of the memorial, just past the entrance, there is a long wall on which the names of 750 prisoners are inscribed in Chinese characters. The records of all these prisoners have been checked, and against the names of the many who were executed there is a small mark. By all accounts, this is only a tiny fraction of the total number of those executed. If the real total were at the upper end of the range of Wang Sheng's estimate at about 10,000, it would be the statistical equivalent of about 500,000 executions in China during the same 40 years. Even the communist regime's own account acknowledges that there were more executions than that in the early 1950s alone. But there is no memorial in China like the one on Green Island.

Far from Green Island, in the heart of Taipei, there is another memorial to the victims of Guomindang repression. The 2/28 Peace Park and Museum commemorates the fearful bloodletting that occurred between 28 February and late March 1947 when the citizens of Taiwan rose up against misrule by mainlanders and were crushed in a brutal military operation by Chiang Kaishek's armed forces. For decades the history of these events was politically suppressed by the Guomindang, but the Taiwanese did not forget. The museum records a general outline of what happened at the time. (We should remember that this massacre took place in the era before the White Terror, and before the prison system had been established.)

For many mainlanders it is deeply upsetting to confront this history, and there are some who still dismiss it as Taiwanese nationalist propaganda. They are mistaken. There were many witnesses to the events at the time, including an American diplomat, George Kerr, who set down an account of what he saw.[14] Taiwanese exiles also kept the matter alive, claiming that

20,000 people had been massacred. In 1991, two U.S.-based Chinese researchers and an American scholar published a detailed examination of the matter, in which they estimated that the number of deaths—almost all Taiwanese—was between 8,000 and 10,000.[15] This was a conservative figure. In 1995, the Guomindang itself apologised for the terrible excesses of 1947, and admitted that the number of Taiwanese killed in 1947 was between 18,000 and 28,000.[16]

These are numbing statistics. A proportionally equivalent level of bloodshed in Australia today would be the execution of some 75,000 or more people in a matter of weeks; in the United States, the equivalent figure would be over 800,000; while a proportionate number for China's population would be two to three million executions—the number Schram estimated were executed by the communists between 1949 and 1954. Small wonder that even the pro-Guomindang Ramon Myers and his colleagues described the 1947 massacres as being followed by a 'glooming peace' which 'covered Taiwan like a blanket of ashes laid down by a forest fire.'[17] The Green Island memorial and the 2/28 Memorial Museum, however, elevate the dead above statistics. They also rub away some of the numbness by physically signifying that the truth has come out, that the cause has been vindicated, and that repression as a means for resolving political differences has been repudiated. The 'glooming peace' has been supplanted by a vigorous green growth without further violent upheaval. Furthermore, the heirs of those executed in 1947 have taken office in recent years as the legitimate government of Taiwan.

This is a human-rights story which should be much more widely known and better understood. It is a paradigm case of what democratisation can accomplish that merits emulation in a world still grievously beset by ruthless political violence. It is a shining example, within the Chinese world, of what is possible when traditional authoritarianism and ideological bloody-mindedness are replaced by magnanimity, imagination, and principle. And it is dramatic proof that human rights are not an ethic confected by Western civilisation, to interfere in the cultural and political domains of other states. They are fundamental and universal principles, without which barbarous violence and arbitrary government will occur and go unchecked. This is, of course, what Hu Yaobang's circle and Wei Jingsheng, and his ilk, already understood in China by 1978.

When Taiwan was handed back to the Chinese government in 1945, following the defeat of Japan in World War II, Taiwan was in excellent condition. The Japanese had been savage conquerors in China and elsewhere in Asia between 1937 and 1945; but in Taiwan, which they had taken from the Chinese empire in 1895, they had been remarkably constructive colonial masters. The Japanese had developed rail and port infrastructure, industries and agriculture, public health, responsible administration, and general education. Thousands of Taiwanese received a good education in Japan and played dignified roles in the life of the island under Japanese rule. As a result, they found the contrast with Guomindang rule after 1945 a shock. It was especially shocking because they had hoped that the political philosophy of the Guomindang—Sun Yatsen's 'Three Principles of the People'—would entail sound and democratic government. Instead, they found that the dictatorship under Chiang Kaishek was ruthless, corrupt, and wholly uninterested in their expectations.

By 1946, educated Taiwanese had invented a wry pun to characterise Guomindang rule. The *San Min Chu-I* (Three Principles of the People), they quipped, had turned into *Ts'an-min Chu-I* (Cruel Personism).[18] Nothing the Japanese had done in Taiwan prepared the Taiwanese for what happened when they rebelled against their mainland rulers. The civil war between the Guomindang and the communists had just entered its final phase in February 1947, and the Guomindang acted ruthlessly to root out opposition on their southern flank in Taiwan. Thousands of regular troops were put ashore at Keelung and Kaohsiung. Shooting indiscriminately even as they landed, they then proceeded to round up and slaughter hundreds of civic leaders and thousands of ordinary citizens. There were scenes of barbarism reminiscent of the Boxer Rebellion.

> Not least among the victims were countless idealistic young students. George Kerr wrote:
>> We saw students tied together, being driven to the execution grounds, usually along the river banks and ditches about Taipei, or at the waterfront in Keelung. One foreigner counted more than thirty young bodies—in student uniforms—lying along the roadside east of Taipei; they had had their noses and ears slit or hacked off and many had been castrated. Two students were beheaded near my front gate. Bodies lay unclaimed on the roadside embankment near the Mission compound ... For days the dead continued to be washed up in Keelung Harbor ... The atrocities perpetrated at Kaohsiung were (if possible) even more revolting than the mass executions and torture used at Taipei ...[19]

The White Terror that followed throughout the 1950s did not involve massacres on this scale. It lasted longer, but was more discriminating in its suppression of opposition to the Guomindang.[20] The terror began in 1949, as Chiang Kaishek's Guomindang fled from defeat on the mainland, and sought both to consolidate their hold on the island against the Taiwanese and to root out real or suspected communist infiltrators in their chaotic ranks. It was in these years that the Green Island prisons were built and filled.

The process was wretchedly similar in character to what was happening on the mainland at the same time as Mao Zedong's communists purged the country of counter-revolutionaries, warlords, Guomindang officers and officials, and feudal reactionaries. It can have been no consolation to the Taiwanese to have known (if indeed they did know) that things were even worse on the mainland, where hundreds of thousands were being rounded up and executed as counter-revolutionaries. The contrast with China became more acute throughout the 1950s, 1960s, and early 1970s, when China became appalling under Mao Zedong. Taiwan under Chiang Kaishek was highly repressive by any measure, but it wasn't nearly as bad as mainland China.

Of the thousands of cases of repression from this era, those of Lei Chen, Su Tingchi, and Peng Mingmin are almost paradigmatic cases of political persecution. Lei Chen was a leading liberal journalist who was arrested in 1961, along with three of his colleagues, for advocating clean and fair elections. He was sentenced to ten years in prison for this heinous offence. When a young student, Su Tingchi, organised a petition for clemency on Lei's behalf, he was arrested, tortured, tried for sedition, and executed in May 1962. His wife was sentenced to life imprisonment for refusing to denounce him. Peng Mingmin, a brilliant, young, Japanese-educated political scientist at National Taiwan University, was arrested in 1964 for appealing to all the people of Taiwan—both Taiwanese and mainlanders—to work together to establish a democratic state.[21] He and two of his students were sentenced to prison terms of eight to ten years.

These case histories provide a sense of perspective. They invite searching comparisons with the persecution of democratic dissidents in China right up to the present. The dissent of Lei Chen and Peng Mingmin in the early 1960s directly anticipated the dissent of Liu Binyan, Fang Lizhi, Wei Jingsheng, and a great many others in China one or two decades later.[22] Lei, Su, and Peng were not firebrands, but individuals who sought to make the Guomindang live up to and fulfil its charter to bring democracy, not dictatorship, to the Chinese world. It was in precisely this spirit that Wei Jingsheng challenged the Communist Party from his prison cell for so many years.[23]

The core problem that all these individuals faced, whether under the Guomindang or the communists, was the repressive nature of Chinese political culture, and its inveterate lack of recognition of the dignity of the individual and the rights of the citizen. Bo Yang was a mainlander who fled communism in the 1940s, only to be jailed by the Guomindang on Taiwan in 1967 for 'defaming the leadership'. (He eventually became the director of the Human Rights Education Foundation in Taipei under the democratic order.) Following his release from Green Island in 1984, Bo delivered a speech at Iowa University, which was later published as *The Ugly Chinaman*. It still cannot be openly published in China, but has gone through numerous reprints in democratic Taiwan.

'During my incarceration', Bo reflected, 'I spent a lot of time contemplating my fate. What crimes had I committed? What laws had I broken? I continued pondering these questions after I was released and began to wonder whether mine was an abnormal or special case.' Mainlanders he met in America, who had escaped communist China, told him, 'Someone like you would never have made it as far as the Red Guards or the Cultural Revolution. You'd have been lucky to survive the anti-Rightist Movement'. This is nothing but the sombre truth, for a great number of individuals like Bo Yang perished or endured years in China's prison system during those horrific times.[24]

Given the antiquity and richness of Chinese civilisation, Bo Yang found this a dismal reality at the end of the twentieth century. 'Why', he asked, 'must a Chinese person with the courage to speak an iota of truth suffer this sort of fate? I've asked a number of people from the mainland why they ended up in prison. The answer was invariably, "I spoke the truth" ... But why does speaking the truth lead to such unfortunate consequences? My answer is that this is not a problem of any particular individual but rather of Chinese culture as a whole.'[25]

We now know better. We know that the lack of human rights has a long history in China, but that it is neither peculiar to Chinese culture nor ineradicable within Chinese culture. We also know that the transition from abuse of human rights to systematic respect for them can be brought about constitutionally and peacefully from within a Chinese polity. We know that individual Chinese citizens, free of prompting by any external power and proceeding only on the basis of reason and experience and the few good examples on offer around the world, can aspire to these rights and bring them into being. We know all this because it has happened on Taiwan. We are still waiting for the big breakthrough in mainland China, but the time has passed when any sort of cultural fatalism or ideological rationalisation can serve to excuse the abuses still practised by the Chinese Communist Party. The Guomindang, long overtaken by the Communist Party in the violence stakes, has shown it a clean pair of heels in the democratisation stakes since the death of Chiang Kaishek.

The breakthrough on Taiwan is, therefore, of world historical significance. No single aspect of its transformation is quite so remarkable as the fact that it was initiated by none other than Chiang Chingkuo, the son of the old dictator and, for many years, one of the chief guardians of his dictatorship. In his admirable biography of the younger Chiang, Jay Taylor did a great service to the cause of historical transformation in Chinese political culture. He told a story that few people can have known through all the years that Chiang Chingkuo ruled the Republic of China on Taiwan, either as his father's regent between 1955 and 1975, or in his own right until his death in January 1988. It is a story of deep political learning under the most testing of circumstances and, as such, should become required reading in every Chinese home and for everyone attempting to think through the modernisation and democratisation of Chinese political culture.

Chiang Chingkuo was Deng Xiaoping's contemporary. Were Plutarch himself to have written a modern, global *Parallel Lives* he would have found a suitable analogy in these two lives. The two were classmates together in Moscow in 1926, where they learnt to be good communists. Chiang's girlfriend in Moscow was the daughter of the warlord Feng Yuhsiang, for whom Deng went to work on his return to China. Deng organised the anti-Rightist campaign for Mao Zedong in the 1950s, while Chiang Chingkuo organised the White Terror and the Green Island 'New Life Institute' for his father at the same time.

Both saw the need for reform in the early 1970s but could do little at the time.[26] Deng imprisoned Wei Jingsheng in 1979–80 even as Chiang imprisoned Shih Mingte and Annette Lu, the leaders of the Taiwanese democracy movement (later to become the Democratic Progressive Party).[27] But then came the great divergence: Deng recoiled from democratic liberalisation in the 1980s, while Chiang embraced it. Deng turned against his enlightened liberal heirs apparent, Hu Yaobang and Zhao Ziyang, while Chiang ushered his—Lee Tenghui—into office.[28] And so, as the new century opened, peaceful democratisation took place in Taiwan with the Guomindang conceding ground in successive clean elections, while in China the Communist Party clings to power still.

It was the confident view of leading Guomindang liberal Shaw Yuming, in 1985, that China could and would reform itself. At the same time, it was the conviction of the recalcitrant Iron Blood Patriots, hardline Guomindang rightists, that Chiang Chingkuo had gone soft on the democratic opposition. They asserted bitterly that he should have done as his father would have done, and thrown the democratic oppositionists 'into the sea', as the Argentine colonels did during the notorious dirty war of the mid-1970s. Chiang Chingkuo—raised as a Leninist, tempered as a Stalinist, seasoned as an anti-communist secret police chief—chose instead, at the end of a long political life, to throw Leninism into the sea.

And when his old classmate, Deng Xiaoping, wrote to him in the last decade of his life, urging that they work together to reunify China, he replied that, while China remained as it was, this would mean 'pouring spoiled wine into old bottles'. The Chinese people, he declared to Deng's messengers, were sick of communism.[29] They aspired, in its place, to freedom, democracy, and prosperity. He could not give these things to China, but he did give them to Taiwan and, in doing so, he set a wonderful example to his old classmate. But Deng could not find it in himself, or his party, in his last years, to follow his example.

In 1988, a six-part TV mini-series called *River Elegy* was screened in China to great popular acclaim. It advanced the argument that Chinese political culture faced a profound choice. It could cling to all the imperial traditions symbolised by the Yellow River (which was drying up) and the Great Wall, (which was an old ruin representing unsuccessful defensiveness against the outside world). Or it could look to the deep blue sea, from which the democracy, science, and industry of the modern world had come, and embrace an open future instead of the xenophobic past. The Communist Party reacted badly to the program, suppressing it even before the disastrous events of June 1989.

Like Bo Yang, however, the makers of the TV series were speaking the truth. It is a truth whose time has come, and which might best be expressed in a new program called *Island Elegy*, to take up where *River Elegy* left off. It could begin with the statement by Yao Chiawen, then chairman of the Democratic Progressive Party, in 1988: 'Taiwan is not part of China, but an island which stands at the intersection of the world's greatest continent and the world's greatest ocean.'

At this intersection, Taiwan now embodies the challenge to China and all that is regressive in its political culture. A precise measure of whether China is able to rise to the challenge will be the manner in which it chooses to deal with the island in the next decade or two. Will it continue to attempt to impose its will by force and censorship, as the Guomindang imposed itself on Taiwan in the 1940s and 1950s? Or will it, like Chiang Chingkuo in the 1980s, renounce *Ts'an-min Chu-I* for *San Min Chu-I*, replacing threats with recognition of the rights, dignity, and freedom of the people of Taiwan? Gazing out from the memorial on Green Island at the deep blue of the Pacific Ocean, one can see that the better choice is at least conceivable for the new generation of communist leaders, as it was for the Guomindang leadership. The greatest task in the Chinese world in the years ahead is to draw them in this direction.

Chapter 14

Of Beethoven and Chinese Democracy

Hail to the day, hail to the hour, so long awaited, so long denied, when justice allied with mercy appears before the gate of our tomb!

—Chorus, finale to Beethoven's *Fidelio* (1814)

If Chiang Chingkuo opened the door to political freedom in Taiwan, it was Lee Tenghui who walked through it and introduced genuine democratic reforms to the island state. Lee is the elder statesman of political freedom in the Chinese world. Given that freedom in China is yet to be realised, no mainland leader can stand comparison with him in this regard. Yet he is largely denied international recognition, because the rulers of China are afraid of him, and because too many politicians and businessmen in liberal democracies are afraid of upsetting them.

Nevertheless, in Taiwan itself one can now talk candidly about freedom in a manner that is simply not possible in China. On a visit to Taiwan in 2002, I had the pleasure of talking privately with Lee (then 79) in the quiet of his pleasant and unpretentious residence. The difference between the political systems of China and Taiwan could be summed up by the striking contrast between the freedom granted a foreign visitor to meet privately with a former president of Taiwan for a frank conversation, and the fact that people trying to visit Zhao Ziyang in his last months (or, for that matter, trying to publish his private thoughts after his death) risked being beaten up or arrested. No one who wishes China well should feel comfortable with this discrepancy.

During the same visit, I also met three other elderly champions of freedom in the Chinese world: Peng Ming-min, a long-time leader of the Taiwanese independence movement; Bo Yang, the colourful and tenacious human-rights advocate referred to in the previous chapter; and Ruan Ming, an adviser in the 1980s to Hu Yaobang, the reformist general secretary of the Chinese Communist Party. Having left China for the United States after the defeat of Hu's reform program, Ruan Ming is now a citizen of democratic Taiwan.

To underscore the contrast with China, this was like being able to go to China and meet with veteran democratic dissidents and exiles Wei Jingsheng, Fang Lizhi, and Yan Jiaqi, all living peacefully in their homeland and free to speak their minds.

The roads to freedom travelled by these four old men converged in the democratisation of Taiwan between 1988 and 2000. Lee led the process. Having grown up under Japanese rule in Taiwan, he kept his head down during Chiang Kaishek's dictatorship, and ended up rising through the ranks of the Guomindang to become mayor of Taipei, then vice-president and, finally, president of Taiwan. His extraordinary political odyssey did not end with his retirement from the Guomindang leadership in 2000. He has since helped in founding the Taiwan Solidarity Union, which is the political rallying-point for those most outspokenly determined to defend the island's freedoms.

Peng Mingmin, born in the same year as Lee Tenghui, also grew up under the Japanese. Unlike Lee, however, Peng refused to accept the harshness of Guomindang dictatorship after 1945. His resistance landed him in political detention for five years and then in exile for 23 years. He returned from exile during the presidency of Lee Tenghui. By 2002, he had an office in the Presidential Palace as a special counsel to President Chen Shuibian. Meeting him there seemed to me rather like meeting Andre Malraux in Paris in the mid-1960s, when the famous novelist had become President De Gaulle's minister of culture (except that, unlike Malraux, Peng had never been a fellow traveller; he had never compromised his principles). It was almost like a hypothetical meeting with Wei Jingsheng, triumphant in a democratic China after many years in exile.

Bo Yang (originally Kuo Yitung), the eldest of the four children, was born in China in 1920. He grew up during the decades of civil war and the Japanese invasion of China, and was still on the mainland in 1947 when, as he puts it, 'the Americans dropped the Guomindang on Taiwan like an atomic bomb'. But he experienced the communists at the height of the civil war as 'cruel and hypocritical', and so fled to Taiwan in 1949. There he assumed his identity as the writer Bo Yang. Bo's prolific and biting criticisms of the corrupt and dictatorial Guomindang finally got him arrested in 1968. He was accused of being part of a communist conspiracy, was severely tortured, and served nine years of imprisonment in Taipei and on Green Island.[1] While in prison on Green Island, Bo concluded that Chinese political culture was all but fatally flawed by its lack of any tradition of representative government or free political discourse. This view was reinforced in his published work.

When I met Bo, he spoke of his admiration for England, America, and Australia, 'because they are the oldest democracies'. This is the voice of experience, not that of some naïve young activist. As it happens, the same view was expressed by Hu Yaobang, in 1986, when he told interlocutors in Europe that China needed to jettison the outdated ideas of Marxism and 'adopt the political philosophy of Montesquieu'—which is to say, a division of powers and the rule of a law that cannot be overridden by the party at its own discretion. The difference is that Hu was sacked by Deng Xiaoping for his views, whereas Bo's were expressed as a free man.

Sitting in the restful surrounds of his Taipei apartment, Bo told me how he had returned to China for the first time in 1987 and met old friends whom he had left behind almost forty years before. 'You made a good decision in 1949', they told him. All those who had chosen to stay in communist China had suffered humiliation and brutality as the communists continually set citizens against each other. Given his own experiences in Taiwan, their reaction must have struck him as ironic. Yet they were right. China under Mao Zedong had been a far worse place to live than Taiwan under Chiang Kaishek; just as Stalin's Russia had been far worse than, say, Franco's Spain.

When Hu Yaobang was dismissed from his position as general secretary in January 1987, it was the beginning of the end of Ruan Ming's allegiance to the Communist Party. Ruan and Hu were long-time friends and colleagues. They had known each other since the early 1950s, when they had worked together in the Communist Youth League. They had both suffered during the Cultural Revolution, and laboured together after the death of Mao Zedong to humanise Marxism in China. Under Deng Xiaoping, the writing was on the wall that the party was not going to undertake serious political reform. Ruan decided it was time to leave. Others stayed on to work with Zhao Ziyang; only to flee China after the political debacle of Tiananmen Square.

I found Ruan to be a slender, gentle scholar in the best Chinese tradition—a tradition that has somehow endured ever since the First Emperor's notorious book-burnings and scholar-killings. There was a keen twinkle of humour and humane intelligence in his eyes. He was neither a broken nor a cynical man. He had, however, left China and become a citizen of Taiwan, after spending some years in leading universities in the United States. To renounce the country of his birth was his ultimate judgement on the political movement to which he had dedicated almost his entire life. There are many, similarly disaffected, whom the Communist Party has sought to isolate, suppress, and even crush.

Ruan told me that democratic reform in China is still a long way off. The Communist Party leaders around Jiang Zemin, he told me in 2002, were as corrupt and inept as the Soviet leaders around Leonid Brezhnev had been 20 years earlier, but they were exploiting China's economic growth in an opportunistic effort to cling to power. Jiang Zemin's much-vaunted rhetoric about all classes being represented by the party was mere window-dressing. It did not come close to fulfilling the hopes of the reformers, like Ruan, who had rallied around Hu Yaobang. What they had hoped for was a fundamental renovation of the Chinese polity, incorporating both Western democracy and the rule of law.[2] But this was the crucial point at which Deng Xiaoping had baulked in 1979, in 1987, and again in 1989. The regime had not moved beyond this point under Jiang Zemin, nor has it done so under Hu Jintao.

This renovation is precisely what Lee Tenghui initiated in Taiwan, with Chiang Chingkuo's blessing, from 1987 onwards. Looking back on his presidency in 1998, Lee wrote: 'In the past ten years Taiwan has undergone unprecedented changes: democratization of its political system, diversification of its social fabric, and liberalization in many aspects of public life.'[3] Any honest biography of Jiang Zemin would have to state that, during his term as China's president through the same period of the 1990s, democratisation and liberalisation were relentlessly *suppressed*. And, for all his assertions that China is 'vigorously building democracy', the early signs under Hu Jintao are that suppression remains unrelenting.

After the Sixteenth Congress of the Chinese Communist Party in late 2001, the power of the cadres in the repressive one-party dictatorship was further entrenched. Those who have taken office in the recent years, as the 'fourth generation' of communist leaders, have so far given little indication that they intend to embrace 'the fifth modernization'—democracy. By contrast, Lee Tenghui has been actively involved in the rapid diversification of political parties in Taiwan since he stepped down from the presidency, and the leadership of the Guomindang. His successor, following democratic elections in 2000, had been the leader of the political opposition, Chen Shuibian. Lee was then replaced by Lien Chan, democratically, as leader of the defeated Guomindang. In both cases, there was open campaigning free of any police interference.

Independently of Chen or Lien Chan, Lee inspired the rise of a third political party, the Taiwan Solidarity Union, which won 13 seats in the national legislative elections of December 2001. Now more than 80 years old, he remains full of vitality and is actively committed to the flowering of civil society in Taiwan. Jiang Zemin, on the other hand, having never undertaken any striking initiatives to compare with those of Lee, is in no position to take a fresh approach now. Now that his political life is over, nothing he has to say is likely to be of broad interest.

(Unless he should unexpectedly, and uncharacteristically, write a set of candid memoirs in the manner of Nikita Khrushchev. *That* would be interesting.)

Because Lee relies wholly on free and open public debate to contribute to the future of his country, he is able to help shape public opinion and take political initiatives in a manner that is impossible within the Chinese Communist Party. His ideas are not locked away within the secretive compartments of the party, as even those of Hu Yaobang and Zhao Ziyang were, but are openly mooted. One way he is encouraging debate is through Taiwan Advocates, a policy forum he created in 2001, which he likes to call a 'do-tank' rather than a think-tank. It is designed to bring together leading political and business figures from across Taiwanese society to generate a new public-policy agenda the twenty-first century.

The crossover point in Taiwan's shift to freedom came in 1986, when Chiang Chingkuo, confronted by the formation of the Democratic Progressive Party (DPP), was urged by hardliners in the Guomindang to crush the fledgling opposition. Importantly, he chose to accept it and thereby open the way to democratic politics in Taiwan. This is precisely the opposite of what happened in China under Deng Xiaoping and Jiang Zemin. Even so, the shift was not confirmed in Taiwan until 1996 when Lee Tenghui became the first democratically elected head of state in the history of the Chinese world. Nothing like this had been attempted in China since the 1912 constituent assembly elections. (Fortunately, this time there was no coup or assassination, as there had been in 1913, when democratic leader Song Jiaoren was killed). Lee Teng-hui took office and, in everything but name, the Republic of China on Taiwan started to become the liberal, democratic Republic of Taiwan.

'As long as I live I will never forget my inaugural day, May 20, 1996,' Lee wrote in 1999. 'Following a suggestion by my wife, Tseng Wenfui, the ceremony opened with the 'Ode to Joy' from Beethoven's Ninth Symphony, as an expression of my gratitude to the people.'[4] Lee declared in his inaugural address at the time:

> 'This gathering today does not celebrate the victory of any candidate, or any political party, for that matter. It honours a triumph of democracy for 21 million people. It salutes the confirmation of freedom and dignity—the most fundamental human values ... We in Taiwan have realised the Chinese dream.'[5]

It is worth dwelling on the wider significance of the Taiwanese president playing 'Ode to Joy' at his inauguration. This choral climax to one of the most famous creations of Western culture is so commonly performed that its use risks seeming clichéd. But to dismiss it as such in this case would be both an error and an injustice. 'Ode to Joy' was inspired by *An die Freude*, a poem written by Friedrich Schiller in 1785, that went to the heart of Enlightenment hopes for the liberation of oppressed and impoverished mankind. It is the most passionate statement of Beethoven's humanism in a symphony widely understood, in Maynard Solomon's words, as 'the unsurpassable model of affirmative culture.'[6]

Writing of the 'Ode to Joy' as rendered by Beethoven, the young Nietzsche declared: 'Now the slave is a free man, now all the rigid and hostile boundaries that distress, despotism or "impudent fashion" have erected between man and man break down. Now with the gospel of world harmony, each man feels himself not only united, reconciled and at one with his neighbour, but *one* with him ...'[7] Schiller himself had written, 'To arrive at a solution even in the political problem, the road of aesthetics must be pursued, because it is through beauty that we arrive at freedom.'[8] Thus, the playing of 'Ode to Joy' at Lee's inauguration was not only a celebration of the beauty of freedom, but also a repudiation of the Chinese tradition of tyranny, and a demonstration that the joy of liberty is not merely a Western experience, but can be experienced wherever liberation is achieved.

The sheer difficulty of achieving liberation throughout the twentieth century, and the dark visions of the human future to which this difficulty gave rise, led many to reject the kind of aesthetic humanism espoused by Schiller and Beethoven. 'I want to revoke the Ninth Symphony', declared Thomas Mann's composer of the darkness, Adrian Leverkuhn, in *Doctor Faustus*. In his *Essay on Liberation*, Herbert Marcuse, that Pied Piper of 1960s activists, wrote 'Today's rebels against the established culture also rebel against the beautiful in this culture, against its all too sublimated, segregated, orderly, harmonizing forms ... The refusal now hits the chorus which sings the 'Ode to Joy', the song which is invalidated in the culture that sings it.'[9]

But the song was not invalidated, whatever one might have thought of certain aspects of 'the culture'. On the contrary, 'Ode to Joy' has been validated again and again, both by the struggle for freedom, and by the many forms freedom has taken worldwide, despite the countless obstacles and challenges it has faced. Marcuse and many of his acolytes believed that repudiation of the beauty of classical forms and humanist culture would open a way to liberation. There is, however, at least as much reason to believe that it was this very repudiation, in fascist and communist states as well as in the Dadaist and Marcusean 'counter-culture' of the West, that did great harm to the cause of human liberation in the twentieth century.

Certainly, the Maoist Cultural Revolution of the 1960s took Marcuse's repudiation of classical beauty to its nadir. Indeed, it has often been remarked that it is just as well Chiang

Kaishek's supporters took so many priceless Chinese art treasures with them to Taiwan, where they are now securely housed in the National Palace Museum, because they would almost certainly have been destroyed in the name of 'liberation' under Mao Zedong. It was, therefore, all the more significant and moving to see the standard-bearers of freedom in the Chinese world heralding and affirming beauty, form, and hope as a political statement, by playing Beethoven's 'Ode to Joy' at the end of the twentieth century.

We should consider what it took to bring about freedom in Taiwan, for it did not come easily, and its heroes remain largely unknown and unsung outside Taiwan. Meanwhile, the Chinese government has denounced Lee Tenghui, because the manner in which he has brought freedom to Taiwan shows up the glaring deficiencies in its own political practices. Another reason he is persona non grata in China is that, since leaving office in 2000, he has become an outspoken champion of the right of the Taiwanese people to choose the terms on which they might agree to political unification with China. What is needed in the present situation is a Chinese statesman of the calibre of the English Whigs of the late eighteenth century who stood up and declared their sympathy for the spirit of liberty espoused by the rebels in the American colonies.

The elder William Pitt, Earl of Chatham, and Edmund Burke both spoke freely in the British parliament during 1774–75 in defence of the freedom claimed by the Americans. Burke, so often attacked by the Left in the twentieth century for his denunciation of the Jacobin terror in France in 1793, praised what he dubbed 'the fierce spirit of liberty' of the American revolutionaries. Pitt's defence was even more striking, and has a certain resonance in the case of China in the early twenty-first century. 'This glorious spirit of Whiggism,' he declaimed in the House of Commons, 'animates three millions in America, who prefer poverty with liberty to gilded chains and sordid affluence; and who will die in defence of their rights as men, as free men. What shall oppose this spirit, aided by the congenial flame glowing in the breasts of every Whig in England, to the amount, I hope, of double the American numbers?'[10]

There are educated people in China who feel the same way about democratic change in Taiwan, but they are not free to stand up in the National People's Congress or the central committee of the Chinese Communist Party, and declare it in the bold and inspiring manner of Pitt the Elder. While this says a great deal about the failure of China's modern 'revolution' to bring liberty to China, it also shows what genuine liberty within political institutions would mean for China. It would mean political leaders seeing, appreciating, and being free to champion the practice of liberty both in and outside of China. It would mean, for example, that Wen Jiabao would be free, should he feel so inclined, to speak in defence of Taiwan's independence movement in terms that could resemble those used by Burke or Pitt about the American separatists all those years ago.

True free speech could begin with sympathy—even admiration—for Lee Tenghui. What Chinese nationalists have yet to come to terms with is that, when he was president, Lee saw himself as a *Taiwanese*, not as a Chinese citizen. His ancestors had migrated to Taiwan from China several generations before. Growing up under Japanese rule, he developed a view of China that is literally foreign to that of the Chinese themselves. Moreover, these characteristics make Lee *typical* of the people of Taiwan. Yet Chinese policy regarding Taiwan is repeatedly articulated as if the majority of people on Taiwan are self-consciously Chinese, and feel artificially separated from the mainland by the fact that the Guomindang had held out there after 1949. Any constructive future policy on China's part will have to recognise that this is a false perception.

The majority of Taiwanese were neither born on the mainland nor born of parents from the mainland. Their history has only ever been marginally influenced by government from China. When it intruded forcefully after 1945 in the form of the Guomindang, it catalysed a desire for democracy and independence which the Guomindang eventually recognised. Few individuals can claim to have played a more central and principled role in Taiwan's transformation than Peng Mingmin—a real Taiwanese Florestan to Lee Teng-hui's Leonore, to extend the *Fidelio* analogy.[11] Peng's account of his struggle against the Guomindang, *A Taste of Freedom*, continues to be the single most lucid introduction to the case for Taiwan's independence.[12]

A Taste of Freedom is a rich and poignant memoir. At a time when the questions of Taiwan's future, and of freedom for China's citizens, are among the most important facing the Asian and Pacific world, it should be required reading for political leaders right around the Pacific basin, beginning with China's leaders. The vision that Peng Mingmin put forth from exile in America more than 30 years ago still speaks to China:

> Once the [Taiwanese] people free themselves from the Nationalist Chinese regime and form a genuine representative government of their own … I believe they will declare to the world their *de facto* and *de jure* severance from past Chinese internal conflict. I believe the new [Taiwanese] government will spare no effort to establish close economic, commercial and cultural relations with China. It may even be willing to explore the possibility of working out with China a formula through which the basic national and foreign policies of the two countries could be coordinated, provided China does not meddle in the domestic affairs of the island and does not interfere with its free social, political and cultural development.[13]

For the present, China seems intent on continuing such interference. For example, since 1996 China has made futile efforts to dissuade Taiwanese voters from backing first Lee Tenghui, then Chen Shuibian, and then, more generally, the DPP. Its relentless stockpiling of ballistic missiles on the coast opposite Taiwan, and its threats of force to compel Taiwan to accept unification, can only affect the situation negatively. Moreover, China may be heading for a major internal crisis within the decade that could have unsettling repercussions for relations with both the United States and Taiwan. Now is the time to think about such possibilities; and, as we do, the victory of freedom and reform in Taiwan should be uppermost in our minds. Taiwan has prosperity with institutionalised freedom, which is surely what we all want for China—including millions of members of the corrupt and politically bankrupt Communist Party.

Lee Tenghui, Peng Mingmin, Bo Yang, and Ruan Ming are genuine heroes in this great cause of democratisation in the Chinese world. What is now called for is a common commitment to fully vindicate the cause, just as peacefully in China as in Taiwan. As Ruan Ming remarked to me, there have been at least three attempts at democratic reform in China since 1908, and all have been defeated by authoritarians with guns. Never before, though, have the preconditions been so ripe as they are now for its political transformation. Is it too extravagant a thought to imagine the overture from Beethoven's *Fidelio*—an opera about faithful love and liberation from tyranny heralding a transition to democratic rule in Beijing in January 2012, to mark the anniversary of the founding of the Republic of China? It seems to me that only the defining moment of the Tiananmen Square debacle in 1989 stands between the Communist Party and a resolute move toward such a transition in China.

The Chiang Kaishek Memorial sits in the heart of Taipei much as Tiananmen Square is central to Beijing. At the centre of each square is the mausoleum of a dictator responsible for the deaths of masses of people between the years 1927 and 1975. But here the parallels end. When thousands of people stood in Tiananmen Square on 3 June 1989 demanding democratic reforms in China, the tanks were sent in. On 30 November 2001, thousands of people gathered in Chiang Kaishek Memorial square, free of military intimidation, to celebrate democratic reforms in Taiwan. The Taiwanese elections then yielded a stunning victory to the party of reform and imagination.

On the eve of the election, Chen Shuibian, leader of the DPP and president of Taiwan since March 2000—and winner of the European Union's Freedom Medal—stood on a modest podium in the Chiang Kaishek memorial square amid a festival of green banners, horns, streamers, and television cameras. He made a passionate appeal to the citizens of Taiwan to bestow on him their confidence; to give his minority government the mandate to govern in its own right; and to endorse his program of economic reform and dignified autonomy for Taiwan.

It was extraordinary to witness his speech in that setting. Yet the talk in coffee houses and think-tanks in the week prior to the election was that he would probably fail to gain his mandate. After all, Taiwan was in the middle of its worst recession in living memory, after enjoying decades of remarkable economic growth under the Guomindang. Unemployment had climbed to the unheard-of level of 5.3 per cent. China had made it clear that it did not wish to treat with Chen because of his quiet insistence that it respect Taiwan's political autonomy. Only his integrity and energy, together with that of his DPP colleagues, seemed likely to save them from a sapping defeat.

As history attests, integrity and energy won the day. Two days before his speech, I was among an international group of specialists who met with Lien Chan, leader of the Guomindang, to discuss his outlook on the forthcoming election. He was so wooden, so vague, and so devoid of any vitality or vision that one could sense impending doom. When asked what he would regard as a good electoral result, he stated flatly that if the Guomindang won 85 to 90 seats he would consider it 'a major victory'. The implications of his declaration were stunning. The leader of the once totally dominant party, with an existing outright majority in the legislature of 113 out of a possible 225 seats, was facing a minority government beset by economic woes, and telling a group of specialists that it would be a great 'victory' if his party only *lost* 20 or 30 seats in the election!

The Guomindang's party headquarters is an imposing edifice, rich in marble and statuary, and fine furniture. As we left these grand surrounds, I remarked to my companions that Lien Chan had the dazed dignity of the captain of a great old ship who, standing on the bridge as it is slowly sinking beneath the waves, reminisces about how it has, in its time, sailed the oceans of the world. Another member of the group likened the condition of the Guomindang to that of the Russian space station *Mir*, slowly coming apart at the seams and perhaps fated to crash to earth. The Guomindang seemed a moribund political force, and its leaders appeared bereft of the capacity to arrest its decline.

By comparison, the DPP's headquarters was simple and unadorned, but brisk and alive. We met there with the party's director of international affairs, an energetic young computer scientist called Wilson Hsin Tien. When Wilson was asked what he would view as a good electoral result, he stated that all the circumstances militated against the party winning a clear majority, but that careful polling suggested they could win 85 seats, which would represent an increase of 20 seats. He went on to say that more than this would be outstanding, especially if the new, pro-independence Taiwan Solidarity Union (TSU) party could, as expected, win eight to ten seats, and join the DPP in a coalition government.

The crispness and candour of this man's answers contrasted so markedly with Lien Chan's response that one had the inescapable sense of witnessing the future of Taiwan as compared with its past. And so it transpired. When the election returns came in, the DPP had won 87 seats, the TSU had 13, and the Guomindang received a dismal 68. The People First Party (PFP), a breakaway group from the Guomindang, also did remarkably well, increasing its number of seats from 20 to 46. The so-called New Party, which had based itself on strong support for reunification with China, was almost annihilated, losing all but one of its 13 seats; the one it retained was on Kinmen, immediately off the coast of China's Fujian province, and very closely tied to its coastal economy.

What did these results mean? First, that Taiwan's transition to democracy had been strongly confirmed. Fresh air was blowing through the corridors of power in Taiwan as never before. Democracy was not an illusion or an elaborate charade, or a fragile blossom: the results demonstrated it to be real and vigorous. Whereas the Guomindang rallies seemed mechanical and contrived, DPP rallies sparkled with spontaneous energy as its supporters grasped at tangible freedom. Whereas the Guomindang seemed loaded down with financial assets, like Midas with his excess of gold, the DPP ran on lean resources, relying on its members' belief in the transformation of their island country. They envisaged the creation of a 'green silicon island'—a frontrunner in both wealth creation and quality of life in the twenty-first century.

Second, the results indicated that Taiwanese democracy was mature, not feverish. The citizens of Taiwan had assessed the situation their country's situation, and had voted with insight and discrimination. This was tremendously encouraging. Ironically, they also showed that the democracy that had taken root in Taiwan had emerged in a manner consistent with the Guomindang's own founding charter. This was something of which the old revolutionary party could be proud—even if it had to accustom itself to being a truly democratic party, rather than being in a position of permanent governance.

After all, Sun Yatsen, the old party's founder, had believed that republican institutions and economic development would prepare the ground for the flowering of democracy in the Chinese world. Although the 50-year dictatorship of Chiang Kaishek (1925–1975) threatened to leave the ground barren, his son, Chiang Chingkuo, replanted it in the 1980s by putting an end to martial law and anointing Lee Tenghui as his successor. Lee, in turn, watered the ground and has watched the flowers grow. What happened in Taiwan at the end of 2001 was, in every sense, the flowering of a democratic polity. It was the fulfilment of the vision held by Sun Yatsen and Liang Qichao 100 years ago, before the assassination of Song Jiaoren and the dispersal of the democratically elected Chinese parliament in Beijing by the old imperial general Yuan Shikai.

Third, this full flowering of democracy on Taiwan gave a strong mandate to the DPP to pursue its agenda of economic reform and dignified negotiations with China over the island's future. That the Communist Party in China has refused to enter into such negotiations is a sign only of its own obduracy and lack of political imagination. Until this election in late 2001, there was some scope for critics of the DPP to argue that it was not an effective governing party, or that it did not have the confidence of the people of Taiwan. These claim have now been put to rest. Taiwanese voters were faced with a clear choice between the DPP, with its 'green silicon island' agenda, and the agenda shared by the Guomindang and the New Party of economic conservatism and accommodation with China. The voters wiped the floor with the Guomindang, wiped out the New Party, and handed a resounding vote of confidence to the DPP. Nothing in the few years since then has fundamentally altered this clear preference.

Fourth, the election result presented the leaders of China with a two-fold challenge. It signalled to them that their anachronistic determination to win the civil war of 1946–49 and take Taiwan from the Guomindang should finally be cast into the famous 'dustbin of history' into which twentieth-century communists used to like to think they would soon cast all their ideological opponents. The Chinese civil war is now ancient history. The modern-day Taiwan that China's leaders need to deal with is not a recalcitrant province or the refuge of a warlord; it is a vibrant, progressive, democratic polity. This status was reinforced by the results of the 2004 legislative elections, in which the DPP held its ground.

Finally, the flowering of democracy in Taiwan should make a deep impression on the leaders and citizens of Western democracies. For too long, Taiwan has been seen through the lenses of historical scepticism that focus on Chiang Kaishek and his corrupt, repressive version of anti-communism. For too long, it has been seen merely as a little island off the coast of the real China, and has been treated geopolitically as a problem to be handled with diplomatic discretion and polite evasions. The 2001 legislative elections demonstrated that it was time for the Western democracies to rethink their position on Taiwan. The task is particularly important for Australia, because of the rising importance to Australia of China.

There are two island democracies off the main land mass of Asia, each with around 20 million citizens: Taiwan and Australia. One is a geographically small island-democracy, and one is a geographically continent-sized island-democracy, but demographically they are roughly equivalent. Moreover, each has a modern economy that is faced with continuing challenges of structural adjustment in a globalised world. And each credibly aspires to being a leader in both sustainable development and quality of life during the twenty-first century.

Both Taiwan and Australia depend in fundamental ways on a strategic alliance with the United States for their security. Both have a very large and growing stake in trade with China, as well as a chief foreign policy challenge of coming to terms with the demographic size, economic rise, and geopolitical ambitions of China. Those commonalities are all thrown into high relief by the maturing of the DPP as a serious political party, the emergence of the Taiwan Solidarity Union, and the obliteration of the pro-unification New Party, in 2001. It's time they were reflected on more seriously in Canberra. The 2004 legislative elections, correctly understood, would drive this point home further. The electorate voted cautiously, but demonstrated that there is no constituency now for advocates of reunification—only for advocates of the responsible handling of Taiwan's *de facto* independence.

The day after the 2001 elections, I attended a conference on the significance of the election results for the future of Taiwan and China, at Taipei's Grand Hotel. The location was loaded with meaning, for the Grand Hotel is a spectacular building that was built for Madame Chiang Kaishek, decades ago, in the style of a Chinese imperial palace. It still expresses the spirit of that greatest of all 'dragon ladies'. It was also where the DPP held its founding congress in 1986. In a powerfully symbolic manner in 2001, it had become the venue for discussing both the decline of the Guomindang, and the rise of to power of the DPP in Taiwan.

The conference was addressed by a woman different in almost every respect from Madame Chiang; a woman who embodied the freedom and integrity and vigour of the new, democratic Taiwan—the then director of the Mainland Affairs Council, Dr Tsai Ingwen. She spoke of how the DPP government was committed first and foremost to responsibility, stability, and flexibility in both economic policy and cross-Strait affairs. As with the other DPP people with whom we met, there was nothing aloof, stiffly bureaucratic, or ideologically hidebound about Tsai—only clarity of diction and evidence of abundant intelligence.

Her message was plain. Taiwan was seeking a natural place in the comity of nations. It was seeking a rational and constructive dialogue with its China, in which the economic and political relations between the two polities could be put on a sound, productive footing, free of antagonism. It sought the respect, empathy, and goodwill of other nations in realising these outcomes. Perhaps, in times past, it did not deserve these things by right. There is no doubt, given the results of its democratic elections in 2001 and 2004, that it does now. The time has come for the international community to acknowledge the freedom and achievements of the people of Taiwan, and to urge China to do likewise.

Conclusion
Setting China Free

A French bastard landing with an armed banditti, and establishing himself king of England against the consent of the natives, is in plain terms a very paltry rascally original.—It certainly hath no divinity in it.

—Thomas Paine, *Common Sense* (1776)[1]

History drips with irony—often of the most savage kind—and few histories do so more than that of modern China. One is struck by it at almost every major turning point in the country's history, from the fate of political reform under the late Qing (1898–1911) to the death of Zhao Ziyang in 2005. Indeed, the repetitive cycle of historical irony might best be encapsulated by drawing a parallel between the Empress Dowager Cixi placing the Emperor Guangxu under house arrest for attempting political reform in 1898, and the 'Emperor Dowager' Deng Xiaoping placing Premier Zhao Ziyang under house arrest in 1989 for essentially the same 'crime'. What had the intervening 90 years of revolution been for, if not to rid China of tyranny and give it a fully modern constitution?

Of course, on paper, it has a more or less fully modern constitution. But the Communist Party stills stands above the constitution in the role of an absolutist monarch. The realisation of democratic freedoms in China is incompatible with it exercising such a role, and only the legitimisation of political opposition can change this fateful state of affairs. Although Cixi first crushed the reform movement in 1898, she then saw the need for political reform and, in 1905, initiated moves towards a constitutional monarchy, albeit she still kept the Emperor Guangxu confined for the rest of his life. Ironically, Cixi's ten-year-plan for the political reform of the Chinese empire created provincial constituencies so impatient for more rapid and radical change that they brought down the monarchy altogether in 1911. The plan that had been intended to give the empire greater flexibility and strength precipitated its fragmentation and consequent weakening. This, in turn, contributed in no small measure—along with the illusion of 'success' in Lenin's Russia from 1917–21—to many of the empire's erstwhile democratic dissidents deciding in the 1920s that the nascent Chinese nation state needed one-party rule to pull it together.

It was Sun Yatsen who led the shift towards one-party rule, following a violent betrayal of the fledgling democratic republic by those who should have protected it. Having perceived in early 1912 that the empire was fragmenting and that a republic could not hold things together without military force to back it up, he offered the presidency to the old Qing general, Yuan Shikai. Under Yuan's supposed protection, democratic elections were held in December 1912—just as they were to be held five years later in the former Russian empire, under supposed Bolshevik protection. A National Assembly was elected by forty million voters and Sun's party (the Guomindang) won 269 of the 596 seats, which was less than an absolute majority, but roughly equivalent to the plurality enjoyed in 2005 by the DPP in Taiwan. Democratic politics had begun in China, but they were almost immediately aborted by men with guns.

On 20 March 1913 Song Jiaoren, the thirty-year-old wunderkind of the Guomindang, was on his way to Beijing, to head the new National Assembly and form a Guomindang coalition government, when he was assassinated at Shanghai's central railway station by agents of Yuan Shikai. The old general then disbanded the National Assembly and arrested many of its elected members. He believed—or so he propagated the story—that the new Chinese state needed strong, centralised government in order to achieve unity and progress. There were those even among the most enlightened of the reformers—chiefly Liang Qichao, whose Progressive Party had won many seats in the National Assembly—who bowed to this assertion and tried to work with the usurper, but their attempts failed. The old empire fragmented, and regional generals took power in the absence of any central authority.

The unfortunate conclusion that almost all China's republican revolutionaries drew from this sequence of events was not that democracy should be more vigorously protected, but that the country was not ready for democracy and that the republic would need to establish a centralised government, as Yuan had proposed, with a monopoly of force and power. Sun Yatsen's reasoning in this regard was that the new republic, with its immense, impoverished, and largely illiterate population, *needed a period of 'political tutelage' before it would be ready for democracy*. There seems to be no basis for a suspicion that he was being cynical and self-serving in making this claim (though that could not so easily be said of others before and since). Yet it was an argument based on a counter-intuitive interpretation of the events that had just occurred. Sun's judgment was that a citizenry who had just elected a 596-member multi-party National Assembly and then seen it arbitrarily disbanded needed instruction in the workings of democracy, but surely the events of 1912–1913 demonstrated that it was the men wielding guns who needed such instruction.

In any case, this argument entailed a corollary that should have set strong limits on the exercise of the tutelage, for whatever term of years it persisted. The logical corollary was that the Chinese people would be instructed in the responsible practice of citizenship under the law, with the gradual extension of the franchise as the vital institutional infrastructure was put into place. Did this process fail to occur because Sun Yatsen died prematurely, aged 59, in March 1925? Perhaps, but he had already set in train both an alliance with Leninists and the creation of a military force, imperiling his uncertain regime from two sides. Within two years of his death, those two sides were at one another's throats, fighting not over the best principles of tutelage but over the monopoly of raw power. If anyone among his lieutenants could have held the project together, it would likely have been Liao Zhongkai—brilliant, independently wealthy, a fluent English speaker, an outstanding labour organiser and financier—but Liao's assassination by conservatives, in August 1925, ended that possibility.

A year after Sun Yatsen's death in March 1926, Chiang Kaishek asserted control of the Guomindang by military force and set out to achieve a kind of synthesis of the political projects begun by Yuan Shikai and Sun Yatsen: a dictatorship in the name of *political tutelage* and the repression of those on the Left, as well as warlords on the Right, who stood in the way of his plan. For the following 23 years he pursued the project in the belief that it would make China unified and strong. But, as history shows, it kept China divided and weak, narrowed the talent available to him to develop or mobilise the country, and ended with the thorough corruption and ultimate downfall of his regime.

Had the Chinese people rejected the idea of democracy in allowing Chiang and his corrupted Guomindang to fall? Not at all, for he had denied them democracy. Had they rejected political tutelage by the Guomindang? Not at all, for they had been given repression, corruption, and misrule in place of tutelage in democracy. Had they chosen proletarian dictatorship in preference to bourgeois democracy? Not at all, for the former was imposed on them by the Communist Party, and the latter had long since been denied them by Chiang Kaishek.

The irony of Chiang Kaishek's downfall, then, was that he failed precisely because of the means he adopted in his determination to succeed. Had the Communist Party come to power determined to make restitution for Chiang Kaishek's failures and his consequent distortion of the idea of political tutelage, the 'New China' they boldly proclaimed might have truly liberated its people, and set them on the path to the freedom that modern constitutions and democratic processes espouse and enshrine. Of course, in a sense they saw themselves as doing exactly this, but only in a narrow sense, constricted by the same presumption that had twisted Sun Yatsen's reasoning after the dispersal of the National Assembly by Yuan Shikai. Instead of seeing that their power needed to be circumscribed in order to avoid a descent into tyranny, the party acted on the assumption that so long as it controlled the guns and used them to unify the country, all was well.

At least, that would be the most charitable interpretation of the implicit ideological reasoning behind the creation of the communist dictatorship in 1949, and its sweeping campaign of terror in the early 1950s to root out all 'counter-revolutionaries' and 'bad elements'. Politically speaking, what the Communist Party did was to 'succeed' in creating a one-party dictatorship on a scale that put the dreams of Sun Yatsen and the rule of Chiang Kaishek's corrupted Guomindang entirely in the shade. So overwhelming was their power that the American 'Trotskyist' Harold Isaacs wrote in the preface to the 1951 edition of his 1938 classic, *The Tragedy of the Chinese Revolution*, 'between their defeat in China in 1927 and their victory in 1949, the Chinese Communists grew into a force capable only of imposing a new totalitarian dictatorship upon China.'[2] Ten years later—but still well before the Cultural Revolution was inflicted on China—he added, in new edition, 'there is at least one matter on which all accounts seem to agree: the totalitarian system laid upon China by the Communists in the first years of their power has outdone anything ever produced by the Russians.'[3]

This was a verdict from the Left, not the Right. Even so, it was not the judgment that much of the mainstream Left accepted until well after the death of Mao Zedong. Isaacs, one might argue, was himself something of a sentimental Leftist who believed that the Marxist–Leninist approach to politics contained the seeds of emancipation, rather than being hopelessly vitiated by its inbuilt and intractable errors. Nonetheless, given all that has transpired in the years since he wrote those lines, it is worth pondering his account of where his political odyssey had left him, as early as 1951. He was uncomfortable with the label 'Trotskyist' and considered that the term had been 'much-abused'—quite an understatement, given the appalling abuse of it by Stalin. He added, however, 'Although I reject the Bolshevism of which Trotsky became the most authentic spokesman, I still have great respect for some of Trotsky's conceptions of what the socialist revolution was meant to be.'[4]

What *was* the socialist revolution 'meant to be'? Even while denouncing both Stalinism and Maoism in 1951, Isaacs still paid obeisance to the pieties of Leftist mythology, by doffing his cap to 'Lenin's uncompromising internationalism' and the 'proletarian roots' and 'socialist premises' of the Bolshevik revolution. While he wrote that the socialist and working-class features of the revolution 'barely survived the Russian civil war' and that, as early as 1922, Lenin 'saw an abyss yawning at Russia's feet', he laboured under a tenacious Leftist illusion in presuming that the revolution had ever been innocent of those pernicious features that later overtook it.[5]

The moment at which 'the revolution' went astray in Russia was not when Stalin effected control of the party, but when Lenin himself insisted on seizing power from the Provisional Revolutionary Government in 1917. In another of history's ironies, Stalin had opposed this step. It was not the abandonment of 'socialist' ideals that was the downfall of the communist movement; it was the radical incapacity of those very ideals to deal with human nature intelligently by framing laws and a constitution that would inhibit the worst proclivities of human beings from dominating the political process. This lesson remains to be applied in China now, almost thirty years after the death of Mao Zedong. Only by applying it—intelligently—will China finally be set free.

Still the Communist Party clings tenaciously to a monopoly of political power on the basis of vaguely defined 'socialist' ideals; still it rationalises its arbitrary extra-constitutional exercise of power on the basis that political tutelage is necessary to maintain unity and further China's progress as a modern nation-state. These could be described as propagandist lies, given the Communist Party's record in both suppressing disgruntled workers, and violating every right of the citizenry under its own constitution. But it isn't necessary to accuse the party of lies. In some ways, it would be more powerful to point out that, in so far as they sincerely believe their own propaganda, they are laboring under what were the most destructive delusions of the twentieth century.

The communist revolution in China—radically flawed as it was from the start—had, finally, only one justification: setting China free. This meant ending reactionary forms of social hierarchy that led to the abuse of working people, the suppression of women, the retardation of education, science and economic endeavour, the stultification of moral imagination, and the violations of human dignity implicit in archaic penal codes. If there was any justification for the communist overthrow of Chiang Kaishek in 1948–49, it was that the party might do better at setting China free than he had done. If there is any residual justification for it clinging to power now, it could only be that it is better at setting China free in these specific respects than any feasible alternative government would be. This is the only criterion by which its legitimacy should be judged.

But here is the crunch: the party has no justification for presuming that it alone can be the judge of whether it is, indeed, best qualified for this fundamental task. Such a judgment can only be made by those who are the subjects, not merely the objects, of the freedom that is at stake: the citizens of what has always called itself the People's Republic of China. There is a transparent fraud entailed in asserting that the party is the only feasible guarantor of the country's freedoms, and then taking the most condign measures to prevent any other guarantor from emerging into the realm of legitimate politics with protection under the law. That it should, in the process, actively violate the freedoms of its own citizens by arbitrarily imprisoning scholars, journalists, labour organisers, religious activists, democratic dissidents, environmental activists, human-rights activists, retrenched workers claiming their rights, and peasants protesting against abuse by corrupt officials is merely the concrete proof of the fraud.[6]

Yet, however well-documented and earnest this argument is, it does not, perhaps, exert as powerful an effect on the political imagination as the laughter that should by now greet any claim by the Communist Party to political legitimacy in China. The humour springs from the sense of irony that the party's posture must inspire in any but the most historically illiterate or politically obtuse observer. This irony is three-fold. First, as sketched out above, the party claims political legitimacy as the governing power that is setting China free, but finds itself compelled to censor and repress all but the most rudimentary political freedoms in order to 'achieve' this self-appointed task. Second, having come to power in the name of setting China free from the presumed evils of capitalism, the party has only been able to generate impressive economic growth in the country by embracing capitalism. Now all its leaders feel it is de rigueur to dress like Western businessmen and Western 'bourgeois' politicians, while clinging by their teeth to the threadbare notion that they have the right to rule China as a 'communist' party. Viewed from a wholly detached perspective, this is surely a matter for the most side-splitting laughter.

But the greatest irony is the third one. The communists now face dilemmas remarkably reminiscent of those that confronted the Empress Dowager Cixi a hundred years ago exactly—and they don't know what to do. Like her, they have sent scholars abroad to study 'world's best practice' and, like her, have concluded that political reform is necessary. But they cannot bring themselves to go even as far as she did in allowing a substantial franchise and the creation of fully elected provincial legislatures. It seems that they fear such reforms will bring about their downfall in the same way that they, unintentionally, brought about the downfall of the Qing Dynasty. This, then, is the most delicious irony of them all. To paraphrase Karl Marx, a spectre is haunting communist China—the spectre of the Empress Dowager. That things should, in this specific sense, have come full-circle, after all the upheavals of the twentieth century and all the overblown pretensions of Chinese Marxism, should be the cause for great bemusement. Historical irony does not get richer than this.

Nonetheless, there are still two hard inferences to be drawn. The first is that, if the party fears political reform will bring about its own downfall, it implicitly confesses that it does not have legitimacy in the eyes of the people, in which case it has no justification to do anything but gracefully relinquish power. The second inference is that, by its own account, it has failed despite decades of 'people's democracy' to prepare the Chinese people for the responsible exercise of power. If it had succeeded, it would have nothing reasonable to fear from democratisation, even should it lead to its loss of a monopoly of political power. Yet, since it has not done so, it has surely forfeited any right to persist in the exercise of power, unless it moves openly to enable China's people to exercise their political rights, instead of continuing to inhibit them from doing so.

This is the logic of the situation. The psychology of it is not altogether convergent with the logic, of course, which is why the party persists in exercising arbitrary power and resisting the need for serious political reform. But there is another reason which only the well-informed can know: the party's leaders and minions are exploiting arbitrary power to enrich themselves by any means they can while the going is good. Corruption is rampant, and the party is at the centre of it. Given a reasonably ironical perception of their historical circumstances, their political rhetoric, and their sartorial transformation we might feel a certain amount of perverse sympathy for the confused and venal motives that have them still trying to eliminate all political dissent. But this is only because we can view the situation from a safe distance and under the protection of those Western 'bourgeois' constitutions that the Communist Party insists are not 'Chinese' enough to be gifted to the long-suffering people of China. Moreover, it ignores the pressing need for the rule of law, the protection of civil rights, and the freer circulation of information in China on purely pragmatic grounds—that is, for the sake of sound, stable economic and social development.

In short, political reform in China, far from being a dubious Western imposition, or a luxury that can be allowed to eventually come about, is the key to China's modernisation. It has been sought and frustrated for more than a century. It has been denied in the past for invalid reasons. There is now no rational ground—only historically confused and politically hypocritical excuses—for denying reform. It goes to the heart of what modernity is about: the emancipation of human beings from the bonds of natural necessity and political tyranny.

A democratic movement in China, of the kind that has existed and been repressed again and again, would have as its raison d'etre what was the only tenable basis for the foundation of the Communist Party in 1921, and its seizure of power in 1949: setting China free. The party's only reasonable justification now for prolonging its time in office is to serve that end, and it can do so only by relinquishing dictatorship and working to undo the insidious political consequences of Yuan Shikai's assassination of Song Jiaoren. That much is common sense. The rest is politics.

Notes

Preface to the Second Edition

1   Yang Jisheng *Tombstone: The Great Chinese Famine 1958-1962* (Farrar, Straus and Giroux, New York, 2008) and Frank Dikotter *Mao's Great Famine: The History of China's Most Devastating Catastrophe, 1958-1962* (Bloomsbury, London, 2010), chapter 37 'The final tally'. Dikotter points out that there have been many estimates, ranging from 23 million to 60 million, but that the Party keeps its archives sealed against 'the eyes of prying historians'. His own reasoning, based on the testimony of a senior Party historian and member of a large working group that assessed the matter internally, estimates that the death toll could well have been 55 million. One can only hope that the Party will fall from power and the archives opened.

2   There were honourable exceptions, among them James Mann and Aaron Friedberg in the United States, John Lee in Australia and Jonathan Fenby in the United Kingdom. Mann's *The China Fantasy* (2007) was an early call-out. He had, like me, the advantage of being an independent writer, not weighed down by institutional groupthink. Friedberg, dug in at Princeton University, has made a career of studying the challenges confronting first the British Empire (in the decades before the First World War) and then the United States (in the decades after the Cold War) as a 'weary titan'. After examining the emerging challenges, he called out the situation with a major study, (in 2011): *A Contest for Supremacy: China, America, and the Struggle for Mastery in Asia*. He followed this up, in 2022 with a long essay forthrightly called *Getting China Wrong*. John Lee's *Will China Fail? The Limits and Contradictions of Market Socialism* Centre for Independent Studies, (Sydney, 2007) was another insightful contribution.

3   Stefan Halper *The Beijing Consensus: How China's Authoritarian Model Will Dominate the Twenty-First Century* (Basic Books, New York, 2010). See, also, Kellee S. Tsai *Capitalism Without Democracy: The Private Sector in Contemporary China* (Cornell University Press, 2007) and Giovanni Arrighi *Adam Smith in Beijing: Lineages of the Twenty-First Century* (Version, 2007). Arrighi dedicated this book to veteran Marxist economic development theoretician Andre Gunder Frank (1929-2005). He himself died in 2009, aged 72.

4   See https://www.piie.com/blogs/realtime-economic-issues-watch/what-washington-consensus

The main Washington Consensus policies included maintaining fiscal discipline, reordering public spending priorities (from subsidies to health and education expenditures), reforming tax policy, allowing the market to determine interest rates, maintaining a competitive exchange rate, liberalizing trade, permitting inward foreign investment, privatizing state enterprises, deregulating barriers to entry and exit, and securing property rights. This set of elements was classically set out in 1989 by American economist John Williamson.

He noted that such policies contradicted conventional wisdom in developing countries, not least in Latin America, many of which had had state dominated systems, loosely inspired by the Soviet example, since the 1950s. It was very clear, well before the GFC, that China did not adhere to these policies in important respects, especially the matter of subsidies, interest rates, sustaining state owned enterprises and interfering with property rights.

5   Shortly after this book was first published, I was invited to a lunch with the board of one of Australia's largest banks. Each member of the board had been given, in advance, a copy of the book. I found no evidence, over lunch, that any of them had read it. Their only real question was, 'When will China open up its financial institutions?' I remarked that that was a question worth a substantial consulting contract rather than a mere lunch, but that I wouldn't hold my breath on the Party liberalizing its financial institutions any time soon and, if I was (as their bank was) contemplating an investment in those institutions I would hedge my bets very carefully. They disregarded my advice and lost a good deal of money investing in Chinese banking. China has still not opened up its financial institutions. In fact, under Xi Jinping, it is regressing in that regard.

6   Ho-fung Hung *The China Boom: Why China Will Not Rule the World* (Columbia University Press, New York, 2017), Carl Minzner *End of an Era: How China's Authoritarian Revival is Undermining Its Rise* (Oxford University Press, 2018), George Magnus *Red Flags: Why Xi's China is in Jeopardy* (Yale University Press, 2018), Dinny McMahon *China's Great Wall of Debt: Shadow Banks, Ghost Cities, Massive Loans and the End of the Chinese Miracle* (Little Brown, London 2018), William H. Overholt *China's Crisis of Success* (Cambridge University Press, 2018). There were others, but these half-dozen are a good sample.

7   Ezra F. Vogel *Deng Xiaoping and the Transformation of China* (Belknap Press of Harvard University, 2011) and Frank Dikotter *China After Mao: The Rise of a Superpower* (Bloomsbury, London, New York 2022), not least Chapter 10 'Hubris (2008-2012'.

8   *Thunder From the Silent Zone: Rethinking China* (Scribe, Melbourne, 2005, Introduction, p. 7)

9   Should such a scenario occur, Taiwan by 2025 to 2029, would be taken backwards by eighty years to the time when it was invaded and brutally subjugated by the Chinese Nationalists. Far too few people outside Taiwan are acquainted with this history. George H. Kerr *Formosa Betrayed* (Eyre and Spottiswoode, London, 1966) and Peng Ming-min *A Taste of Freedom: Memoirs of a Formosan Independence Leader* (Taiwan Publishing Co., Irvine, California, 1972) are indispensable reading on the subject.

10 Joshua Wong with Jason Y Ng *Unfree Speech: The Threat to Global Democracy and Why We Must Act Now* (Penguin, London, 2020); Antony Dapiran *City on Fire: The Fight for Hong Kong* (Scribe, Melbourne, 2020); and Louisa Lim *Indelible City: Dispossession and Defiance in Hong Kong* (Text Publishing, Melbourne, 2022).

11 The Necker cube is an optical illusion that was first published as a Rhomboid in 1832 by Swiss crystallographer Louis Albert Necker. It is a simple wire-frame, two dimensional drawing of a cube with no visual cues as to its orientation, so it can be interpreted to have either the lower-left or the upper-right square as its front side. https://en.wikipedia.org/wiki/Necker_cube

12 Jim Molan *Danger on Our Doorstep* (Harper Collins, Sydney, 2022).

13 Paul Monk 'Wake Up and Smell the CCP' *IPA Review* Volume 74 No. 4, Summer 2022-23 pp. 63-67.

14 William H. Honan *Visions of Infamy: The Untold Story of How Journalist Hector C. Bywater Devised the Plans That Led to Pearl Harbor* (St Martin's Press, New York, 1991).

15 One of the finest accounts of the wars of the early 20th century in East Asia is that by Sarah C. M. Paine *The Wars For Asia 1911-1949* (Cambridge University Press, 2012). But the three-volume history of the Pacific War by Ian Toll—*Pacific Crucible: War at Sea in the Pacific, 1941-1942*, *The Conquering Tide: War in the Pacific Islands, 1942-1944* and *Twilight of the Gods: War in the Western Pacific, 1944-1945*—is indispensable.

16 https://en.wikipedia.org/wiki/Cai_Xia

17 Her move away from Communist Party orthodoxy appears to have begun at the very time I was writing this book, in the early 2000s. According to an August 2020 article in *The Guardian*, she had been assisting the then-CCP general secretary, Jiang Zemin, in drafting his Three Represents theory. She was already advocating liberal views in the press, including opening of the CCP to more businesspeople and professionals. Her faith in the Communist Party was apparently shaken up on a trip to Spain where she studied the Spanish transition to democracy after the death of Francisco Franco. She observed that Mao and Franco had died at similar times but Franco's successors had quickly and successfully transitioned to a stable democracy while Mao's had created a muddled hybrid economy and completely ignored political reform.

18 The literature on the quest for democratic governance in China is large, but too widely neglected. Among the most useful and insightful accounts are Edmund S. K. Fung *In Search of Chinese Democracy: Civil Opposition in Nationalist China 1929-1949* (Cambridge University Pres, 2000) and *The Intellectual Foundations of Chinese Modernity: Cultural and Political Thought in the Republican Era* (Cambridge University Press, 2010); Merle Goldman *Sowing the Seeds of Democracy in China: Political Reform in the Deng Xiaoping Era* (Harvard University Press, 1994), Dali Yang *Remaking the Chinese Leviathan: Market Transition and the Politics of Governance in China* (Stanford University Press, 2004) and Ian Johnson *Wild Grass: China's Revolution From Below* (Penguin, 2021). Strikingly, the expectations of all these scholars have been disappointed by what has (not) taken place since the 1980s. This is especially striking in the case of Dali Yang, an unusually acute and incisive analyst, who pointed clearly to the structural logic of reforms that have simply not been implemented by the Chinese Communist Party.

19 The single finest analysis of this phenomenon in the recent past is surely John Fitzgerald's *Cadre Country: How China Became the Chinese Communist Party* (UNSW Press, Sydney, 2022). Fitzgerald's specialty, over a long career, has been the roots of China's modern political institutions. He was awarded the Levenson Prize a generation ago for his brilliant study of the Chinese revolution of 1912 and its political fate over the succeeding decade, in *Awakening China: Politics, Culture and Class in the Nationalist Revolution* (Stanford University Press, 1996). I reviewed the book without ever having met Fitzgerald and hailed it as something that anyone seriously interested in modern Chinese history and the prospects for political reform there simply must read. It's not clear that

a great many did. But my review was read widely enough that my remarks about it were cited by the Levenson committee, in *Foreign Affairs* and on the back cover of the paperback edition of the book. 'China Stretches', *Quadrant* September 1997, pp. 85-86.

20 Geoff Raby *China's Grand Strategy and Australia's Future in the New Global Order* (Melbourne University Press, 2020).

Preface to the First Edition

1 Andrew J. Nathan & Perry Link, eds, *The Tiananmen Papers*, Little, Brown and Co., London, 2001, pp. 453–54.

2 This is my own rendering. Kowallis (p. 313) offers two alternative translations, but both of them seem rather wooden; the first because it is too literal and stilted, the second because, in an effort to construct rhyming couplets in English, it seems forced and somewhat trite. The first reads:

> *Ten thousand families' ink-dark faces sunken in underbrush*
> *Dare there be songs sung to move the earth in sorrow?*
> *Heart's concerns boundless, connecting vast expanses*
> *In without sounds place hear tremorous thunder.*

The second version, apparently Kowallis's own, reads as follows:

> *The dark and haggard faces of a countless host*
> *Are sunken in the bushes, living still, at most.*
> *Yet who among us dares with song burst forth*
> *A sorrow that could move the very earth?*
> *Troubles boundless in my heart expand,*
> *Ranging the vastness of our land,*
> *And in this place without a trace of sound,*
> *I hear tremorous thunder raging round.*

3 Hu Yaobang (1915–1989) was general secretary of the Chinese Communist Party from 1980 until 1987, when he was removed from that post by Deng Xiaoping for being too supportive of calls for fundamental political reform in China. His death on 15 April 1989 set off the social explosion that led to the declaration of martial law by Deng Xiaoping, and the Tiananmen Square bloodshed of 4 June.

4 Hu Jiwei (1916–2012) was the editor of the *People's Daily* from 1977 to 1983, and a champion of political reform and the protection of individual rights. At the March 1989 meeting of the National People's Congress (NPC) he openly criticised the State Council for not opening the way to structural political reform. He called for freedom of the press, and declared that democratic norms, not autocratic authority, would give political stability to China. Without them, he warned, the situation could become 'explosive'. He was sacked from the NPC for opposing the declaration of martial law and the suppression of the protests on 4 June 1989. (See Merle Goldman, *Sowing the Seeds of Democracy in China: Political Reform in the Deng Xiaoping Era*, Harvard University Press, 1994, pp. 298–99.) In January 2005, when a frail old man of 88, he circulated a letter calling on

the party to give the deceased Zhao Ziyang a grand memorial, and rejected its claims that Zhao had erred in opposing the Tiananmen Square crack down. (See Xin Fei, 'Hu Jiwei Requests Zhao's Reputation Be Restored', *The Epoch Times*, 25 January 2005.)

5   Qin Benli (1918–1991) was closely associated with Hu Yaobang's intellectual network, and a prominent advocate of political reform in China. He was the founder and editor of the *World Economic Herald*, an independent and liberal newspaper in Shanghai between 1980 and 1989. The paper was shut down by Jiang Zemin, then mayor of Shanghai, in May 1989, for demanding 'an environment where we can speak freely'. (See Goldman, op. cit., pp. 308–09.)

6   Wei Jingsheng, *The Courage to Stand Alone: Letters From Prison and Other Writings*, Viking, New York, 1997. See especially the biographical essay by Sophia Woodman 'Wei Jingsheng's Lifelong Battle for Democracy', pp. 249–71.

7   Fang Lizhi (1936-2012) was China's Andrei Sakharov, a distinguished physical scientist who suffered abuse and, after 1989, exile from China (to the United States) for his open criticism of the Communist Party's abuse of power.

8   Liu Binyan (1925-2005) was a journalist for the *People's Daily* until 1987, after which he was sacked and then exiled for demanding freedom of the press as 'the first step toward true political reform'. Goldman, op. cit., p. 239. In exile, Liu published his memoir, *A Higher Kind of Loyalty*, Pantheon, New York, 1990.

9   Yan Jiaqi (1942–) was director of the Institute of Political Science of the Chinese Academy of Social Sciences from 1985 until 1989, when he was forced to flee to exile in the United States because of his support for political reform, and his opposition to the bloody suppression of the democracy movement.

10 Ruan Ming (1931–) was the editor from 1977 until 1982 of *Theoretical Trends*, the in-house journal of the Communist Party's Central School. Like many others, he fled China after the 1989 suppression of the democracy movement, and now divides his time between the United States and democratic Taiwan.

11 Goldman, op. cit., p. 241. The original text was printed in the *People's Daily*, 23 May 1988, p. 5, and in English translation in the U.S. government's Foreign Broadcast Information Service, 8 June 1988, p. 30.

12 Kowallis, op. cit., pp. 311–15.

13 For a detailed analysis of democratic dissent in the Nationalist era, see Edmund S. K. Fung, *In Search of Chinese Democracy: Civil Opposition in Nationalist China 1929–1949*, Cambridge University Press, 2000.

14 On the Hundred Flowers campaign, see Jonathan Spence, *The Search for Modern China*, Hutchinson, London, 1990, pp. 569–73.

15 Ibid., p. 93

16 Ibid., p. 80.

17 Ibid., p. 94.

18   Stuart Schram, *Mao Tse-tung*, Penguin, Harmondsworth, 1967, p. 267. Schram estimated that between one and three million people were executed in the revolutionary terror in China between 1950 and 1953.

19   Spence, op. cit., p. 572.

20   The key scholarly pieces on the toll taken by the famine are two papers that were published in *Population and Development Review* in 1984: John S. Aird & Ansley Coale, 'An Analysis of Recent Data on the Population of China', vol. 10, no. 3, June 1984; and Basil Ashton, Kenneth Hill, Alan Piazza & Robin Zeitz 'Famine in China, 1958–1961', vol. 10, no. 4, December 1984. For a full-length account of the matter, see Jasper Becker, *Hungry Ghosts: Mao's Secret Famine*, The Free Press, New York, 1996; Dali L. Yang, *Calamity and Reform in China: State, Rural Society and Change Since the Great Leap Famine*, Stanford University Press, 1996; and Frederick C. Teiwes & Warren Sun, *China's Road to Disaster: Mao, Central Politicians and Provincial Leaders in the Unfolding of the Great Leap Forward 1955–1959*, M. E. Sharpe, New York, 1999, Frank Dikotter *Mao's Great Famine* (Bloomsbury, 2010) and Yang Jisheng T*ombstone: The Great Chinese Famine 1958-1962* (Farrar, Straus and Giroux, New York, 2012).

21   Willy Lam, 'Hu's Reforms and the Zhao Ziyang Fiasco', Association for Asia Research (AFAR), 14 February 2005, http://www.asiaresearch.org/articles/2504.html. The piece was originally written for the Washington-based Jamestown Foundation.

Chapter 1: The Clash of Civilisations and the Chinese Empire

1   Samuel P. Huntington, *The Clash of Civilizations and the Remaking of World Order*, Simon & Schuster, New York, 1996, p. 231.

2   Lee Kuan Yew, as quoted by Huntington, op. cit., p 231.

3   Gerald Segal, 'Does China Matter?', *Foreign Affairs*, vol. 78, no. 5, Sept/Oct 1999, pp. 24–36.

4   Stuart Harris, *Will China Divide Australia and the US?*, Australian Centre for American Studies, Sydney, 1998.

5   Hugh White, 'After Britain and then the US, China is in line to be our new best friend', *Sydney Morning Herald*, 24 March 2005.

6   Ross Garnaut, writing in the *Australian Financial Review*, 21 February 1997.

7   Paul Kennedy, *The Rise and Fall of the Great Powers: Economic Change and Military Conflict from 1500 to 2000*, Unwin Hyman, London, 1988.

8   This subject is taken up in robust fashion by John M. Hobson in *The Eastern Origins of Western Civilization*, Cambridge University Press, 2004.

9   China is rapidly approaching those dimensions again, in aggregate terms. According to a report released in February 2005 by the US-based Earth Policy Institute, China overtook the United States in 2004 as the world's largest consumer of food, energy, and minerals, as well as of many consumer durables, such as refrigerators, televisions and cell phones. (*Associated Press*, 17 February 2005.)

10 John W. Dower, *Embracing Defeat: Japan in the Wake of World War II*, W. W. Norton & Co., New York, 1999.

11 The agreement of 1985 under which Japan agreed to end its policy of Yen stability and, bowing to American pressure, allowed the Yen to rise relative to the dollar.

12 Herman Kahn, *The Emerging Japanese Superstate: Challenge and Response*, Penguin, Harmondsworth, 1973, dedicatory epigraph.

13 George Friedman & Meredith Le Bard, *The Coming War With Japan*, St Martin's Press, London, 1991.

14 Dali L. Yang, *Calamity and Reform in China: State, Rural Society and Change Since the Great Leap Famine*, Stanford University Press, 1996. See especially the introduction 'The Great Leap Famine, the Rise of Reform and the Cognitive Basis of Institutional Change', pp. 1–20.

15 William H. Overholt, *China: The Next Economic Superpower*, Weidenfeld & Nicolson, London, 1993, pp. 216–17.

16 Mark Elvin, *The Pattern of the Chinese Past: A Social and Economic Interpretation*, Stanford University Press, 1972, p. 319.

17 David Hale & Lyric Hughes Hale, 'China Takes Off', *Foreign Affairs*, November/December 2003, pp. 36–53. The quote is from p.39.

18 Bernard Lewis, 'The Roots of Muslim Rage: Why So Many Muslims Deeply Resent the West and Why Their Bitterness Will Not Be Easily Mollified', *The Atlantic Monthly*, no. 266, September 1990, p. 60.

19 Bernard Lewis, *Islam and the West*, Oxford University Press, New York, 1993, pp. 8–9.

20 Marco Polo, *The Travels*, Penguin, Harmondsworth, 1974, p. 149.

21 Jonathan Spence, *The Chan's Great Continent: China in Western Minds*, W. W. Norton & Co., New York, 1998, p. 1.

22 Ibid., p. 3.

23 Bernard Lewis, *Islam and the West*, Oxford University Press, New York, 1993, pp. 15–16.

24 Louise Levathes, *When China Ruled the Seas: The Treasure Fleet of the Dragon Throne 1405–1433*, Simon & Schuster, New York, 1994, is the standard account. For a brief description of the voyages, see Ann Paludan, *Chronicle of the Chinese Emperors*, Thames & Hudson, London, 1998, p. 166

25 Gavin Menzies, *1421: The Year China Discovered the World*, Bantam Books, New York, 2002. Menzies argued that Chinese fleets had, in fact, circumnavigated the world, charted the coasts of Australia and Antarctica and colonised the New World. His arguments have not been well received by more seasoned scholars. See, for example, the caustic review by Natalie Danford at www.salon.com/books/feature/2003/01/07/menzies.

26 Ibid., p. 19.

27 Arthur Waldron, *The Great Wall of China: From History to Myth*, Cambridge University Press, Melbourne, 1990.

28 Merle Goldman, *Sowing the Seeds of Democracy in China: Political Reform in the Deng Xiaoping Era*, Harvard University Press, 1994, p. 257.

29 Samuel P. Huntington, *The Clash of Civilizations and the Remaking of World Order*, Simon & Schuster, New York, 1996, pp. 20–21

30 Ibid, p. 29.

31 Ibid., p. 70.

32 Bernard Lewis, op. cit., p. 5

33 Huntington, op. cit., p. 103.

34 Ibid., 82.

35 Ibid., p. 88.

36 Ibid., p. 223.

37 Ibid., p. 229.

38 Ibid., pp. 232–33.

39 Ibid., pp. 312–16

Chapter 2: Chinese Grand Strategy and American Hegemony

1 Michael Mann, *Incoherent Empire*, Verso, New York, 2003; Niall Ferguson, *Colossus: The Rise and Fall of the American Empire*, Allen Lane, London, 2004.

2 Chalmers Johnson, *The Sorrows of Empire: Militarism, Secrecy and the End of the Republic*, Henry Holt & Co., New York, 2004.

3 Chalmers Johnson, *Blowback: The Costs and Consequences of American Empire*, Metropolitan Books, New York, 2000, p. ix.

4 Ibid., p. 5.

5 Ibid., p. 228.

6 For a searching account of America's grand strategy and move to global primacy after 1945, see Melvyn P. Leffler, *A Preponderance of Power: National Security, the Truman Administration and the Cold War*, Stanford University Press, 1992. Leffler did not counsel withdrawal from primacy after the defeat of Communism, only a prudent and creative use of it (p. 518).

7 Robert B. Strassler (ed.), *The Landmark Thucydides: A Comprehensive Guide to the Peloponnesian War*, Simon & Schuster, New York, 1998, p. 126.

8 Ibid., p. 127. (Book Two 65:5-7 of *The Peloponnesian War*.)

9 For a recent and quite characteristic example of this view of American foreign policy, see Dan Briody *The Halliburton Agenda: The Politics of Oil and Money*, John Wiley & Sons, Inc., New Jersey, 2004.

10 Joseph S. Nye Jr, *The Paradox of American Power: Why the World's Only Superpower Can't Go It Alone*, Oxford University Press, 2002; Ivo H. Daalder & James M. Lindsay, *America Unbound: The Bush Revolution in Foreign Policy*, Brookings Institution Press, Washington D.C., 2003.

11 Johnson (2000), p. 228.

12 Alastair Iain Johnston, *Cultural Realism: Strategic Culture and Grand Strategy in Chinese History*, Princeton University Press, 1995.

13 Michael D. Swaine & Ashley J. Tellis, *Interpreting China's Grand Strategy: Past, Present and Future*, Project Air Force, RAND, 2000, p. 241.

14 Johnston, op cit., p. 266.

15 Johnston's book repays a close reading. He examines the strategic doctrine embodied in the seven great military classics of imperial China and the strategic behaviour of the Ming dynasty (1385–1644). He concludes that what he calls the parabellum paradigm—the assumption that 'conflict is a constant in human affairs' and a preference for offensive strategies over accommodation—has been dominant in both Chinese history and Chinese theory. He argues that this has been preferred to the 'Confucian-Mencian paradigm'—the assumption that 'conflict is aberrant, or at least avoidable through the promotion of good government' and a preference for defensive strategies, in which force is used 'only under unavoidable conditions, and then only in the name of the righteous restoration of a moral-political order' (p. 249).

Chapter 3: Variations on the LAM

1 George Gilboy, 'The Myth Behind China's Miracle', *Foreign Affairs*, July/August 2004, p. 48.

2 David Hale & Lyric Hughes Hale, 'China Takes Off', *Foreign Affairs*, November/December 2003, pp. 39–40.

3 George Gilboy, op. cit., pp. 33–48.

4 Paul Dibb, *The Soviet Union: The Incomplete Superpower*, MacMillan/IISS, London, 1986, p. 30.

5 Paul Kennedy, *The Rise and Fall of the Great Powers: Economic Change and Military Conflict From 1500 to 2000*, Unwin Hyman, London, 1988, p. 477. Kennedy went on to state that 'it is difficult to see Russia relinquishing its many controls over eastern Europe' (p. 509) and that its many economic problems did not 'mean that the USSR is close to collapse' (p. 513).

6 Vaclav Smil, who is of Czech origin and fled Czechoslovakia after the Soviet invasion of 1968, is Distinguished Professor at the University of Manitoba. He is a specialist on world energy and food systems and the author of 19 books, including *Feeding the World* (MIT Press, 2000), *Enriching the Earth: Transformation of World Food Production* (MIT Press, 2001), and *Energy at the Crossroads* (MIT Press, 2003). His work on China includes *China's Environment: An Inquiry Into the Limits of National Development*, M. E. Sharpe, New York, 1993, and most recently *China's Past, China's Future: Energy, Food, Environment*, Routledge Curzon, London, 2004.

7 Gordon Chang, *The Coming Collapse of China*, Random House Business Books, London, 2001, p. xvi.

8   Joe Studwell, *The China Dream: The Elusive Quest for the Greatest Untapped Market on Earth*, Profile Books, London, 2002. The remarks quoted are those of James Kynge, China Bureau Chief for the *Financial Times* of London. David Murphy, Beijing correspondent for the *Far Eastern Economic Review*, remarked, 'This book will cause blushes in boardrooms around the world.'

9   Studwell, op. cit., pp. 154–55.

10 Peter Schwartz, Peter Leyden & Joel Hyatt, *The Long Boom: A Vision For the Coming Age of Prosperity*, Orion Business Books, London, 2000. Their prognostications, of course, are every bit as optimistic as LAM forecasts for China, but they are based on the prospects for the American and global economies, whose problems are not quite so serious or politically straitjacketed as are those of China.

11 George Gilboy, op. cit., pp. 38–39, points out that foreign-funded enterprises (FFEs) accounted for 55 per cent of China's exports in 2003. Such dominance is even more apparent in advanced industrial exports where, over the decade to 2003, it grew from 35 per cent to 79 per cent. For computer equipment, one of the most rapidly growing of all such sectors, exports shot from $US716 million to $US41 billion in the decade to 2003, with the FFEs' share of these rising from an already high 74 pre cent to a staggering 92 per cent. Gilboy concludes that 'this pattern repeats itself in almost every advanced industrial sector in China'.

12 Yenping Hao, *The Commercial Revolution in Nineteenth Century China: The Rise of Sino-Western Mercantile Capitalism*, SMC Publishing Inc., Taipei, 1986, especially pp. 277–357.

13 Yenping Hao, op. cit., p. 351. Hao's concluding chapter is an excellent general introduction to the economic history of late Qing China.

Chapter 4: Kinmen and Kinship

1   'China's Dangerous Leap Backwards', editorial, *Taipei Times*, 20 December 2004.

2   Ibid.

3   Ibid.

4   John Wilson Lewis & Xue Litai, *China's Strategic Seapower: The Politics of Force Modernisation in the Nuclear Age*, Stanford University Press, 1994, p. 219.

5   Thomas J. Christensen, *Useful Adversaries: Grand Strategy, Domestic Mobilisation and Sino-American Conflict 1947–1958*, Princeton University Press, 1996, p. 69, n. 149.

6   Ibid., p. 109.

7   Ibid., p. 113.

8   Ibid., p. 118.

9   For a close analysis of the complexities in American policy at that time, see David Finkelstein, *Washington's Taiwan Dilemma, 1949–1950: From Abandonment to Salvation*, George Mason University Press, 1993.

10 Christensen, op. cit., p. 177.

11. In a biography of Mao Zedong published before the Cultural Revolution had made its devastating impact, and before all but a few specialists realised how catastrophic the Great Leap famine of 1959–61 had been, Stuart Schram estimated that a 'reasonable estimate' of the number of people executed by the communists in the period 1949–52 would be two to three million. See Schram, *Mao Tse-Tung*, Penguin, Melbourne, rev. ed., 1967, p. 267.

12. See Lowell Dittmer, *Sino-Soviet Normalisation and Its International Implications, 1945–1990*, University of Washington Press, 1992, p. 173. Dittmer argues that it was Mao's intention to seize the islands, however new archival evidence indicates that this was not so.

13. Ibid., p. 327, n. 27.

14. A memorandum from the director of the policy-planning staff, Gerard Smith, to secretary of state, Christian Herter, dated 13 August 1958 (and declassified only on 14 February 1995), describes plans by the joint chiefs of staff to defend Kinmen (Quemoy) and Mazu (Matsu) with nuclear strikes deep into China, and indicates estimates of millions of Chinese civilian casualties. President Eisenhower and Secretary of State Dulles had warned several times since 1955 that they would use nuclear weapons against China in defence of Taiwan.

15. Christensen, op. cit., pp. 220 and 228–29.

16. Ibid., pp. 231–233. Mao certainly had Khrushchev puzzled in 1958. In his memoirs, Khrushchev remarks that Mao told him that having Chiang Kaishek's forces on Quemoy (Kinmen) and Matsu (Mazu) was useful, whereas 'if we'd occupied the islands, we would have lost the ability to cause him discomfort any time we want'. See Khrushchev, *Khrushchev Remembers*, vol. 2, Penguin, Melbourne, 1977, p. 312.

17. Steven Mufson & Helen Dewar, 'Pentagon Issues Warning to China: U.S. Officials Criticise Beijing White Paper Backing Use of Force Against Taiwan', *Washington Post*, 23 February 2000.

18. These are two of Christensen's observations, in the final pages of *Useful Adversaries*. The following 'third point' is my own.

19. That they do collide seems to be the burden of John Mearsheimer's argument in his major work, *The Tragedy of Great Power Relations*, W. W. Norton & Co., New York, 2001. For his brief remarks on the possibility of Sino-American conflict over Taiwan, see pp. 373–77.

20. Interview with Wu Chengtien, Taipei, December 2001.

21. Tatan literally means 'liver'. To the Chinese the liver denotes courage or, more colloquially, guts. An alternative translation of Tatan, would therefore be Guts (Island), but Boldness (Island) is less uncouth.

22. President calls for expanding three small links during return visit to island of "boldness", *Taipei Journal*, 24 May 2002, p. 7.

Chapter 5: Conceiving a Paradigm Shift

1. See Gabriel Gorodetsky, *Grand Delusion: Stalin and the German Invasion of Russia*, Yale University Press, 1999 (especially chapters 13 and 14). The quotes are from pp. 299 and 311.

2   See Ernest R. May, *Strange Victory: Hitler's Conquest of France*, Hill and Wang, New York, 2000 (especially chapters 17–18 and 24–25).

3   For further discussion of this fascinating 'intelligence failure' see Abraham Rabinovich, *The Yom Kippur War: The Epic Encounter that Transformed the Middle East*, Schocken Books, New York, 2004. The quote is from the prologue, p. 3.

4   For a thoughtful reflection on the rise of such an emotional sense in China in the past decade, see Peter Hays Gries, *China's New Nationalism: Pride, Politics and Diplomacy*, University of California Press, 2004.

5   W. J. F. Jenner, *The Tyranny of History: The Roots of China's Crisis,* Allen Lane, London, 1992.

6   Lee Kuan Yew, *From Third World to First: The Singapore Story, 1965–2000*, HarperCollins, New York, 2000, p. xiv.

7   George Steiner, *The Death of Tragedy*, Faber & Faber, London, 1961, p. 6.

Chapter 6: Looking at the Taiwan Strait from 'Down Under'

1   For a systematic account of this matter, see Paul Monk, 'Secret Intelligence and Escape Clauses: Australia and the Indonesian Annexation of East Timor, 1963–1976', *Critical Asian Studies*, vol. 33, no. 2, June 2001, pp. 181–208.

2   Top secret cablegram to Canberra from Spender, in London, 8 September 1950. Documents on Australian Foreign Policy, *Australia and Recognition of the People's Republic of China, 1949–1972*, Department of Foreign Affairs and Trade, Canberra, 2002, p. 25.

3   Ibid. Spender himself, in the same cablegram remarked, 'Chiang Kai-shek's regime is rather lamentable, to say the least. In any event, it can hardly be said to represent a democratic choice of the Formosans.'

4   Ibid., pp. 23–24. At a cabinet meeting in Canberra on 25 August 1950, the prime minister, Robert Menzies, explained that Douglas MacArthur's opinion that Taiwan was strategically vital had been accepted in Washington. The chief of the naval staff, Admiral Collins, concurred with this view, but the chief of the general staff, Lieutenant General Rowell, and the chief of air staff, Air Marshal George Jones, disagreed. All such assessments, of course, were premised on the idea that it was important to strategically contain China.

5   Ibid., p. 819.

6   This possibility had long been foreshadowed. It is articulated explicitly in a letter from Hugh Dunn, Australia's last ambassador to the Republic of China (1969–1972), to the secretary for foreign affairs (1970–74), J. K. Waller, in which he stated that 'it would be most desirable … not to appear to abandon the ROC completely and precipitately' and that this could be achieved *'provided that we do not specifically endorse the PRC's claim to Taiwan'* [Emphasis added]. Letter from Dunn to Waller. SECRET Personal. 30 June 1972, ibid., p. 737.

7   Ibid., p. 509.

8   Ibid., p. 486.

9   Ibid., p. 487.

10 Ibid., p. 513.

11 Ibid., p. 513, n. 3.

12 Ibid., p. 510.

13 Ibid., p. 503.

14 Secret AUSTEO Priority Cablegram from Renouf to Canberra, 20 July 1971, ibid., p. 517.

15 Ibid., p. 517.

16 Harold Anderson, First Assistant Secretary, Asia Division, Submission to Bowen, 25 August 1971, ibid., pp. 588–90.

17 Sterling Seagrave, *The Soong Dynasty: The Extraordinary Story of the Richest and Most Powerful Family in Modern China*, Sidgwick & Jackson, London, 1985, p. 457. Madame Chiang, Mayling Soong, then aged 78 and very sick, left Taiwan after the death of her husband, and went into permanent exile in the United States. She lived there in seclusion at the Long Island estate of her nephew, David Kung, passing into legend well before her death at the great age of 106 in 2003.

18 See Chienmin Chao & Bruce J. Dickson, eds, *Remaking the Chinese State: Strategies, Society and Security*, Routledge, New York, 2001, especially the essay by Dali Yang, 'Rationalizing the Chinese State: the political economy of government reform', pp. 19–45. See also Andrew J. Nathan, *China's Transition*, Columbia University Press, 1997, especially chapter 5, 'Chinese Democracy: The Lessons of Failure', and chapter 15, 'The Constitutionalist Option'.

19 For a particularly nuanced reflection on this problem, see Peter Hays Gries, *China's New Nationalism: Pride, Politics and Diplomacy*, University of California Press, 2004, especially chapter 8, 'Chinese Nationalism and US-China Relations in the Twenty-first Century'.

20 'Developments in Sino-American Relations: Implications for Australia', Policy Planning Paper, SECRET ECLIPSE, ibid,. pp. 518–25.

21 Ibid., p. 518, repeated with deliberate emphasis on p. 524.

22 Ibid., pp. 519–521.

23 Ibid., p. 523.

24 Ibid., p. 524.

25 Ibid., p. 525.

26 Malcolm Cook & Craig Meer, *Balancing Act: Taiwan's Cross Strait Challenge*, Lowy Institute for International Policy, Sydney, April 2005.

27 Michael O'Hanlon, 'Why China Cannot Conquer Taiwan', *International Security*, vol. 25, no. 2, Fall 2000, pp. 51–85, provides an excellent overview of the military balance.

28 Robert S. Ross, 'The 1995–96 Taiwan Strait Confrontation: Coercion, Credibility and the Use

of Force', *International Security*, vol. 25, no. 2, Fall 2000, pp. 87–123, explores the Chinese strategy with admirable sensitivity to its nuances.

29 For an interesting reflection on American interests in the matter, see Nancy Bernkopf Tucker, 'If Taiwan Chooses Unification, Should the United States Care?', *The Washington Quarterly,* Summer 2002, pp. 15–28.

30 Thomas J. Christensen, 'Posing Problems Without Catching Up: China's Rise and Challenges for U.S. Security Policy', *International Security*, vol. 25, no. 4, Spring 2001, pp. 5–40. The quote is from p. 40.

31 On the Great Leap 'Forward' famine as a watershed event in the history of the People's Republic of China, see Dali L. Yang, *Calamity and Reform in China: State, Rural Society and Change Since the Great Leap Famine*, Stanford University Press, 1996. There are other excellent introductions to the catastrophe: notably, Jasper Becker, *Hungry Ghosts: Mao's Secret Famine*, Free Press, 1996, and Frederick C. Teiwes & Warren Sun, *China's Road to Disaster: Mao, Central Politicians and Provincial Leaders in the Unfolding of the Great Leap Forward 1955–1959*, M. E. Sharpe, New York, 1999.

32 Nancy Bernkopf Tucker, 'If Taiwan Chooses Unification, Should the United States Care?', The *Washington Quarterly*, Summer 2002, p. 19, quotes 'a Chinese official who handles Taiwan affairs' as having declared in 2001, "Once we said we would liberate Taiwan, then we said Taiwan was just a province of China, now we are saying Taiwan can be our equal. For the mainland to make these kinds of adjustments in policy is not an easy thing."

Chapter 7: Can Rationality Save Us?

1 Central News Agency, 8 April 2004, 'Election Dashed Beijing's Dream—UCLA Professor'.

2 Reuters, 28 February 2004.

3 Ibid.

4 *Taipei Times*, 6 April 2004.

5 Willy Lam, CNN.com, 19 May 2004.

6 Lam, loc. cit..

7 'China's Rapid Missile Build-up No Empty Threat', Reuters, 12 August 2004.

8 For a particularly useful assessment of the balance of forces, see Michael O'Hanlon, 'Why China Cannot Conquer Taiwan', *International Security*, vol. 25, no. 2, Fall 2000, pp. 51–86.

9 James Mulvenon, quoted in 'China's Rapid Missile Build-up No Empty Threat', Reuters, 12 August 2004.

10 Wendell Minnick, 'The Year to Fear for Taiwan: 2006', *Asia Times*, 10 April 2004.

11 Martin L. Lasater, 'Why China May Elect to Use Force in the Taiwan Strait', 13 August 2004. For the full text, see http://taiwansecurity.org/IS/2004/Lasater-130804.htm.

12   Robert Karniol, quoted in 'China's Rapid Missile Build-up No Empty Threat', Reuters 12 August 2004.

13   *The Fog of War* won the 2003 Academy award for best documentary and was voted best documentary feature by the National Board of Review, the Los Angeles Film Critics Association, the Chicago Film Critics Association, the Washington D.C. Film Critics Association, and the Village Voice Film Critics Poll. The DVD release by Sony Pictures Classics includes two dozen scenes not previously seen in the cinema version, and Robert McNamara's own list of ten lessons from his life, which are not the same as the 11 lessons Errol Morris draws in the feature.

14   Graham Allison & Philip Zelikow, *Essence of Decision: Explaining the Cuban Missile Crisis*, 2nd ed., Longman, 1999, p. viii: '… managers in government, business and the non-profit sector have found the argument in the original edition more valuable than its author had anticipated. The book has been used in graduate schools of government and public policy, business and other professional training programs where the objective is preparation for practice, rather than theory. At Harvard's John F. Kennedy School of Government, it has served as a text in the political and institutional analysis curriculum for almost a quarter century.'

15   For a critical review of the book, in both editions, see Barton J. Bernstein, 'Understanding Decisionmaking, U.S. Foreign Policy and the Cuban Missile Crisis: A Review Essay', *International Security*, vol. 25, no. 1, Summer 2000, pp. 134–64.

16   The ideas for the original edition of *Essence of Decision* began with the deliberations of the May Group at Harvard in 1966. Headed by Ernest R. May (1928-2009), who had become one of the leading scholars in the Western world on the uses of history and intelligence in the making of national security policy. The group included many notable contributors. As a result, the conceptual lenses developed in the book are a real work of collaborative social science, not simply the idiosyncratic views of an individual scholar.

17   Graham Allison & Philip Zelikow, op. cit., p. 7.

18   Ibid., p. 3.

19   'We speak of occurrences not as unstructured happenings but rather as "the Israeli decision to attack", "the Chinese policy toward Taiwan", and "American action in the Persian Gulf". To summarize the relevant aspects of a state of the world as a nation's "decision" or "policy" is—at least implicitly—to slip into the rational-actor framework. Decision presupposes a decider and a choice among alternatives with reference to some goal. Policy means the realization in a number of particular instances of some agent's objectives. These concepts identify phenomena as actions performed by purposeful agents. This identification involves a simple identification of the pervasive everyday assumption that what human beings do is at least intendedly rational. This everyday assumption of human purposiveness is common in the social sciences. As Seymour Martin Lipset has noted, "The major assumption in the social sciences generally … is that people seek ego gratification—that this is their goal or end." Thus economics, political science, and, to a large extent, sociology and psychology study human behavior as purposive, goal-directed activity.' Ibid., pp. 16–17

20. Ibid., p. 24.
21. Ibid., pp. 24–25.
22. Douglas McEachin, P*sychology of Intelligence Analysis*, Center for the Study of Intelligence, Central Intelligence Agency, 1999, pp. 5–6.
23. Ibid., p. 20.
24. Ibid., p. 143.
25. Ibid., p. 159.
26. Ibid., p. 162. Allison and Zelikow were quoting from a study by Diane Vaughan of the Challenger disaster.
27. Ibid., p. 164.
28. Ibid., p. 177.
29. Ibid. p. 255.
30. Ibid. pp. 296–97.
31. Ibid. p. 299.
32. Ibid. p. 302.
33. Ibid. pp. 302–03.
34. Lasater, loc. cit., pp. 1–2.
35. Ibid. p. 2
36. Ibid. p. 4.
37. 'Beijing Starts Soul Search: Who Lost Taiwan?', *Straits Times*, 7 April 2004.
38. Ibid.

Chapter 8: Ancient History, Modern Cinema, and Political Allegory

1. Sima Qian', *The Grand Scribe's Records, Volume 1: The Memoirs of Pre-Han China*, SMC Publishing Inc., Taipei, 1994, p.

2. Ian Kershaw, *Hitler 1889–1936: Hubris*, Allen Lane, London, 2001, p. 526.

3. *The Cambridge History of Modern China, Volume 1: The Qin and Han Empires, 221 BC–AD 220*, Caves Books, Taipei, 1986, pp. 85–86.

4. A synopsis of the story is provided in *The Cambridge History of China Volume 1*, p. 45. Dirk Bodde writes, 'In 227, in a desperate effort to halt the quickening advance of the Qin military machine, the state of Yan (located in the present Peking [Beijing] area) sent an envoy, Jing Ke, to the Qin court, bearing as a token of submission and the head of a self-immolated renegade Qin general, who had sought refuge in Yen. At the ensuing audience, Jing Ke seized a dagger which had been

concealed within the map, and with it attacked the future First Emperor, whom he very nearly succeeded in assassinating before he himself was cut down.'

5 One of the odd things about the film is the way in which it confuses the chronology of historical events. It opens with a statement in English announcing that in 221 BCE, after centuries of strife between the feudal warring states, there were just seven states remaining. But, in fact, by 221 BCE there was only one state remaining. The other six had been subdued by the King of Qin in the preceding decade: Han, (230 BCE), Zhao (228), Wei (225), Zhu (223), Yan (222), and Qi (221). The attempt to assassinate King Zheng took place after the fall of Zhao and the sack of its capital, Handan, in 228 BCE.

Moreover, the death of Lu Buwei and some of the other events depicted in the film—notably the attempted palace coup by the Marquis Lao Ai—took place a decade before the sack of Zhao, but one would never guess this from the film. The need for 'dramatic unity' cannot explain these discrepancies, since the film is divided into five 'chapters' or acts. These could quite readily have been made to accommodate a clearer sense of the timeframe involved in historical reality. The chronological inaccuracies could be taken to mean that Chen and Wang do not know their ancient history, but it seems more probable that they deliberately reworked the history into a dramatic screenplay with a powerful, if subtle, political meaning.

6 It has been computed, according to the Grand Scribe's Records, that the total number of enemy soldiers slaughtered by the Qin armies between 364 and 234 BCE was 1,489,000. Modern historians have cast doubt on the accuracy of these numbers, but their magnitude testifies to the reputation of Qin for ruthless extermination of its enemies, not only in battle, but following surrender. See *The Cambridge History of China Volume 1*, pp. 99–100.

7 The state of Qin originated in the early ninth century BCE, in what is now Gansu province. Its rise as a powerful state is normally dated from the mid-fourth century BCE and, thereafter, parallels the rise of Roman power in Italy and the Western Mediterranean, between the Samnite wars and the Punic wars. The Romans had to fend off the Gauls, to the north-west, before they could proceed to consolidate their primacy in Italy. Similarly, the Qin had to fend off the Jung to their north-west, in the fifth century BCE, before consolidating their power. The systematic development of that power dates from the prime ministership of Shang Yang, under King (or Duke) Hsiao, 361–338 BCE. According to Dirk Bodde's judgement, however, 'Events during the period of little over a century between the death of Shang Yang in 338 and the unification in 221 (BCE) give no indication that the latter was reached as the result of any consciously devised long range strategic plan or design.' *The Cambridge History of China Volume 1*, .38.

8 *The Cambridge History of China Volume 1: The Qin and Han Empires, 221 BC–AD 220*, Caves Books, Taipei, 1986, p. 43.

9 Ibid.

10 Ibid.

11 Oddly enough, King Zheng's great grandfather was called Zhao Ziyang. He was the King of Qin from 306 to 251 BCE, and was a conqueror every bit as ruthless as his grandson.

12 Ronald Hingley, *Pasternak: A Biography*, Weidenfeld & Nicolson, London, 1983, provides a nuanced account of the poet's struggles with Marxism and the idea of modern revolution.

13 Boris Pasternak, *Doctor Zhivago*, trans. Max Hayward & Manya Harari, Fontana, London, 1976, p. 373.

Chapter 9: Overcoming the Confucian

1 Simon Leys [Pierre Ryckmans], *The Analects of Confucius*, Norton, 1997.

2 Lee Kuan Yew, *From Third World to First World: Singapore and the Asian Economic Book*, HarperCollins, New York, 2000, p. 491.

3 Donald Johanson & Blake Edgar, *From Lucy to Language*, Weidenfeld and Nicolson, London, 1996, p. 46: 'The earliest erectus specimens in East Asia include the cranium from Gongwangliang (Lantian), China, which may be a million years old or closer to 800,000 years old, and some isolated sites from Yuanmou and other Chinese sites that probably date to around 700,000 years ago.'

4 Gina L. Barnes, *The Rise of Civilization in East Asia: The Archaeology of China, Japan and Korea*, Thames & Hudson, London, 1999.

5 *Good News Bible*, Ecclesiastes i: 9–10.

6 Recent archaeological finds in Indonesia suggest that remnants of both Homo erectus and a new, hitherto unknown, species of smaller hominid may have survived until relatively recently.

7 Garniss Curtiss, Carl Swisher, & Roger Lewin, *Java Man*, Little, Brown & Co., Boston, 2001.

8 For an interesting thesis on the invention of agriculture, see Mark Nathan Cohen, *The Food Crisis in Prehistory: Overpopulation and the Origins of Agriculture*, Yale University Press, 1977.

9 Denise Schmandt-Besserat, *How Writing Came About*, University of Texas Press, 1996.

10 For two excellent introductions to the emergence of theoretic thinking among our ancestors, see Merlin Donald, *Origins of the Modern Mind: Three Stages in the Evolution of Culture and Cognition*, Harvard University Press, 1991; and Steven Mithen *The Prehistory of the Mind*, Thames & Hudson, London, 1996.

11 Arnaldo Momigliano, 'The Fault of the Greeks', in '*Wisdom, Revelation and Doubt: Perspectives on the First Millennium BC*', Daedalus, vol. 104, no. 2, Spring 1975, pp. 9–20. The quote is from p. 9.

12 For a useful brief account of the so-called 'Hundred Flowers Campaign' and the sweeping repression that followed, see John Byron & Robert Pack, *The Claws of the Dragon: Kang Sheng— The Evil Genius Behind Mao and His Legacy of Terror in Mao's China*, Simon & Schuster, New York, 1992, pp. 225–29.

13 Colin A. Ronan, *The Shorter Science and Civilization in China, vol. 1*, Cambridge University Press, 1978, p. 30.

14 Letter to the author from Mark Elvin, 30 May 2001.

15 Simon Leys [Pierre Ryckmans], *The Analects of Confucius*, Norton, 1997, pp. xv–xxii.

16 For a good introduction to the latest scholarship on this considerable archaeological challenge, see Geza Vermes, *The Authentic Gospel of Jesus*, Allen Lane, London, 2003.

17 Joseph Needham, *Science and Civilization in China, vol. 2*, Cambridge University Press, 1961, p. 29.

18 Karl Popper, *The World of Parmenides: Essays on the Pre-Socratic Enlightenment*, Routledge, London, 1998. See especially his remark on p. 5: ' ... I think that with Aristotle's theory, that science, episteme, is (demonstrable and therefore) certain knowledge, it may be said that the great enterprise of Greek critical rationalism came to an end. Aristotle killed the critical science to which he himself had made a leading contribution. The philosophy of nature, the theory of nature, the great original attempts in cosmology, broke down after Aristotle, owing mainly to the influence of his epistemology, which demanded proof (including inductive proof).' Popper was not, of course, arguing that scientific theories do not need testing, but rather that they need to be seen precisely as testable and therefore in principle falsifiable, rather than 'proven' once for all.

19 See Mencius, trans. D. C. Lau, Penguin, Harmondsworth, 1970, and Kwongloi Shun, *Mencius and Ancient Chinese Thought*, Stanford University Press, 1997.

Chapter 10: Hu's Rhetoric

1 For a brilliant evocation of the world and times of Liang Qichao, see John Fitzgerald, *Awakening China: Politics, Culture and Class in the Nationalist Revolution*, Stanford University Press, 1996. Fitzgerald, one of Australia's leading Sinologists, received the Levenson Prize of the American Historical Association for this book. For his specific reflections on Liang Qichao's visit to Australia see 'The Slave Who Would Be Equal: The Significance of Liang Qichao's Australian Writings', in Billy So, John Fitzgerald et al, eds, *Power and Identity in the Chinese World Order*, Hong Kong University Press, 2003, pp. 353–75.

2 For an excellent biographical study of Kennedy, including a judicious assessment of his presidency, see Robert Dallek, *John F. Kennedy: An Unfinished Life 1917–1963*, Allen Lane, London, 2003.

3 Andrew J. Nathan & Bruce Gilley, eds, *China's New Rulers: The Secret Files*, Granta, London, 2003, p. 191.

4 George Leggett, *The Cheka: Lenin's Political Police*, Clarendon Press, Oxford, 1981, pp. 463–68.

5 Since the fall of the Soviet Union and the partial opening of Soviet archives, the figures for excess deaths under Stalin have been reviewed. In comparison with earlier estimates in the tens of millions, the best research now suggests that the total number was probably in the vicinity of five to seven million, including three million deaths by starvation in the Ukraine famine, one to two million executions and one to two million deaths by cold, hunger, disease, and brutal treatment in the Gulag or in deportations between 1925 and 1953. Anne Applebaum, *Gulag: A History of the Soviet Camps*, Allen Lane, London, 2003, calculates still higher figures, ranging from 12 to 20

million; but see also Oleg V. Khlevniuk, *The History of the Gulag: From Collectivization to the Great Terror*, Yale University Press, 2004, pp. 287–327, whose figures are more systematic and closer to the lower end of the spectrum.

6 Michael A. Santoro, *Profits and Principles: Global Capitalism and Human Rights in China*, Cornell University Press, 2000.

7 Abraham Ascher's magisterial work, *P. A. Stolypin: The Search for Stability in Late Imperial Russia*, Stanford University Press, 2001, is the best study in a very considerable literature on the man.

8 Stolypin 'placed on the political agenda a series of reform proposals that touched on virtually all aspects of Russian society and were designed to reshape the country in a fundamental way'. Lenin saw him as 'an astute statesman whose dual program of repression and reform might well have succeeded in undermining the revolutionary cause'. He was also, in the interests of his reform agenda, 'unbending in his determination to keep Russia out of foreign entanglements that could embroil the country in war'. Ascher, op. cit., pp. 3–10.

9 Ibid., pp. 396–97.

10 Qin Hui, 'China's Stolypins', *New Left Review*, March/April 2003. See also the extended interview with Wang Hui, then chief editor of China's leading monthly journal *Dushu (Reading)* : 'Fire At the Castle Gate', *New Left Review*, Nov/Dec 2000, pp. 69–99.

11 Wen Jiabao, quoted in Andrew J. Nathan & Bruce Gilley, eds, op. cit., p. 191. For a searching critique of this interesting, but somewhat loosely written, book, see Alfred Chan's review essay in *The China Journal*, no. 50, July 2003, pp. 107–119.

12 Nathan & Gilley, eds, op. cit., p. 194.

13 Moshe Lewin, *Lenin's Last Struggle*, Pluto, London, 1975, is a crucial documentary source here; but an indispensable corrective to any sentimental interpretation of Lenin's politics is Richard Pipes, *Russia Under the Bolshevik Regime, 1919–1924*, Harvill, London, 1994.

14 A good overview of intellectual debates in China between 1989 and 2000, and their policy implications, is Joseph Fewsmith, *China Since Tiananmen: The Politics of Transition*, Cambridge University Press, 2001. On the controversies of the 1980s, it is hard to improve on Merle Goldman's *Sowing the Seeds of Democracy in China: Political Reform in the Deng Xiaoping Era*, Harvard University Press, 1994.

15 Joe Studwell, *The China Dream: The Elusive Quest for the Greatest Untapped Market on Earth*, Profile Books, London, 2002, is the must-read book on the question of the 'vast market', and the propensity of Western investors to pour money into China in the hope of economic returns that are yet to materialise.

16 Gordon G. Chang, *The Coming Collapse of China*, Random House, New York, 2001, p. xvii.

17 Arthur Waldron, *The Great Wall of China: From History to Myth*, Cambridge University Press, 1990 (Canto, 1992), is an excellent example of his work as an historian.

18 *Commentary*, July/August and October 2003, vol. 117, no.8. For more sanguine views of China's economic prospects, see Laurence J. Brahm, *Zhu Rongji and the Transformation of Modern China*, Wiley & Sons, Singapore, 2002, and various remarks in Joseph Stiglitz, *Globalisation and Its Discontents*, W. W. Norton & Co., New York, 2002. Stiglitz was the winner of the 2001 Nobel Prize in economics.

19 Ross Terrill, *The New Chinese Empire*, UNSW Press, Sydney, 2003, p. 21.

20 Nicholas D. Kristof, 'A Clampdown in China', *The New York Times*, May 17 2005.

21 Hugh Thomas, *Cuba: The Pursuit of Freedom*, Pan, London, 2002, is the richest resource on the history of Cuba and its Castroist revolution. For Kennedy's problems with Cuba see Lawrence Freedman, *Kennedy's Wars: Berlin, Cuba, Laos and Vietnam*, Oxford University Press, 2000, pp. 123–248, and Dallek, op. cit., pp. 373–574.

Chapter 11: Wei Jingsheng and the Communist Party

1 Catherine Armitage, 'Under the scab of Tiananmen, China still bleeds', *The Weekend Australian*, 4–5 June 2005, p. 15. On 21 June, Reporters Without Borders sent a petition, signd by 10,500 people worldwide, calling for Ching Cheong's release and the dismissal of 'spying' charges against him.

2 For a monumental treatment of the impact of both men, see Michael Scamell, *Solzhenitsyn*, Hutchinson, London, 1985.

3 Andrei Amalrik, *Will the Soviet Union Survive Until 1984?*, 2nd ed., Penguin, Harmondsworth, 1980. Amalrik himself did not live to see the collapse of the USSR; he died in a car accident in France in 1980, shortly after the publication of the second, revised edition of his book.

4 Natan Sharansky, *The Case for Democracy: The Power of Freedom to Overcome Tyranny and Terror*, Public Affairs, New York, 2004.

5 'The Fifth Modernization: Democracy' in Wei Jingsheng, *The Courage to Stand Alone: Letters From Prison and Other Writings*, Viking, New York, 1997, p. 202.

6 Ibid., p. 203.

7 Ibid., p. 255.

8 Sophia Woodman, 'Wei Jingsheng's Lifelong Battle for Democracy' in *Wei Jingsheng*, op. cit., p. 258.

9 Ibid., p. 259.

10 Ibid., p. 262.

11 *Wei Jingsheng*, op. cit., p. 215.

12 Ibid., pp. 215–16.

13 Ibid., pp. 218–19.

14 Ibid., p. 220.

15 Ibid., pp. 222–23.

16 Ibid., pp. 223–25.
17 Ibid., p. 226.
18 On the May Fourth Movement and the origins of the Communist Party in China, see Arif Dirlik, *The Origins of Chinese Communism*, Oxford University Press, London, 1989.
19 Wei Jingsheng, op. cit., p. 130.
20 Ibid., p. 132.
21 Ibid., pp. 132–36.
22 Ibid., p. 138.
23 Ibid., pp. 138–39.
24 Ibid., p. 264.
25 Ibid., p. 265.
26 Ibid., p. 266.
27 Ibid.
28 Robert Horvath, *Soviet Dissent and Russia's Transition to Democracy*, Routledge Curzon, London, 2005.
29 *Wei Jingsheng*, op. cit., p. 267.
30 David Lague, 'Beijing Frees Leading Dissident', *The Age*, Melbourne, 17 November 1997. 'Human rights groups and other dissidents welcomed his release after about 16 years in communist prisons. Mr Wei, 47, became the leading symbol of the struggle for democracy in China. His freedom is believed to be linked to the China-US presidential summit in Washington last month at which the US president, Mr Bill Clinton, strongly criticised Beijing's abuse of human rights and called on his Chinese counterpart, Mr Jiang Zemin, to release political prisoners.'
31 Wei Jingsheng, 'The Fifth Modernization: Democracy', in *Wei Jingsheng*, op.cit., p. 209.
32 The classic study of this terrible upheaval is Jonathan Spence's *God's Chinese Son: The Taiping Heavenly Kingdom of Hong Xiuquan*, Flamingo, London, 1996. The Taiping rebellion lasted for 20 years, and 20 to 30 million people are estimated to have died as a direct result of the conflict. In fact, the period from 1850 to 1873 saw the empire's population fall by a staggering 60 million as a result of rebellion, drought, and famine in various parts of China.
33 Ha Jin, *Waiting*, Pantheon, New York, 1999.
34 Ibid., p. 15.

Chapter 12: The Truth about Tiananmen

1 Mike Chinoy, 'The Tiananmen Papers: An Exclusive Interview' (June 2001), http://edition.cnn.com/SPECIALS/2001/tiananmen/papers.html.
2 Andrew J. Nathan & Perry Link, eds, *The Tiananmen Papers*, Little, Brown & Co., London, 2001, p. xxix.
3 Dali Yang, *Calamity and Reform in China*, Stanford University Press, 1996, p. vii.

4   Ibid., p. 11.
5   Andrew J. Nathan & Perry Link, eds, op. cit., pp. 4–5.
6   Ibid., pp. 6–7, 8, and 11–15.
7   Merle Goldman, *Sowing the Seeds of Democracy in China: Political Reform in the Den Xiaoping Era*, Harvard University Pres, 1994, p. 287.
8   Ibid., p. 288.
9   Ibid., pp. 289–91.
10 Nathan & Link, op. cit., p. 19.
11 Goldman, op. cit., p. 307.
12 Ibid., p. 29.
13 Ibid., pp. 34–35.
14 Nathan & Link, op. cit., p. 31.
15 Ibid., pp. 19–20.
16 Ibid., p. 71.
17 Ibid., p. 73.
18 Ibid., p. 76.
19 Ibid., p. 81.
20 Ibid., p. 82.
21 Ibid., p. 107.
22 Ibid. p. 116.
23 Ibid., pp. 127–28.
24 Ibid., p. 128.
25 Ibid., p. 141.
26 Ibid., p. 150.
27 Ibid., p. 189.
28 Ibid., pp. 372–77.
29 Ibid., pp. 389–91.
30 Xin Fei, 'Hu Jiwei Requests Zhao's Reputation Be Restored', *The Epoch Times*, 25 January 2005.

Chapter 13: Green Island

1   Simon Leys, *The Burning Forest: Essays on Chinese Culture and Politics*, Holt, Rinehart and Winston,

New York, 1986.

2   Richard Walker, *China Under Communism*, George Allen & Unwin, London, 1956, p. 219.

3   Stuart Schram, *Mao Tse-tung*, Penguin, rev. ed., Harmondsworth, 1967, p. 267.

4   Oleg V. Khlevniuk, *The History of the Gulag: From Collectivization to the Great Terror*, Yale University Press, 2004, p. 328.

5   Anne Applebaum, *Gulag: A History of the Soviet Camps*, Allen Lane, London, 2003, p. 515.

6   Richard L. Walker, 'The Human Cost of Communism in China', Senate Committee on the Judiciary, Internal Security Subcommittee, 92nd Congress, 1st session, 1971, Committee Print., p. 16.

7   Stephen Rosskam Shalom *Deaths Due to Communism in China: Propaganda versus Reality*, Occasional Paper no. 15, Centre for Asian Studies, Arizona State University, 1984.

8   R. J. Rummel, *China's Bloody Century: Genocide and Mass Murder Since 1900*, Transaction Publishers, New York, 1991, figure 8.1 and appendix II:1.

9   Harry Hongda Wu, *Laogai: The Chinese Gulag*, Westview Press, Boulder, Colorado, 1992.

10 Fan Shidong, 'Shattering Harry Wu's Western Funhouse Mirror', *Sing Tao Daily*, 24–29 June 1998.

11 Richard Anderson & James D. Seymour, *New Ghosts, Old Ghosts: Prisons and Labor Reform Camps in China*, M.E. Sharpe, New York, 1998.

12 Jay Taylor, *The Generalissimo's Son: Chiang Ching-kuo and the Revolutions in China and Taiwan*, Harvard University Press, 2000, p. 212.

13 Ibid., p. 479, n. 27.

14 George H. Kerr, *Formosa Betrayed*, Eyre and Spottiswoode, London, 1966. See especially chapter XIV, 'The March Massacre'.

15 Lai Tsehan, Ramon H. Myers & Wei Wou, *A Tragic Beginning: The Taiwan Uprising of 28 February 1947*, Stanford University Press, 1991, pp. 164–66.

16 Jay Taylor, op. cit., p. 148.

17 Lai Tsehan, Ramon Myers & Wei Wou, op. cit., p. 193.

18 Murray Rubinstein, ed., *Taiwan: A New History*, M. E. Sharpe, New York, 1999, p. 291.

19 George H. Kerr, op. cit., pp. 300–03.

20 See Ho Chingtai, *White Archives*, Taipei, 1991, and Lan Pochou, *The White Terror*, Taipei, 1993. These publications (available only in Chinese) provide detailed overviews of the period, including oral histories of both Taiwanese and mainland political prisoners.

21 Peter Chenmain Wang, in Murray Rubinstein, ed., op. cit., p. 335.

22 For an excellent introduction to the democratic movement in China, see Merle Goldman, *Sowing the Seeds of Democracy in China: Political Reform in the Deng Xiaoping Era*, Harvard University Press, 1994.

23 Wei Jingsheng, *The Courage To Stand Alone: Letters From Prison and Other Writings*, Viking, New York, 1997.

24 See Anne Thurston, *Enemies of the People*, Pantheon, New York, 1987, for a sound introduction to the repression of intellectuals under communist rule in China.

25 Geremie Barme & John Minford, eds., *Seeds of Fire: Chinese Voices of Conscience*, Bloodaxe Books, Newcastle-upon-Tyne, 1989, p. 171.

26 In 1972, Chiang Chingkuo 'told his cabinet that the Chinese people had suffered thousands of years of arrogant treatment from officials'. He told the US ambassador in 1973 that he was committed to a more open society, which would contrast favourably with China's closed society. See Taylor, op. cit., pp. 311, 313.

27 Annette Lu remained in prison until 1987. She is now the vice-president of Taiwan.

28 According to Taylor, Chiang decided 'before the end of 1983' that 'his successor would be a native Taiwanese'. Taylor, op. cit., p. 379.

29 The chief go-between from 1980 to 1987 was none other than Lee Kuan Yew, who became a close friend and confidant of Chiang Chingkuo in these years. Taylor, op. cit., pp. 382–84.

Chapter 14: Of Beethoven and Chinese Democracy

1 For a good profile of Bo Yang, see Margaret Scott's story 'Stuck in the soy sauce vat of Chinese culture', *Far Eastern Economic Review*, 3 September 1987, pp. 38–40.

2 Jiang Zemin's 'Three Represents' purports to show that the Communist Party represents all 'classes' in Chinese society. In fact, it represents nothing but its own interests. Democracy will come to China only when the 'Three Represents' becomes the 'True Represents', whereby constituencies are represented according to their will, and not that of political commissars of the current order.

3 Lee Tenghui, *The Road to Democracy: Taiwan's Pursuit of Identity*, PHP Institute, Tokyo, 1999, p. 10.

4 Ibid., p. 197.

5 Ibid., pp. 197–98.

6 Maynard Solomon, *Beethoven*, Schirmer Books, New York, 1998, p. 411.

7 Friedrich Nietzsche, *The Birth of Tragedy Out of the Spirit of Music*, trans. Shaun Whiteside, ed. Michael Tanner, Aphorism #1. Penguin, Harmondsworth, 1993, p. 17.

8 Johann Christoph Friedrich von Schiller, *Letters on the Aesthetic Education of Man*, Letter 2, quoted by Solomon, op. cit., p. 412.

9 Both the Mann and Marcuse citations are borrowed from Solomon, op. cit., p. 411. His discussion of the place of von Schiller's poetry, and *An die Freude* in particular, in Beethoven's creative vision is one of the high points of his celebrated biography of the great composer.

10 Max Beloff, ed., *The Debate on the American Revolution*, Nicholas Kaye, London, 1949, p. 193.

11　Peng Mingmin, *A Taste of Freedom: Memoirs of a Formosan Independence Leader*, Holt, Rinehart & Winston, New York, 1972.

12　Ibid., p. 246.

13　Joshua Kurlantzick, 'Is China's Economic Boom a Myth?', *The New Republic*, December 2002. Kurlantzick draws on the recent work of Thomas Rawski, Joe Studwell, and Nicholas Lardy to suggest that China could well be riding for a fall, due to radical weaknesses in its economic and legal systems and the sheer incapacity, or unwillingness, of the communist leadership to do anything fundamental about them.

Conclusion: Setting China Free

1　Thomas Paine, *Common Sense*, Penguin, Harmondsworth, 1976, pp. 78–79.

2　Harold R. Isaacs, *The Tragedy of the Chinese Revolution*, 2nd rev. ed., Stanford University Press, 1961 [includes preface to the 1st rev. ed., 1951], p. xvii.

3　Ibid., p. viii.

4　Ibid., p. xviii.

5　Ibid., p. xvi.

6　Perry Link, 'China: Wiping Out the Truth', a review of He Qinglian's 152-page report 'How the Chinese Government Controls the Media', *The New York Review of Books*, 24 February 2005, pp. 36–39.

Index

A

Academia Sinica (Taiwan) xxxi
Academy of the Gate of Qi 124, 130
Acheson, Dean 49, 50-51, 52
Aeschylus 123
Albanese, Anthony xx
Alliance for Democracy in China 162
Allison, Graham xxii, 96, 98, 99, 100
Amalrik, Andrei 144
Ang Lee (film director) 109
Anti-Rightist Campaign (1957) xxxv, 5,
April Fifth Forum (journal) 145
Aristotle 120, 121, 123, 125, 126, 128, 129
Ascher, Abraham 135
AUKUS xviii
Australia 195
    Neutralism and 79-80
    Policy on Taiwan 75
    Taiwanese plebiscite idea 71
Australian Outcome (to Taiwan question) 69, 71, 91-92
Australian Secret Intelligence Service (ASIS) xxv
Australian Strategic Policy Institute (ASPI) xx

B

Bacon, Francis 159
Bao Tong 161, 168
Barton, Edmund 132
Beckley, Michael xxi-xxii
Beethoven, Ludwig 188, 189, 191
Beijing Consensus xiv, xxi
Bodde, Dirk 114
Bolt, Robert (playwright) 117
Bounded rationality (see Simon, Herbert)
Boxer Rebellion (1899-1901) 19
Bo Yang 178-79, 181, 183, 191
Brands, Hal xxi-xxii
Bundy, McGeorge 99
Burke, Edmund 189-90
Bywater, Hector xviii

C

Cai Xia (Chinese scholar in exile) xix, 207
Canetti, Elias 126
Castro, Fidel 139
Chang, Gordon 37, 43, 137, 138
Checkpoint Charlie 48
Chen Kaige 109, 112, 113, 114, 115
Chen Qitian xxxiv, xxxv
Chen Shuibian 56, 64, 86, 93, 101-2, 184, 191
Chiang Chingkuo 82, 179, 180, 181, 183, 187, 194
Chiang Kaishek xxxii, xxxiii, xxxv, 52, 55, 74, 177, 193
    Asserts control over Guomindang 199
    Holds Kinmen against communists 49-50, 53-54
    2/28 massacre in Taiwan 50, 93, 175-77
    White Terror xxxiii, 177

Death of 77
Chiang Kaishek Memorial 191
China (People's Republic of)
  Defence budget xiii-xiv
  Economic growth 5, 33
  Executions in 133
  Financial institutions 40
  Internal security budget xiv
  Territorial claims 65, 88
Chinese Academy of Social Sciences (CASS) 163
Christensen, Thomas 53, 81, 85, 89, 94, 95, 96, 97, 98
Cixi, Empress Dowager 131, 149, 197, 202
Confucius 122, 123, 124, 125, 126, 127, 128
Cotton, James xxviii
COVID-19 xv, xix
Cuban Missile Crisis 95, 98, 99
Cultural Revolution xxxv, 5, 172
Curran, James xx

D

Defence Intelligence Organization (DIO) x, xxi, xxiii, xxv, xxvi-xxviii, xxix, xxx, xxxi
Defence Intelligence Thesaurus xxvi
Deng Xiaoping ix, xv-xvi, xxxii-xxxiii, 5, 8, 9, 10, 15, 20, 33, 36, 69, 78, 82, 83, 85, 89, 116, 134, 145, 149, 155-169 passim, 185, 186
Democracy Wall Movement 138, 144, 145, 160
Democratic Progressive Party xvi, 82, 104, 181, 187, 192-3, 194
Democritus 123
Department of Foreign Affairs and Trade (DFAT) xxix, xxx, 37
Deutscher, Isaac 117
Diamond, Larry xix
Dibb, Paul 28, 30, 35

E

Eisenstein, Sergei 116
Elvin, Mark xxix, xxx, 9-10, 119, 124, 126
Emperor and the Assassin, The (film) 110, 111, 112, 113, 115, 117
Essence of Decision (book) 95, 102
Exploration (Democracy Wall journal) 144, 147

F

Fang Lizhi 161, 184
Fingar, Thomas 37
Fitzgerald, John xx, xxxi, 152, 153, 207, 223
Fitzgerald, Stephen xx
Fog of War, The (documentary film) 95, 103
Fraser, Malcom 4, 72, 86
Friedberg, Aaron 205
Friedman, Edward 65, 66
Friedman, George 8
Fukuyama, Francis 4

G

Gang of Four 5, 147, 148, 162
Garnaut, Ross 5, 20
Global Financial Crisis (GFC) xiv, xv
Goddess of Democracy (statue) 112, 160,
Goldman, Merle 15
Gong Li (actress) 112, 117
Goodman, David (database) xxix
Great Leap Forward famine xii, xxxv, 5, 87, 89, 172

Great Wall of China 14-15, 19
Green Island 171-81 passim, 184
Green, Michael xxi
Guam 24
Guns of August, The (book) 98

H

Ha Jin 153
Hawke, Bob 4
Hegel, G.W.F. 160
Hero (film) 109, 111, 112, 115, 117
Hitler, Adolf 60
Hong Kong xvi, xxx, 82, 150
Hong King Gambit 68, 69, 81
Howard, John 132
Hu, Jason xxx-xxxi
Hu Jintao xi, xxxv, 43, 56, 87, 131, 132-33, 135, 138, 186
Hu Jiwei 163, 208
Hume, David 106
Hundred Flowers Campaign (1957) xxxiv
Huntington, Samuel xi, 3-21 passim, 23, 29, 35, 40, 119, 120
Hu Qili 162, 165, 166
Hu Shih xxxiv, xxxv
Hu Yaobang xxxi, xxxiii, xxxvi, 9, 91, 160, 161, 162, 163, 167, 180, 183, 185, 186

I

Isaacs, Harold 200

J

Japan 48,
    Colonial policy in Taiwan 176-77
    Defeat in the Second World War 7
    Meiji Restoration 7, 8
    Pearl Harbor and xviii
    San Francisco Treaty of 1951 83
    Treaty of Shimonoseki 83
Jiang Zemin 56, 131, 138, 151, 152, 186
    Suppression of democracy movement and 151, 186
Johnson, Chalmers 24-25, 28
Johnson, Lyndon Baines 99
Johnston, Alastair Iain 27, 30
Jung Chang 172
Justinian (Roman Emperor) 124

K

Kahn, Herman 8, 9,
Keating, Paul xx
Kennan, George F. 52
Kennedy, John F. 98, 132-33, 139, 140
Kennedy, Paul 6, 23-24, 29, 35
KGB xxiv, xxviii
Khrushchev, Nikita 187
Kim Il-sung 51
Kinmen (Quemoy) 48-57 passim, 64, 193
Kissinger, Henry 75-76, 77
Korean War 51, 55
Kurosawa, Akira 116

L

Labour Camp System (Laogai) 173-74
LAM (Linear Ascent Model) xi, 31-44 passim
Lean, David 116
Lee Kuan Yew 4, 8, 24, 27, 34, 35, 120
Lee Tenghui xxx, 64, 82, 84, 85, 180, 183, 184, 186, 187, 189, 190, 191, 194
Lei Chen 178

Lenin, Vladimir 134, 136, 197, 201

Lewis, Bernard 11, 14, 16

Leys, Simon (see also Ryckmans, Pierre) 171, 173

Li Hongzhang 84

Li Hongzhi (Falun Gong) 153

Lin Biao 53

Linear Ascent Model (LAM) xi, xii,

Li Peng 148, 157, 163, 164, 165

Liang Qichao 89, 114, 131, 169, 194

Liao Zhongkai 140, 199

Lilley, James 137

Liu Binyan 161

Liu Huaqing (Admiral) 17-18

Lu, Annette 180

Lu Xun xxxii, xxxiii, xxxiv, xxxv, 169

M

MacArthur, Douglas 51, 52

McEachin, Douglas 97

McMahon, William 75-76, 79

McNamara, Robert 95, 99, 104

Mandela, Nelson 86

Mann, James xxii, 205

Mao Zedong xv, xvii, xxiii, xxxii, xxxiv, xxxv, 8, 49, 50, 52, 53, 55, 67, 89, 104, 110, 114, 131, 171, 172, 177-78, 189

Marco Polo 11

Marcuse, Herbert 188

Marx, Karl 202

May, Ernest R. 60

May 4th Movement (1919) xxiii, xxxiv, 161

Mencius 121, 123, 124, 125, 126, 129

Molan, Jim xviii

Momigliano, Arnaldo 123

Monroe Doctrine xx

Montesquieu 185

Morris, Errol 95

Muggeridge, Malcolm xxiv-xxv

Myers, Ramon 176

N

National socialism with Chinese characteristics 78-79

NATO (North Atlantic Treaty Organization) 19

Necker Cube xvi-xvii, 59, 62, 65

Needham, Joseph 7, 124, 127

Nietzsche, Friedrich 188

Nobel Peace Prize 151

North Korea 51, 52, 165

O

Office of National Assessments (ONA) xxvi-xxviii

Okinawa 24

Organization for Economic Cooperation and Development (OECD) xiii, 40

Overholt, William H. 9

P

Paine, Thomas 197

Panmunjom 48

Pasternak, Boris 117

Pax Americana x, 8,

Peng Mingmin 47, 179, 183, 190, 191

Pentagon Papers, The 99

People's Daily, The 163, 164

Pericles 25-26

Perkins, Dwight 10

Peter the Great 110
Pipes, Richard 138
Pitt, William (Earl of Chatham) 189-90
Plato 120, 121, 122, 124, 125, 126, 128, 129
Plaza Accord 8
Plutarch 180
Popper, Karl 127
Putin, Vladimir xiii,

Q

Q Conference xxviii
Quad (Quadrilateral Security Dialogue) xviii, xix, xx
Qiao Shi 166
Qing reforms 197, 202
Qin Shih-Huangdi (First Emperor) 110

R

Raby, Geoff xx, xxi, xxix
RAND Corporation xxx, 94
Rational actor model, assumptions of 95, 97, 99-100
Renouf, Alan 76-77
Riefenstahl, Leni 109, 110
River Elegy (film) 181
Roh Tae-woo xxviii-xxix
Rowen, Henry 137
Ruan Ming xxxiii, 183, 185-6, 191
Ryckmans, Pierre (Simon Leys) 126

S

Saddam Hussein 97
Sakharov, Andrei 144
Schiller, Friedrich 188
Schram, Stuart 172
Shakespeare, William 112
Shanghai Triad (film) 109, 111
Sharansky, Natan 143, 144, 150
Shaw Yuming 180
Shiji (The Grand Scribe's Records) 111
Shih Mingte 180
Sima Qian 3, 109, 111, 112, 115, 116, 124
Simon, Herbert 97, 98
Singapore Gambit 68-69, 71, 80, 89, 91
Small Group for Research on Reform of the Central Political System 161
Smil, Vaclav 37, 213
Socrates 122, 128
Solzhenitsyn, Alexander 144
Song Jiaoren 140, 187, 194, 198, 204
Sophocles 160
South China Sea xiii, xxvi,
South Korea and China xxvii, xxix
Soviet Union
    Collapse of xviii
    Eastern Europe and xviii, xxiv
    Great Terror in 134
    Red Terror in 135
Sovietology and xvii
Spender, Percy 71, 74, 78
Stalin, Joseph 60, 134, 135, 172, 201
Steiner, George 69
Stolypin, Piotr 135, 136, 139, 140
Studwell, Joe 37, 43
Su Tingchi 178
Sun Tzu 69
Sun Yatsen 89, 114, 193, 198-99, 200

T

Taiping Rebellion 153

Taiwan xi, xv, xvii, xviii, xxi, xxx, xxxi, xxxiii, xxxvi, 47, 171-81 passim,
   China's anti-secession law and 94
   De jure independence and xvi, 67, 89
   Elections in 84-85, 192
   Japan and 62
   Japan hands back to the Republic of China 62
   Mutual Security Treaty with United States 52
   Public support for independence in 63, 78
   Qing dynasty cedes to Japan 62
   Strategic thinking and xviii, 28
   US derecognition of 78
Taiwan Advocates 187
Taiwan Solidarity Union 186, 193, 195
T'ang dynasty 129
Tennyson, Alfred 7
Tetlock, Philip ix, x
Thatcher, Margaret 84
Theory Research Office (Central Party School) 162-3
Thucydides 26, 69-70
Thucydides Trap xxii,
Tiananmen Papers, The (book) 155-57, 164
Tiananmen Square protests and massacre (1989) xxxiii, 69, 116, 139, 143, 145, 155-169 passim, 185, 191
Tong Yi 150
Triumph of the Will (film) 117
Truman, Harry 50-51, 52
Trump, Donald xv
Tsai, Henry xxxi

Tsai Ing-wen xvi, 195

V

Van Ness, Peter xxxi
Vietnam 65
Vietnam War xxiii, xxvii, 99

W

Waiting (novel by Ha Jin) 153
Waldron, Arthur 15, 137, 138
Walker, Richard 172, 173
Wang Hui 88, 168-69
Wang Ruowang 161
Wang Sheng 175
Washington Consensus xiv, xx, 25, 205
Weber, Max 135
Wei Jingsheng xxxiii, xxxvi, 115, 139, 144, 145, 146, 147, 148, 149, 150, 151, 152, 153, 178, 180, 184
   Fifth Modernization and 144
Wen Jiabao 9, 138
White, Hugh xx, 4,
Whitehead, Alfred North 125
White Terror (Taiwan) 174
Whitlam Labor government 73
Whitlam, Gough 75, 77
Wilson, Woodrow 26
World Economic Herald (Shanghai) 165

X

Xiao Qian (Chinese ambassador to Australia) xviii
Xiao Qiang (Human Rights in China) 146
Xi Jinping ix, xi, xiii, xx, xxii
Xinhua News Agency xxxii, 165
Xunzi (Chinese sage) 122

Y

Yan Fu 169
Yan Jiaqi xxxiii, xxxvi, 168, 184,
Yang, Dali 8, 59, 89, 93
Yes, Minister (BBC TV series) 100
Yokosuka (US base in Japan) 24
Yom Kippur War 61
Yuan Shikai 88, 149, 194, 198, 199-200, 204

Z

Zelikow, Philip 29, 96, 98, 99, 100
Zeng Qinghong 165
Zhang Liang (pseudonym) 155-57
Zhang Yimou (film director) 109, 115
Zhao Ziyang xxxvi, 8, 9, 116, 140, 158-169 passim, 180, 183, 197
Zheng He (15th century Ming admiral) 13-14
Zhou Enlai 75-76
Zhu Rongji 8, 9, 113, 131
Zoroaster 123

Acknowledgements

However much labour an author puts into them, books are collaborative endeavours. Like all authors, I owe a debt of thanks to many people for this book coming into existence. The list could be long, but by any measure it begins with my mentors, many years ago, in Chinese politics and history, most prominent among them Mark Elvin and John Fitzgerald, both accomplished scholars and linguists to my amateur sleuth and intelligence analyst cum public intellectual.

It was Mark who was my closest confidante in the DIO years, as I sought to become a competent China analyst. He has remained a friend and interlocutor since. John, whom I met only after having read and reviewed his masterly *Awakening China*, in 1997, provided me with an office at Latrobe University, in 1999-2001 and the opportunity to create and teach a course in 20th century Chinese politics.

That work became the seedbed first for a long string of essays in the *Australian Financial Review* (in collaboration with the then editor of its then Friday Review, Hugh Lamberton) on China and Taiwan and then for the first edition of this book, in 2005. The book, however, arose when Henry Rosenbloom of Scribe, asked would I write a book about North Korea, and I suggested one on China instead.

None of the above, of course, nor any of the many specialists on whose work I have drawn in this second edition of *Thunder From the Silent Zone: Rethinking China*, are in any way responsible for whatever errors of fact or inference I may have committed. Nor, it need hardly be said, is anyone in the Australian government to be blamed for my flagrantly critical and revisionist approach to Chinese politics, geopolitics and the status of Taiwan. I claim the credit for those things myself.

For years, starting with the first edition of this book, I have thanked David Speakman and his team at the Peter MacCallum Cancer Centre (now known as the Victorian Comprehensive Cancer Centre) for keeping me alive and therefore able to write this and a succession of other books. I have now been in complete remission for more than five years, but that does not obviate the debt to their skills and care. This second edition is the fruit, however, of the long resurgence from a besieged and debilitated condition.

I can never sufficiently express my gratitude to my mother, now 90 years of age, who fostered my precocious reading from the earliest years and has always exhibited a lively interest in the very fields in which I have ended up working: history, international politics and poetry. She knows, better than anyone, that this book has its deep origins in her gift to me, when I was a very small boy, of a short biography of Marco Polo, along with numerous other quality children's books on history and the natural sciences.

Two other women warrant mention here, as sources of inspiration and encouragement: Claudia Alvarez, a companion on the road of life since 2004; and Rachael Heinrich, who, in the past few years has, as she said she would, breathed new life into me. Each has urged me to fulfil myself as both an analytic writer and a poet. This book springs from the first aspiration, but the borrowing of the title from Lu Xun, a poet and novelist, adumbrates the link between the two things.

It is with the greatest pleasure that I also express warm gratitude to Badiucao, Chinese artist and cartoonist, dissident and exile, for his creative design of the cover to this second edition. His family have been persecuted by the Chinese Communist Party for three generations for no reason other that their insistence on creative freedom and personal civil and political rights.

Finally, I must thank my friend of almost fifty years and recent generous benefactor, Tim Norton, whose hard work, character and integrity have been rewarded by impressive success in business and who both urged and sponsored the republication of this book, given the times in which we now live and the important debates about national security taking place in Australia and around the democratic world because of the ominous nature of the regime in Beijing. May the book find readers and become a spark—iskra—for radical political liberalization in China.

www.ingramcontent.com/pod-product-compliance
Lightning Source LLC
Chambersburg PA
CBHW060936170426
43194CB00027B/2975